TROUBLEMAKER:

Saying No to Power

Frank Emspak

ISBN: 979-8-218-03891-5

Cover Design by D. Bass
Interior layout by D. Bass

Contact Frank Emspak at frankemspak@gmail.com

*To Dolores, my companion and wife without whom my
activism would not have been possible;
my children Jesse and Freya
who had to put up with a great deal
And to my grandchildren Dexter and Simone,
and their chance to build a better world.*

Contents

Preface by Paul Buhle   vii

Introduction   1

Chapter One: Class Conscious from Birth   7

Chapter Two: The Most Expensive Badger Ever:
       University of Wisconsin 1961-65   27

Chapter Three: What are We Fighting For?   45

Chapter Four: Graduate School Successes
       and Detours   73

Chapter 5: Transitions-Medical School, the Communist
       Party and Joining the Working Class   101

Chapter Six: The World Gone By - The United Shoe
       Machine Company and UE local 271   121

Chapter Seven: Building the Union
       at GE Wilmington Local 201   153

Chapter Eight: Local 201 Confronts the Future:
       Technology and the Workforce   181

Chapter Nine: The Battle for Leadership   207

Chapter Ten: New Technologies Promises
       and Defeats   229

Chapter Eleven: The School for Workers   245

Chapter Twelve: Workers Independent News   273

Chapter Thirteen: IT WAS WORTH IT   299

About The Author   315

Preface

This is a book of life, the life of a unique figure within the US Left from the 1950s all the way into the early decades of the twenty-first century. It tells a story too little heard in the current outpouring of Baby Boomer memoirs. Frank Emspak's journey connects the Old Left with the New Left, unions in the industrial era and beyond, and the struggle to communicate to a wide public with all the modern means available.

Frank Emspak has, within the limited world of the US Left and labor movement, something approaching a royal lineage. His father, Julius, commanded, for crucial early years, the leadership of one of the largest unions in the US and the one with the most women members: United Electrical Workers. The devastating, near-total destruction of UE played out during Frank's early years.

A considerable portion of other "children of the Left," whose parents had been persecuted and blacklisted, chose to go politically quiet in their own lives. The personal cost of political activity had proven too high. Frank never considered such a choice. He organized student workers, was active in the Communist Party, played a leading role in the National Coordinating Committee to End the War in Vietnam and fought for progressive reform as an industrial worker in the 1970s.

Frank is most interested in his own shift to industry, and what he found there, in almost every sense. Radical students' move to "industrialize" during the early 1970s proved a "children's crusade" for thousands of dedicated activists across the US, few of them armed with Frank's political savvy. Deindustrialization effectively wiped out this movement as a movement, but the not minority of determined activists who managed to find a way to dig in. Here and there, activists like Frank joined massive union reform movements. Few efforts succeeded in overturning the heavy bureaucracy, but many worthy projects of mobilization around strikes or fresh unionizing efforts offered high points for the shrinking labor movement.

Frank's grasp of the changing industrial process, with the twinned acceleration of automation and the off-shoring of production, offers something rare among left writings; he knows how it looked from the shop floor. Like the protagonists of Studs Terkel's oral histories of work, or of the famed novel of the work process, *Between the Hills and the Sea* by Katya and Burt (i.e., "K.B") Gilden, the view is intimate and dynamic. But it also updated, approaching the end of the twentieth century.

Here we find hinted, if not spelled out, a deeply historical dilemma for labor in the current century: the problem of Memory. For generations, old line unions firmly held to the belief that the production of goods guaranteed them jobs and offered them a ticket into consumer society and a way of life others in the world presumably envied. The winding down of industry shocked the older generation and impressed upon the younger generation that the end of the narrative left them nowhere in particular, economically or historically. Unions, particularly the industrial unions, practically ceased to have a role in their communities.

Much like the dispersion of older ethnic groups and the physical crumbling of modest older neighborhoods, an accepted way of understanding the world had ended.

Trained as a historian, Frank lived through the experience sharply aware of its larger cultural meanings. A related project to this book, the creation of a GE union archive and exhibit within the Lynn, Massachusetts, city museum, would keep this memory locally safe. But what of the larger meaning, either to the descendants of those industrial workers or to the new ethnic communities of immigrants engaged in post-industrial employment? Where would the memories go? The question is posed suggestively here, without any certainty of an answer, but very much involved Emspak as a School for Workers representative touring the state and meeting working people from all walks of life.

Lastly, we might say, Labor Radio offered the rambling School for Workers lecturer Frank Emspak another venue, one explored with huge success in the days of Chicago's WCFL (ie, Chicago Federation of Labor) or New York's WEVD (i.e., Eugene V Debs) generations earlier. By the turn of the new century, it was all uphill, as the AFL nationally headed downhill. Yet the task remained: continue.

~Paul Buhle, Madison, WI April 2022

Introduction

At 7:55 a.m. the first whistle blew at the Burroughs-Wellcome Company. At 8:00 a.m., the second whistle blew. Any kid going to school in Tuckahoe in East Yonkers in during the 1950s knew exactly where they had to be when those whistles blew if they were to be in class on time.

In the paper-making towns of Maine and Wisconsin, especially on humid days, a particular smell enveloped the place. As the saying went, "That was the smell of money." There was a certain ritual that meant stability, continuity and prosperity in many towns throughout the country. Maybe these were experienced unconsciously — but by the 1980s they were all fast disappearing.

Growing up in these places, my generation absorbed the reality of community disintegration firsthand. Ours was the first generation since the 19th century to experience the slowdown, stop and then the reversal of the upward moving escalator of prosperity.

As activists seeking to improve our society, we were uniquely positioned to observe what was happening in our cities and towns. Whether we were completely conscious at the time or not, we had an almost subliminal baseline that defined where our community and our families had been as we reached maturity.

Having directly experienced this loss, my generation of activists is also well positioned to address the reasons for part of the working class' subsequent significant shift to the right. This memoir is an attempt to do just that. A former union activist and skilled machinist, I pay particular attention to the inability of our unions and the political parties they support to control capital mobility and impede plant closures.

As a younger person, I and many of my generation shared a vision of the future which included abolishing racial discrimination, strengthening a progressive labor movement and a foreign policy directed towards peace rather than war.

Many of us also believed capitalism was the root cause of discrimination, a warlike foreign policy, and an inability to meet the basic needs of working people for decent jobs, adequate housing and an environmentally healthy world. We said "no" to the American war in Vietnam because we had a vision of peace and the right of self-determination for all peoples. We sought to build a socialist movement. We understood that fundamental to both missions was the fight against racism.

The most outstanding example of our generation's optimism was the fight for civil rights, especially in the South. To a great degree, the civil rights movement was a movement of young people who believed in the urgency of "now" and the need to fight for their place in America. Their optimism helped drive the movement. The music of the time reflected that; the biggest rock n' roll hits were of love, optimism and excitement.

Almost immediately, however, the Nixon administration began a calculated campaign to undermine the movements of young people. The administration invented the "war on drugs." The war was fought on two fronts — one against Black people portraying them as drug-crazed addicts who had to be suppressed. The second front was aimed at whites who were portrayed as simply addled young people with too much time and marijuana on their hands. Simultaneously, finance capital withdrew investment in urban areas, ramped up investment overseas and launched a successful offensive against unions in key industries. The concessions movement was born. As the 1970s ended workers' upward mobility came to a halt.

Ronald Reagan astutely took advantage of the ideological weakness of the union movement and broke the air traffic controllers strike (PATCO) — firing and replacing all strikers. The response was a huge demonstration in Washington DC, but no direct actions of any sort to disrupt the economy. In this regard, the PATCO response resembled the "Wisconsin Uprising" 30 years later — huge demonstrations, but no willingness on the part of union leaders to disrupt the status quo. During the 1970s and 80s, working people were able to make significant inroads in the public sector, especially education and health care. But unions were continually on the defensive in the wealth producing sectors of the economy. Finally succumbing to the siren call of corporations and embracing the vision they had to help bring about an increase in share value, or else see employers abandon union workers.

By 2020, a deep pessimism about the future had almost entirely supplanted any optimism that remained. Overall inequality in our society was increasing. Wages had been stagnant for a generation. Almost all employers had eliminated defined benefit pension plans for new employees, and as many current employees as possible. Individual debt was an increasing burden — debts often contracted to pay for an education that did not result in a stable job or income. Medical expenses were an international disgrace. The real upward mobility experienced by the generation of workers from 1945 through 1975 was at an end.

This memoir is about my efforts to realize a vision for the working class. It ends in 2021 with my efforts, along with others, to encourage the organization of the 21st century employers like EPIC, Promega, Google and Amazon.

My intellectual center is the working class and the union movement. "Class consciousness at birth" is probably the best way to summarize my mental framework. My family was the target of the U.S. Government and the destruction of the UE — United Electrical Radio and Machine Workers — was a goal of many in the labor movement. After WWII, the UE was the dominant union in an electrical industry comprised of GE, Westinghouse, Allis Chalmers and others. My father was the secretary-treasurer of the union, a college graduate and a one-time tool and die maker apprenticed at GE. But he was also probably the most educated and philosophically committed left-winger of all the CIO leadership. More importantly, he fought for the political independence of the UE and the right of the membership to elect whomever they wanted to office — including members of the Communist Party.

In academia, I had the opportunity to research the breakup of the Congress of Industrial Organization (CIO) and the destruction of the United Electrical Radio and Machine Workers —and to uncover the documents which directly spoke to the use of the Red Scare, and repressive legislation to break up the UE, and substitute it with a union that essentially accepted the corporate ideological framework and the leadership of the Democratic Party.

In my fifteen years in the workplace, I put this knowledge to use as a skilled metal worker at the United Shoe Machine Company in Beverley, Massachusetts and later at the General Electric Company plant in Lynn, Massachusetts. I became an activist and elected leader within the local unions representing each job site.

Later in my career, I took the knowledge acquired from my workplace, and especially my fellow workers, to the University of Wisconsin-Madison School for Workers. I wanted to teach students to analyze issues through a class-conscious lens — not just militancy and a sense of grievance. In 2011, the failure to achieve this vision of public sector unionism became crystal clear as then Wisconsin Governor Scott Walker eviscerated public sector union rights without any significant disruption to public services. Public sector union membership almost disappeared in most state agencies. Now, ten years later, public sector unionization is barely breathing.

I believe my vantage point regarding the beliefs and aspirations of working people is unique. I entered the blue collar workforce with a PhD in History along with significant skills in biological research. As a skilled machinist, I took my theoretical framework and used it in the fight to apply new technologies in ways that would enhance skills and value people, in addition to fighting discrimination in the workplace and the devastating effects of capital mobility — also known as plant closures.

I describe our movement by my fellow union members to determine how the General Electric Company would invest in a new facility in Lynn, Massachusetts — probably the only time in the latter 20th century that workers went beyond simply discussing the effects of a company's actions to the content of the action itself. In contrast to the top-down manufacturing designs of GE, our starting point was "skills-based automation," a system designed under the influence of German workers to enhance skill and control.

Throughout my education and career, I led efforts to empower members to speak out, in the form of our union newspapers, leaflets, radio and TV interviews and, ultimately, via electronic media.

My participation in the labor movement culminated in a partially successful effort to provide the means for working people to express themselves via a nationwide headline news service — Workers Independent News — which was broadcast on stations throughout the US from 2001 until 2017.

Overall, I remain optimistic. Young working people face daunting challenges. But millions have taken to the streets to demand racial justice and respond to climate change.

Our collective task now, is to look at some of the things the older generation of workers did — and learn how we can all build organizations capable of taking power in our own right.

Chapter One: Class Conscious from Birth

Antecedents: A Family of Troublemakers

My grandfather Frank came to the United States from Hungary in 1902 after his participation in a failed railway workers strike there and the repression that followed. A highly skilled industrial blacksmith, he settled in Schenectady, New York, where he found work at General Electric. Unlike the vast majority of the Hungarian working class, Grandfather Frank's family was strongly anti-clerical, which must have informed his political decisions and the family's relations with the community. For example, when a family member was being interred in the Hungarian Cemetery in Schenectady, the family asked the priest to leave.[1]

Frank's wife Theresa followed eight months later, along with her two children Frank and Vic (Henrick). Anne, my aunt, was born in the United States just a few weeks after their arrival. My father Julius was born in 1906 and thus, a US citizen. This allowed him to escape the deportation fate that was visited upon many of the leaders of the left trade union movement forty years later.

In 1913, my grandfather Frank was killed crossing the railroad tracks on the way to work at GE, depriving his family of their key breadwinner. His eldest son Frank Alexander followed his father into GE, as it was customary for GE to hire family members. Frank became a tool and die maker, the most highly skilled worker. Victor soon joined him, becoming a steamfitter, working with the high pressure steam aspects of turbine assembly. In 1922, Julius, at sixteen, followed his brothers into the factory as an apprentice tool and die maker.[2] My grandmother Theresa was a cleaner at GE. Frank and Vic lived within walking distance to GE and walked to work.

My mother's Jewish family came from what was then the Russian city of Lvov. In 1905, my grandmother Lena and my grandfather Louis along with Louis's two brothers, Sam and Ely, immigrated to the United States immediately after their involvement in the failed First Russian Revolution of 1905. Sam and Ely settled in Holyoke, Massachusetts, while Louis and his family went to Galveston, Texas, where some cousins had established a dry goods store. At that time — the late nineteenth and early twentieth centuries — a network of Jewish merchants settled throughout the South. Neiman Marcus, the high-end department store, grew from this community.

Lena and Louis never married; they believed marriage was a bourgeois institution. My grandmother had four children who survived: Ida, my aunt; Stella, my mother — and Leonard and Adolph — my uncles. My mother was born in 1912, grew up in Galveston and graduated high school when she was a bit over sixteen with the skills of shorthand and typing, which enabled her to earn a living.

In about 1925, my mother told me, a radical organizer visited Galveston, Texas. His vision of a new society, she said, awakened something in her. For the rest of her life she dedicated herself to that vision. Years later, she married Julius Emspak and dedicated herself to the man she believed shared that same vision with her. When she was seventeen, my mother traveled from Galveston to New York City by herself, arriving on October 29, 1929 — the day of the Wall Street crash. Through family connections, she went to work as a clerk in a Brooklyn department store where she dressed professionally, which gave her certain respectability when passing out leaflets. Her skills and political dedication led her to work for a left-wing group of locals within the International Association of Machinist (IAM), organizing in Brooklyn under the leadership of James Matles. Jim Matles was a Romanian immigrant coming to the US when he was nineteen. He worked in various machine shops in Brooklyn becoming an organizer in the IAM. In 1937, Matles, opposing the racial exclusion of the IAM, and a strong supporter of industrial unionism, led a number of locals out of the IAM into the United Electrical and Radio Workers (UE) and became the Director of Organization of the new United Electrical Radio and Machine Workers.

When Jim Matles brought in the Machine Workers, Stella Abrams became the office manager and secretary to my father, the secretary treasurer of the UE. They married in 1938. Today, we don't think much of a marriage outside one's faith, but in 1938, even for people estranged from their religion, Jewish-Catholic marriages were not common. In spite of their radical politics, my paternal grandmother had some objections, but they were overcome thanks to my father's intransigence and also the birth of her grandchildren.

I was born in 1943, and grew up in Yonkers, New York. Later, I would be called a "red diaper baby" — the pejorative term used by right-wing columnists to attack those of us in the anti-war movement who were the progeny of left-wing parents.[3] Shortly before I was born, my maternal grandmother came to live with us, staying until about 1954.

My father was probably the most highly educated industrial union leader in the country. In 1922 at the age of 16 he was hired at GE Schenectady as an apprentice tool and die maker. After

9

graduating from the apprentice program he entered Union College at that time the engineering school for GE, graduating Phi Beta Kappa and pursuing a PhD at Brown University. He left abruptly in 1933 to work in GE's RCA plant in Camden, New Jersey.[4] His goal was to help build the union at GE.

There he began to build what would become the United Electrical Radio and Machine Workers. By the end of World War II, UE had become the third-largest union in the Congress of Industrial Organizations. He remained the founding secretary-treasurer of the UE until his untimely death in 1962.

The UE was the prime target for anti-Communists within the labor movement, companies like GE, and their Democratic and Republican Party supporters. By 1949, the UE represented the vast majority of GE workers. In September of that year, the UE quit the CIO on the same day it was expelled for being Communist-dominated.

There are few papers, letters, or oral histories available that delineate the political or intellectual developments that took place between Julius' entrance to Brown University and his departure to GE.[5] His thesis notes focus on the development of consciousness, and given the family's radicalism, he was probably aware of, or in discussions with people close to the Communist Party. At that time, William Z. Foster, the leader of the CPUSA and one of the most accomplished organizers in the country, advocated industrial unionism and had led the steel and packinghouse strikes of 1919. My father's library had an extensive philosophy collection, but as I discovered upon his death, he also had an extensive collection of writings by Marx and Lenin as well as the leaders of the CP of that time period. He kept some of his tool making equipment at home, including micrometers—which I wondered about at the time. Many years later, I used some of the same tools myself at the United Shoe Machine Company and GE.

How Do You Know You Are Different

Although we lived in suburbia, we were still connected to the respective working class communities of Schenectady, New York and Springfield, Massachusetts, and visited often. In Schenectady we stayed in the family home at 815 Francis Ave. My grandmother ran the household. In fact, even once Frank had become a powerful figure in the UE, the two brothers gave her their paychecks until just prior to her death in 1954. I remember those visits to Schenectady as long and boring stretches of waiting around in the UE offices while my father was in meetings. I entertained myself by looking out from the office at the New York Central Railroad tracks, where the last of the steam engines still operated. My father was often absent from our household for weeks on end as he went from local to local defending the UE. My memory is one of missing his presence.

I was in the second grade in 1952 when my father was jailed for contempt of Congress and spent several weeks in federal custody before being freed by the Supreme Court.[6] I told my second grade teacher about the situation. She probably knew more about him being in jail than I did, as there was constant coverage in the local newspaper.

Fourth grade brought another bit of information about the United Electrical Workers and the controversial nature of my father's work. The principal of P.S.15 refused to let me leave school to go to the UE's convention in New York City with my parents, indicating that, somehow, the event was illegal or immoral. All I remember was that after some hassle, I was permitted to go.

Later, another incident: During the presidential election of 1952, my fourth grade class went to see candidate Dwight D. Eisenhower's motorcade zip by. Back in class, Ms. Sacramento asked who our parents were voting for. The question was innocent and presumably intended to promote the idea of voting. So, I told the class my parents supported Vincent Hallinan, who was running for president on the Progressive Party ticket.

The next thing I knew, the principal of the school, Ms. Rushby, was lecturing me and the class about communism. The class was astounded that I was being singled out for something bad since I was not known as a troublemaker. When I reported this to my father, home recuperating from a cataract operation, he got exceptionally upset. The next day, in our classroom down the hall, we could hear the discussion between my father and the principal. For a kid to have their parent come to school and confront the principal was a big deal. A little later, Ms. Rushby came back and apologized. I don't think any of us understood what she was really apologizing for.

That same year, some of the wealthy kids in class went to sunny places like Florida — on a plane, no less! I went with my father… also on a plane. But instead of a beach vacation, we went to Erie, Pennsylvania to what I now understand was a meeting with UE local 506, the union local representing the workers at the GE locomotive plant.[7]

In spite of their radical politics, our parents raised my brother and me the way almost all first-generation parents from immigrant homes raised their kids. Neither of us was encouraged to learn Hungarian or Yiddish, the two languages spoken by my parents and grandparents. We had a conventional upbringing. I joined the Cub Scouts, my mother went to PTA meetings, and both my parents went to open school nights. But despite the sense of order and normalcy within the family unit, my parents' political lives drew the ire of the U.S. government. On multiple occasions, our family was the target of attacks in the newspaper and surveilled by the FBI and federal marshals.

I only remember one neighbor dropping by our house to visit — Mr. Smyth, of the Irish-Catholic family up the street. Smyth would come down to check on us whenever there was a particularly scurrilous attack in the papers. The people that did come by were part of a close circle of progressive professionals or others living under some anti-communist cloud. Among these families were the Foxes, the parents of my future wife Dolores.

While many families had elderly relatives living at home, even in middle-class and all-white Tuckahoe, most families never had a federal marshal come to the door with subpoena papers for them. That is when my grandmother made it clear that I should never open the door for federal marshals, although I was really impressed when one showed up — I thought he was like the Lone Ranger.

My elementary school was ninety-nine percent white.[8] In the mid-1950s the remnants of the industrial beginnings of Yonkers were still there. Boys had to take shop and mechanical drawing. As it turned out, learning how to read and draw blueprints from Mr. Mathieson in my eighth grade mechanical drawing class allowed me to get a job at the United Shoe Machine Company fifteen years later.

Cultural Immersion Progressive Style: Encountering Racism

Progressive parents sought to have the kids exposed to progressive ideas and beliefs and they did so via discussion groups and summer camps. In the summer of 1953, I started at Camp Juvenile, run by the Federation of Jewish Philanthropies. It was an outpost of Bronx House, a settlement house. The campers were mostly Jewish working- or lower-middle-class kids. At various times during the summer, however, the camp suddenly became integrated with young Black campers joining the camp for a three-week session. Since east Yonkers in 1953 was all white, (and still is) this was a shock. Even though we were all together in the same bunks, I don't remember any Black-white bonding.

Camp Juvenile also believed that integration meant more than just having a Black camper presence. We also had Black counselors and senior administrators.[9] One of those counselors was Greg Moses, who was the older brother of Bob Moses, a future leader of the Student Nonviolent Coordinating Committee. Another was Alvin Poussaint, who became a psychiatrist, well-known for his research on the effects of racism on the Black community. In 1969 he spoke at the University of Wisconsin, delivering an inspirational speech to Black and white students that helped spark what became the "Black student strike." I was a member of the white support organization and presented on the panel discussion initiated by Poussaint discussing white racism in Madison.

The camp also made itself home to progressive cultural leaders, such as the blacklisted musician Pete Seeger. He led us in rousing spirituals and union music. We campers knew "We Shall Overcome" before anyone else in the wider white community ever heard of it.

But the new and powerful "rock and roll" music also came to Camp Juvenile. The camp had an old jukebox that played 45s. People from the Bronx and Brooklyn brought their records — something was playing almost all day. We listened to doo-wop, Frankie Lyman and the Teenagers and the records that would come to make up the New York sound of rock and roll — but two years before anyone else.

In the late fifties and early sixties, something was happening that almost no adult understood, but which was certainly captured by the music. The band Buffalo Springfield said it well: "There's something happening here, what it is ain't exactly clear."[10] The new music was helping to drive a new consciousness. As John Hamilton of Kankakee Illinois attests, "I like to look at the burgeoning rock and roll as the first youth revolution…It was when James Dean was making his movies and Marlon Brando was doing his movie 'The Wild One.'"[11, 12]

As a result of my friendships in camp, there were real parties in New York City. No one else in my high school class went to New

York for parties. The New York adventures raised my social status. At camp I had met M from the prestigious Music and Art High School and went down to the city on dates. The ability to go to the city and grow a bit compared to those stuck in Yonkers began to set me apart.[13]

The "normal" white middle-class camping experience was to become a camper, then counselor, then some sort of professional. I was not judged mature enough to become a counselor. I wound up going to another camp, working as a waiter. But I was no good at that and was transferred to the kitchen.

Over five years, I became a pretty good first cook, a skill that made it possible for me to continue in college. It also introduced me into the bilingual working class.

By 1964, the kitchen was nonwhite, in contrast to the late 50s where it was closer to fifty-fifty. I was the only "white" in the crew. All the other workers were Puerto Rican and spoke Spanish more than English. The racial and cultural chasm was difficult to overcome as I was the first cook working under the bilingual chef, and trying to figure out with him, how to maintain a kosher-style cooking system when the other workers had no idea what was going on.

I was also white and an English-speaker giving work direction to two Spanish-speaking kitchen workers. We were about the same age, but everyone knew sooner or later I would be able to leave the kitchen for good. My job was my ticket out and this contributed to tensions within our crew. But we got the work done because there was no option. We had to get the meals out to 350 or so people three-times-a-day.

But something else also happened. The young white workers in our area (Hancock, New York) did not like the Spanish workers — or any nonwhite people, probably. Even though our small crew was divided, when we went to town we all stuck together.

One night in downtown Hancock we had it out with the locals. We knew some of them — the bread truck delivery person, the LP gas delivery man, the egg guy. The fight didn't last long and no one was arrested — we were probably all too drunk to do much damage. Someone decided enough was enough and we all went home. The next morning, at about 6 a.m., the bread truck driver, the LP gas delivery man and others with whom we had fought the night before, made their deliveries. We all were a little sheepish and looked the worst for wear. But after that, when we went to town everyone got along.

Carrying Dreams Forward

My parents were committed to ensuring their political culture would be passed on to our generation. To accomplish that goal, a group of blacklisted writers, intellectuals and educators from the Jefferson School of the Communist Party, organized the Westchester Discussion group (WDG). It was a way for young people to meet others, end their social isolation and learn about Marxism.

We were taught to unite Marxist theory with practice. We learned about Marxist philosophy and economics, such as the labor theory of value. Direct involvement in political activities took the form of going to New York City or Washington, D.C. to take part in demonstrations against nuclear weapons or in support of civil rights. I picketed Woolworth's in support of students in the South and also against employment discrimination in New York. It was here that I met young people producing the magazine *Common Sense*, which we will discuss in detail.

As we got older, we started throwing parties on Saturday nights before the Sunday events. There was much flirting, some liquor — and as it turned out — pot. We made lifelong friends.

Among other people I connected with was Dolores Fox. We were married in 1964.

The World of High School

Roosevelt High School was a different world. I did all the right things there. I managed the football and track teams, was on the rifle team, wrote for the school paper and even became a sports stringer for the *New York Times*. Our debating team made the local paper, *The Herald Statesman,* after my partner Robert Landau and I won the regional championship. I was the subject of a front page attack a few years later for opposing the war in Vietnam, but at least the editors knew how to spell the name — *Emspak.*

By the end of my junior year, in June 1960, I was part of an identifiable group of people concerned about the world. We focused on racial tensions — picketing Woolworth over their racist employment practices. We also opposed nuclear weapons. The Cold War taught us to duck under our desks and cover our heads in case of nuclear attack. We decided our chances were zero of surviving an A-bomb attack on Columbus Circle, in New York City about fifteen miles way.

In April 1961, our group joined the Committee for a Sane Nuclear Policy's Easter March for Peace. My friend and fellow debating partner Robert decided to make a sign on a longer pole than others so everyone could see that Roosevelt High School was present. Everyone did see; it was on the front page of the *New York Times.* A couple of days later, myself and another participant — a pacifist and Quaker named Susan Andrews —were expelled from school. It was a huge shock for me. But the thought that students could speak for themselves on major issues was a foreign concept to the school administration.

The principal ordered us expelled, but the basketball and track coach, who was also the assistant principal and disciplinarian, did the dirty work. The alleged justification for the expulsion was that I did not have enough gym credits. In fact, I had more credits and letters than most.

After another parental confrontation and without really missing more than one or two days, we were back. A few weeks later, many of us organized opposition to the nationwide civil defense drill as we urged people not to take shelter. [14]

The general acceptance of racism was simply part of the Roosevelt High School landscape. I did not really recognize it at the time, but the social leaders of the class apparently were upset or uncomfortable with my prom date, Dolores, born in Colorado of Japanese descent. Only two couples offered to sit with us for the prom banquet.

Corruption also existed in the supposedly uncontaminated white, college-bound honor class of 1961. A leader of the honor society was caught cheating on the Regents exams, but there was no punishment for him. The president of the class was later indicted in a bank fraud case in California, and another student in a point-shaving basketball scandal at Columbia. A fourth was involved in some real estate scandal in New York. But the biggest scandal of all was that only about sixty students in our class of three-hundred-and-sixty-three actually received a college prep education.

The Student Movement of New York City: Rebirth of a Socialist Left

Starting in 1954, anyone watching television would see teenagers and young college students marching, being arrested and being beaten in their fight to end segregation. But while one could see the public faces of the civil rights movement in the South, almost all of the growing student mobilizations in support of civil rights up North proceeded under the radar of the establishment. That the "establishment" missed the beginnings of the youth movement should not be too astonishing.[15]

Common Sense

One day, picketing at Woolworth we met some high school students passing out their newsletter *Common Sense*.[16] It was really us younger teens meeting older teens. The oldest "leaders" were people who were between eighteen and twenty.

Common Sense was a breath of fresh air. It was a connection to others who believed, as we did, that nuclear war was a bad thing, and that discrimination and poverty were wrong. We also discovered that the parents of the older students were also activists. It was inspirational and also a thrill for me and others in our group to see articles about Westchester and what we were attempting to do.[17] Editor Steve Max evaluated the impact of *Common Sense*: "It is hard to say what the impact of *Common Sense* was as a publication....the impact came more from the stream of FDR Club members who graduated from high school and went off to organize on campus through to about 1963."[18]

Another thread that runs through the movement was self-consciousness. Our vision was captured in an editorial most probably by *Common Sense* Editor Steve Max. *"The new generation of students will only succeed in searching out new answers and bringing them to the nation if we remain independent and learn from the responsibilities of action."*[19] This idea of students as a motivating force was illustrated by the fight in California against the House Un-American Activities Committee [HUAC].[20] In December 1960, the paper's lead dealt with the growing movement to abolish the HUAC. It noted "while several adult groups have been agitating around this issue for a number of years, it has not been until students took up the matter that anything approaching a popular movement has started.[21]

As the youth movement developed in the late 1950s, young people increasingly began to reject red-baiting and anti-communism. Steve Max discussed the impact of the HUAC committee on our constitutional rights.   He pointed out, "If the person has any principles when called before the committee he can take the Fifth Amendment and be labeled a communist for the rest of his life, or he may take the First Amendment and go to jail for contempt of Congress."[22] This hit home because that is precisely what my father did — and was jailed for contempt of Congress.

The Continuity between the Old Left and the New

The FDR Club, just like the Westchester Discussion group, illustrated the continuity between the so-called old left and the new. Steve Max's father had been an editor of the *Daily Worker*, the Communist Party newspaper. When I first came in contact with Steve, my mother immediately recognized the name and asked about his father. A major objective of the anti-communists was to sever connections between an older generation of activists and younger people when it came to Marxism or an understanding of class and race. The events in New York and San Francisco showed that they failed, in part.

Common Sense and the FDR Club that produced it distinguished itself because it fought for the concept of non-exclusion. Non-exclusion meant that anyone who agreed with the objectives of the organization could join even if they were communists or associated with other organizations characterized as communist-dominated. In the New York City of 1960-62, the issue of non-exclusion and a definitive break with the McCarthyism of the fifties played out within the anti-nuclear movement and the Student Committee for SANE Nuclear Policy, which moved to oppose the exclusion of so-called communists. I argued then that a divided peace movement would never get anywhere.[23] I was expressing these views in my capacity as the leader of the student SANE movement in Westchester County. I later championed the same assessment in regards to the anti-Vietnam War movement.

Registering for the Draft

In 1961, all males upon reaching their eighteenth birthday had to register for the draft, even if they declared themselves conscientious objectors. My father made his views clear. He told me that if I wanted to go into politics or do something publicly that I could not be characterized as a draft dodger. Register, he said. And I did, at local board #8 in Yonkers, New York. I was not a pacifist. I was not a conscientious objector. When I was drafted in November 1965, I said the war in Vietnam was wrong, the Vietnamese were right. But in June 1961, all one had to do was register for the draft. I received a student deferment because I was going away to college. At that time, few thought anyone going to college from our city would be drafted. Five years later, it was a different story.

On Wisconsin!

I got into the University of Wisconsin because I was a relatively high scoring out-of-state student paying the full tuition of $362.50 per semester. UW was mildly interested in me because I had managed the high school football team, been a *New York Times* sports stringer and because my uncle had earned his PhD in Chemistry there. All good reasons for acceptance, but the truth was I was going to UW because I did not get accepted at the colleges of greatest interest to my parents — Harvard, Swarthmore, and UC Berkeley. I was accepted at Union College in Schenectady, but I could not conceive of going to an all-men's school. I was also intrigued by Wisconsin as a progressive institution. Two progressive people I knew, Steve Watt and Ann Sterling, were also going UW. Anne was a close friend from the Westchester Discussion Group and Steve Watt was a progressive activist from NYC and the son of a blacklisted Communist Party member. It was probably one of the best decisions I ever made, even if it wasn't fully intentional.

I went off to work that summer and then to college, never expecting to come back to Yonkers — unlike most of my classmates who remained close to home.

My parents' desire for me to be "pro-science and don't get involved in the radical movement campaign" was to spare me the terrible repression they went through. Their plans for me were about one-hundred-percent at variance with what they had done.[24] Yet, Wisconsin was probably one of the last places in the world that one would send someone to be insulated from radical politics.

When, a few years later, I called home to say I had just become the Chairman of the National Coordinating Committee to End the War in Vietnam, my mother cried.

Endnotes For Chapter One

1. Julius Emspak papers, Interview by James Pearlstein, Columbia University 1959. According to Emspak, in about 1920, a relative died and the burial proceeded in the Hungarian Catholic Church in Schenectady (maybe St. Joseph's), my grandmother asked the priest to leave, and later pried the cross off the coffin and threw it into the street. Columbia Center for Oral History, Reminiscences of Julius Emspak 1959; http://id.loc.gov/authorities/names/no2002089284.

2. Skilled workers were often the backbone of the industrial union movement. They were the intellectual leaders in many plants, and their high level of skill insulated them to a degree from layoffs. For example, both Frank and Vic were not laid off during the depression.

3. Kaplan, Judy; Shapiro, Lynn; Eds, "Red Diapers, Growing Up in the Communist Party, (Chicago: University of Illinois Press 1998) ; for a personal history of other progeny of CP members and former members and those who organized their political or social life around the Party, participating in in CP led organizations or in coalitions within which Party members played important roles.

4. In 1940 4.9% of Americans had four or more years of college. My father had a Masters and was working on his thesis when he left Brown University in 1933-34.

5. The oral history conducted by James Pearlstein do not contain any serious discussion of this transition. Columbia Center for Oral History Reminiscences of Julius Emspak.

6. Emspak won a landmark decision allowing the use of the First Amendment to refuse to discuss political affiliations; Emspak vs. United States; 349 US 190, 75 S. Ct. 687, 99 L. Ed. 997 - Supreme Court, 1955 - Google Scholar.

7. It was the GE's main location for diesel electric engine production and the basis for the UE's survival as a representative of GE workers until 2019 when it was sold.

8. "After 27 Years, Yonkers Housing Desegregation Battle Ends Quietly in Manhattan Court" Yonkers was a segregated city. Litigation continued about integrating public housing until 2007 when the last of the lawsuits and injunctions was finally resolved www.nytimes.com/2007/05/02/nyregion/02yonkers.html".

9. When the camp organized reunions in New York City, the racial divisions remained in spite of the efforts in terms of camp staff and a meaningful level of black-white integration at the camper level. This speaks to the depth of racism in the culture and the society. A few weeks in the summer were simply way too little to overcome the other 49 weeks.

10. Buffalo Springfield "For What Its Worth" 1967. Buffalo Springfield was a Canadian band, most productive between 1966-68.

11. Comments by John Hamilton in . Johnson–Bair, K, 400 Saturdays, An Anthology of Vinyl Folklore, (Madison WI; Polyhymia Press,) p.9. K. Johnson-Blair interviewed patrons of a vinyl record shop over 400 Saturdays about their exposure to the "new" music of rock and roll.

12. "The Wild One" a movies starring Marlon Brando as a motorcycle gang leader; 1953.

13. Almost 55 years later, the University of Wisconsin Party with a Purpose commemorating 50 years after the antiwar DOW demonstrations at Madison, I was lucky to meet people from that same circle of New York friends. One of them was a palm reader in Hawaii.

14. For a rundown of the anti "take-cover" demonstrations among high school students in the NY Metro area, see"5000 Defy C.D. Drill" "Common Sense" Vol II, no. 7 May 2,1961" pg. 1; Emspak papers, WHS, Folder 4.200, Common Sense.

15. The organized youth movements of 1959 and 1960 were pretty small-almost microscopic. There was a CP oriented youth group- the Progressive Youth Organizing Committee. The League for Industrial Democracy, a group associated with the Socialist Party had a youth group- the Student League for Industrial Democracy- this eventually became SDS. A Student Peace Union existed- and there was a much larger Students for a SANE Nuclear Policy, the student wing of the National Committee for a SANE Nuclear Policy. I cannot recall any personal connections between the small groups and the teenagers active in the South - for example in the Montgomery Bus Boycott, which started in 1956. But the parents were connected to the Southern struggle and our student groups were out in the street and in the schools doing support work.

16. Steve Max, one of the leaders of the group describes the relationships this way. Common Sense was the publication of the F.D.R. Four Freedoms Club and the Tom Paine Club. Tom Paine was started in the fall of 1959. The initial membership was high school and college students who had been volunteers at the Youth March for Integrated Schools. Tom Paine met monthly to hear a speaker and have a discussion. The largest turnout we had was about 75 kids who came to hear the Cuban Consul General. When the Woolworth Boycott began I pro-

posed that the club get involved, but the majority of members said they wanted it to remain a discussion group.

17. An incomplete collection of Common Sense 1960-1962, as well as the founding documents of the Four Freedoms Club; Wisconsin Historical Society, Frank Emspak papers, folder 4.20.

18. Email, Steve Max to Frank Emspak, March 2019, Wisconsin Historical Society (WHS) Frank Emspak Papers, folder 4.20.

19. Common Sense, vol. II; no. 7 May 2, 1961 pg. 5); Emspak Papers, Correspondence with Steve Max, January 2018, WHS; Folder 4.200.

20. Both President Kennedy and President Nixon had been members of this committee. Not to be left out, v.p. Hubert H Humphry was a member of the Senate Internal Securities sub-committee. The supposedly more conservative Lyndon Johnson was a member of neither.

21. Common Sense, vol. II No. iii December 12, 1960; Emspak papers, WHS, Folder 4.200, Common Sense.

22. Common Sense editorial by Steve Max (12/12/1960 Common Sense December 12,1960 pg. 2; Emspak papers, WHS, Folder 4.200 Common Sense.

23. Common Sense, especially March and April 1961; vol. II no. 7; Letter from Steve Max pg. 6;. letter from Emspak to Common Sense; Emspak papers, WHS, Folder 4.200, Common Sense

24. See the scene in the Godfather when Michael says "you made plans for me?"

Chapter Two: The Most Expensive Badger Ever: University of Wisconsin 1961-65

I arrived in Madison, Wisconsin in September, 1961 as an earnest freshman. My life plan was focused on science. When I arrived back in Madison to start my sophomore year, my life was completely changed. And by the time I finished my undergraduate career at UW I was probably their most expensive student.

After a few months at UW, I recognized that I was not going to emulate my father's performance as a Phi Beta Kappa student. Although I was following the parental direction of becoming a scientist, I did not want to wait for that moment when I received the Nobel Prize to speak out about issues of importance.

In early 1962, I was asked by some supporters of the Communist Party to go to the World Youth Festival to be held in Moscow that summer. I wanted to go, and when I came home for the Easter break I raised the issue with my parents.

My father and I had were having increasingly charged discussions at the time. He opposed the trip, saying that it would come back to haunt me later. I said that he was being hypocritical, referencing his decision to leave Brown University and devote himself to the trade union movement — and in particular, his willingness to stand up to red baiting.

One night, my father went to bed feeling ill, rubbing his arms and jaw. At about 4 a.m. the ambulance arrived. My father had suffered a massive heart attack. He never recovered, barely gaining consciousness the next day before succumbing. He might have survived the attack had it happened just a few years later, but not as things were in 1962. He died a premature death at age 56. My father's death occurred less than two years after his final legal battles and victories.

The funeral resembled the scenes in the movie *The Front.* [1] Hundreds of people came to the Riverside Funeral home. But many did not sign the book indicating their presence. Many others stood across the street afraid to even be in the crowd in the chapel.

My father's passing was a huge tragedy for my mother, brother and me, and for the labor movement at large and for the United Electrical Workers — the union he essentially gave his life for. [2] My mother sacrificed everything for him. She worshiped him. They were looking forward to their 25th anniversary and had planned to retrace the cross-country trip they took in 1938.

But the disaster was even worse for my younger brother Steve. At 14-and-a-half, he was deprived of the nurturing, love and guidance that every young person needs. He inherited the intellectual gifts of our father, as well as the sense of style and design that our father possessed. Steve was also gifted musically and was the smarter of the two of us. In spite of this terrible loss, today he is a vice-president at the leading design & build audio/media systems firm in the United States. He is a natural dealmaker and a musician (with the band Drunk Unkles) still receiving residuals from lyrics he wrote for Aerosmith in the seventies ("Somebody"). My father's death plagued me with guilt. Did our heated argument contribute to his death? By April of 1962, we knew he had heart disease. He was trying to stop smoking. But years of government hounding, investigations, trials and betrayals had taken their toll. Although he died at 56, in photos from the time, he looks at least 10 years older.

The death of my father drew me closer to the UE family. Some officers, including Ernie DeMaio in Chicago and former UE national staffers Russ Nixon and Carl Marzari in New York, mentored Dolores and I. They helped us out in practical ways, too, providing things like a free place to go on vacation. These individuals had either been expelled or left the Communist Party voluntarily, but remained true to the UE. They were my father's closest friends.

Going back to the UW a few weeks later, it was clear going anywhere except to work in the summer of 1962 was now out of the question if I wanted to continue in school. I did not have the necessary grade point average as an out-of-state student to get any scholarships. Luckily, I was at low-cost Wisconsin.[3] That summer, I was able to rejoin my old kitchen crew where my total income equaled tuition plus the first three months of living expenses.

A second blow came later that summer, however. Dolores' parents, using the time-honored parental spying methods of eaves-dropping and reading personal mail, divined that Dolores and I were sleeping together. Her parents were a progressive couple when interracial marriage was still illegal in many states. One would think as progressive people they would have been supportive of a committed relationship. This was not the case. Dolores' parents would not let her return to the University of Chicago unless we agreed to stop seeing each other.

In a tearful scene, Dolores and I agreed. Once we did that, her parents said she could return to the University of Chicago. The split didn't last long, however, and by November Dolores and I had begun to see each other again.

When her parents found out, their reaction was even worse than before, initially refusing to let her out of the house and back to the University of Chicago. But Dolores was determined, and with the emotional support she got from her grandparents, Dolores did graduate from the University of Chicago in 1964. Only at the last minute, as she was going on stage, did her mother arrive at the ceremony. Dolores finished in 3 years, so we could get married. We had discussed our future and Dolores made it clear that living together was not an option. So, on one warm evening in 1963, I proposed and she said yes. We celebrated by going out to Paisan's restaurant, which for us at that time, was a big treat. Dolores reminds me I wore a blue shirt. Given how often I buy clothes, I might actually still have it. Dolores wore a batik dress. Ultimately, it took us another year to actually tie the knot.

For years thereafter, my father-in-law remained hostile, an attitude that sadly deprived him of a relationship with his grandchildren. It was only towards the end of his life that he relented and relations began to normalize. In short — what a waste.

Having worked as a chef saved me from financial disaster and, as it turned out, science saved me from complete depression — and the destruction of any academic future.

In 1962, I became an apprentice scientist in the laboratory of Dr. Walter Plaut, one of the three leading molecular biologists at UW. Working under his guidance gave me direction and allowed me to earn a living as a senior laboratory technician.

My photographs of cell division were recognized in published papers — something that was uncommon for undergraduate lab assistants at the time.[4] Still, I realized I was not cut out for a future as a scientist. Aside from any academic weaknesses, I was too drawn by the outside world of political action. I told Professor Plaut I could not accept the graduate position the department was going to offer me.

Madison: Conventional on the Surface

When I arrived in Madison that day in September of 1961, there were still places that would not rent to Jews — and many more that would not rent to people of color. I was deposited at 422 North Murray street, greeted, assigned a room and began to unpack when another person showed up claiming it was his room. His name was Michael Eisenscher. "Well," I thought. "Emspak or Eisenscher — they all sound the same right?" It turned out (after some panic on my part) that I was supposed to be next door.

It also turned out that Michael was close to the Communist Party, if not a member. We have been friends and comrades ever since, working together on a wide variety of mobilizations and projects.

Culturally, Madison was a pretty conventional place in the autumn of 1961. *In loco parentis* was the rule, meaning women had to be at their place of residence by 10 p.m. weekdays and 12 p.m. weekends unless they had permission to be somewhere else. This was actually taken quite seriously. The drinking age for hard liquor was 21. You could get beer at 18. The UW Memorial Union served low-alcohol beer — what was called "3.2 beer."

While Madison seemed to have more bars than people, most of my real activity took place at various house parties where liquor was freely available. These parties also had music that I had never before heard — especially Big Bill Broonzy's blues, but also good rock and roll. Often there was a party at the home of Danny Kalb, who later developed a national presence with the Blues Project.

On Saturdays and Sundays in autumn, you could walk along the streets of Madison and not miss a single play of either a UW or Packers game. That was good because it cost a couple of dollars to go to the football games and freshmen were urged to buy tickets.

The social hierarchy was set by the fraternities and sororities. Homecoming was a big deal. The left challenged the establishment culture with a Folk Music club led in part by Steve Watt — and a film society led in part by my roommate Bill Fixx. We brought in artists and screened movies that were not then part of the mainstream. Progressive musicians had to fight for space on the Memorial Union terrace — UW had barred musicians from performing there. There were arrests and scuffles, but by 1964 musicians had won the right to play on the terrace.

We also challenged the military culture. The high point of the official social season was the Military Ball — replete with the ROTC officers in their dress uniforms.

An anti-military ball took shape in response under the impetus of Ken Knudsen, a Wisconsin born and bred anarchist. By 1963, the mid-February event was attracting well over 300 people and filling the Great Hall of the Memorial Union. A satirical skit, heavy on the politics and akin to SNL's Weekend Update before it existed, was one of the biggest draws. I did a JFK impression that made me the star of the show, running up on stage in a bathing suit — a knock on JFK's physical fitness campaign. I copied JFK's accent and lampooned his descriptions of Black Muslims. But a couple of years later, as the war in Vietnam escalated, serious political opposition overtook simply making fun of the president, and the event died.

The thriving left wing infrastructure made it possible for me and many others to survive and prosper. The Socialist club was one part of the structure. The Green Lantern Eating Co-op as well as the Groves Co-op for women students was another.

Students who lived in fraternities or dorms ate at their residence. For the hundreds of others, eating co-ops like the Green Lantern was a solution. The co-op served lunch and dinner six-days-a-week. Members took turns serving and cleaning. The Green Lantern plugged me into the progressive political activity of Madison. After dinner, individuals made announcements as to upcoming political activity or the special (and illegal) steam tunnel tour. The Green Lantern offered financial and political support to various progressive organizations especially for activists coming from the South.

The Socialist Club: The Flying Bolsheviks

The UW Madison left was unique as compared to other left stirrings on other campuses. A Socialist Club served as a common home for the left movement. Leaders of the club were a group of very knowledgeable Marxist-oriented graduate students of William Appleman Williams. They also produced the newly-launched publication *Studies on the Left*. The club included an activist wing led by a mixture of Wisconsin radicals and movement people from New York and Chicago. It also had a traveling touch football team — The Flying Bolsheviks.

My participation was welcomed in the club, as well as in Madison's Ban the Bomb movement — a movement to ban atmospheric nuclear testing. Leaders of the Socialist club were prominent for the "non-exclusion" platform in the student's National Committee for a Sane Nuclear Policy. Adult SANE, led by Norman Thomas, expelled student SANE in early 1962 because of our unwillingness to endorse exclusion on the basis of political affiliation — especially communists. Members of the Socialist Club founded SANITY magazine in 1962, which was conceived as the theoretical and practical voice of the new student-led peace movement. The shock of my father's death, however, along with concomitant academic and financial challenges, meant I did not contribute very much to the magazine. Those of the core group that were in Madison in 1965 became the core of the Madison Committee to End the War in Vietnam.

Kentucky

Far from being "just talk," the club believed in action. In 1961, a president of the club was arrested in Mississippi for helping to register Black voters. Within the Socialist Club, the Communist Party wanted to expand the club's focus to support a union struggle that was both a social movement and a union reform movement. The strike by eastern Kentucky coal miners provided that opportunity.

In early 1963, coal miners in Hazard, Kentucky struck to prevent the closing of four United Mine Workers Hospitals scheduled for April. The strikers had asked progressive groups all over the country for aid, specifically, food. The Socialist Club decided to answer that call. [5]

Gene Dennis [6] Michael Eisenscher [7] Roy Lowe, Don Bluestone, and I drove down to Hazard with a station wagon loaded with food. Aside from the direct support, our goal was to interview the miners and other Hazard citizens and report back to the *Daily Cardinal* — the UW student newspaper. The material was ultimately given to the Wisconsin Historical Society, and has found use in films about Hazard.

Arriving in Hazard, we seemed to enter the 19th century. Out of town, on top of a hill stood the Citadel motel. Mine owners stayed there. Down in the valley was the town of Hazard, where the striking miners lived — and voted — so the mayor and police were sympathetic to the miners.

But we were arrested on the way back from our planning meeting with the miners. The police wanted to know what some out-of-town Northerners were doing in Hazard. From their point of view, the best way to find out was to lock us up in jail overnight until we could talk to the police chief the next morning.

The jail was made of big chunks of coal. We were put in a rather large cell and were made comfortable sitting on what looked like long sausages — but which were, in fact, dynamite. It was quite safe as one needed detonators to set them off. One could even smoke. Of course, the dynamite was mostly an ironic touch. In theory, we were being held on "suspicion." Someone had blown up a Louisville and Nashville Railroad bridge a few days before we got there.

That evening, one of the deputies asked what I was studying.

I said, "Zoology."

"What's that? he asked.

I told him, and we got into a discussion of evolution. He informed me that one; we were in the buckle of the Bible belt. And two, evolution was a passing style — sort of like wearing your belt buckle sideways.

The issue of evolution was more controversial than the strike. The deputy urged me not to talk about it with people when we got out. To settle the evolution issue the deputy decided to bring in the town intellectual — the Connecticut General Insurance agent. He had graduated from Yale or Harvard. So, around 6 a.m. we had a philosophical discussion about evolution.

A little later, the deputies informed us the police chief was on his way to see us. They told us this story about the chief: "Sometime earlier in the year, the chief went out for a walk, but tripped on the sidewalk. As he fell, he grabbed his gun, which went off. The bullet went through the window of the bank, setting off the alarm. The deputies rushed out thinking the bank was being held-up. Order was restored a few minutes later and no one was hurt."

Having been thus briefed on the police chief, we awaited his arrival. After introductions he understood that we were in town for the miners, that we had brought supplies for them and wanted to do interviews about the situation. All was forgiven.

He told us, however, not to go outside of the town limits as we would be arrested by the Perry county sheriffs. We usually had a Hazard policeman and an armed miner along with us when we went to meet the striking workers.

Our many interviewees included the anti-mineworker owner of the *Hazard Herald*. She thought people on welfare should be jailed and people like us were essentially vermin.

The Perry County sheriff's department, meanwhile, had learned of our presence. One of the miners and I were walking down the street following an interview, when a Perry County deputy pulled up alongside us and stuck a shotgun out the window of his pickup truck. The miner put his gun on my shoulder. The deputy explained that we had until sundown to get out of town. He said if we did not leave more or less immediately — he could not "protect" us as we wended our way out of Kentucky through Perry County. There was no other escape route.

The miners decided the Perry County sheriff was serious, so we made plans to depart. When we got to the city line, a state police escort took us all the way to Cincinnati —about 4 hours away at a very high rate of speed. So much for Kentucky.

Wisconsin Student Employees Association (WISEM)

I needed to work to stay in school as my summer income was not quite enough to carry me through the semester. Although organizing the working class was discussed theoretically in the Socialist Club — the reality was there were about 3,000 unorganized student workers right there on campus earning seventy-five-cents-an-hour — well below the federal minimum wage of $1.25. Since we were state employees, not federal or private sector employees, we could be paid less than the Federal minimum wage. For those like me who were working to make it through the year, fifty-cents-an-hour was a huge issue.

In September of 1963, Michael Eisenscher and I began the organization of the Wisconsin Student Employees Union (WISEM). From the beginning, we conceived of the organization as a union — not a protest group or a student group which needed university endorsement. We, instead, claimed rights under the National Labor Relations Act.

We initially went to the Madison Federation of Labor for support — but we were treated like a joke and shown the door. Two local unions, however, were sympathetic — the Firefighters and the Teamsters Local 695 as well as District 11 of the UE, led by Ernie DeMaio in Chicago.

Our goal was to raise the UW student employee minimum wage from seventy-five-cents-per-hour to the Federal level of $1.25/hr. Public sector bargaining legislation specifically excluded academic staff and faculty employed by UW from coverage. The UW was under no obligation to recognize a union. The legislation said nothing about student workers. Our view was a worker was a worker — and it did not really matter what the state thought.

The university reacted in what would become typical style. I was told they were going to expel me. We treated threats like this as a violation of labor law, not in reference to the UW code of conduct. Nathan Feinsinger, the GM-UAW national contract mediator, agreed with our view and offered pro bono legal services. While I was sitting in his office he called his "good friend" Fred Harvey Harrington, president of the University. He indicated how much legal trouble he was going to cause his "good friend" President Harrington if the expulsion went through. The issue was dropped.

About three hundred student workers joined the union. The UW's bargaining committee, made up of liberal professors, however, never agreed to recognize the union. A few years later, when the teaching assistants also organized, it took a strike before UW would agree to recognize them.

We won the buck-twenty-five — but no recognition. A rumor got started in May of 1964, shortly before exam week, that the Teamsters were not going to deliver toilet paper. While deliveries did continue, the university also took a new look at the situation. In August, they raised the minimum wage to $1.25. That was really a great victory for us and a big assist to many student workers.

That how I figure I became the university's most expensive undergraduate.

The efforts we made with that small organization illustrated several things:

1) We had the sense under Michael's leadership to go outside the UW and seek progressive trade unions to help us — and the Teamsters local was a progressive union at that time.

2) The liberal professors within the university were fighting us on campus.

3) It was possible to win.

4) The established labor unions would have nothing to do with us (even refusing to give us official NLRB union sign up cards). Ignoring such a huge pool of labor was, to put the best face on it, simply stupid. The UW was, and remains, a low-wage leader in Madison, in part because of the low wages paid to students.

The visit to Kentucky made me think more about the labor movement — and how separate students and entities like the Socialist Club were from that world.[8]

Towards the end of 1963, the Socialist Club was re-evaluating its role and I wrote a guide to our discussions.

A campus-based socialist organization was not enough. Our relationship to the working class was zero. Among other problems, we did not present a believable alternative to capitalism — contributing to the idea Americans "have sunk into apathy and cynicism" and increasing political disengagement. I thought the alienation of many from the political process was a contributing factor to the rise of fascism in Germany.

I did not, at this point, understand the deep effects of racism, but I did recognize the effectiveness of the Taft-Hartley Act in decapitating unions. Especially the use of injunctions, noting JFK had interpreted the injunctive powers granted in Taft-Hartley as widely as possible. Injunctions are a judicial order that restrains a person from beginning or continuing an action threatening or invading the legal right of another, or that compels a person to carry out a certain act. I concluded the strike is the fundamental strength unions have —and without it, and without using it, the individual worker cannot be defended. Eventually, unions would be unable to provide for even the most minimal demands of their members, returning us to the open shop era of the twenties.[9]

I also recognized the peace movement could not succeed without some control over production. The US economy was dependent on arms production — and a large part of the industrial labor movement owed their employment to it.[10]

Early Rumblings

In reality, left wing organizations had only marginal influence on the overall life of the university during the early sixties. But that abruptly changed in the autumn of 1964.

I assumed the chairmanship of the Socialist club — now less of a gathering place for all leftists and more of a coalition of different organizations — right after I left work and returned to the campus in September 1964. But there was no actual organizing activity going on, including mobilizations in support of civil rights.

Then the Berkeley Free Speech Movement (FSM) burst upon the scene. The UC Berkeley administration in California, acting on behalf of the Board of Regents, decided to bar political advocacy inside the traditional student free speech area — and arrested Jack Weinberg, the person manning the CORE (Congress of Racial Equality) table. The action sparked a huge outpouring of student support and blockading of a police car for more than a day — with Jack in it.[11]

Bettina Aptheker,[12] a founder of the DuBois Club and CP member, outlined what happened over the next few weeks (The material is available at the official Free Speech Movement website).

"The Free Speech Movement was born. It lasted through mid-December. In the end, after a sit-in in the main administration building that resulted in the arrests of nearly 800 students, a strike of faculty, graduate students, and staff sanctioned by the local labor council that paralyzed the campus, and the support of the entire leadership of the Black-led Civil Rights Movement, beginning with Dr. Martin Luther King, Jr., we won our central demands."[13]

Because Aptheker was the daughter of one of the leading figures of the American CP and identified as such, it had a positive influence on how students saw both the DuBois Club and the Communist Party. For me, as a red diaper baby, it was a great affirmation. If anything, I was jealous — Bettina was a great leader and doing the right thing at the right time. I wished I could have been at Berkeley.

At Wisconsin, as in other universities, the Free Speech Movement galvanized students and frightened administrators. In Madison, the Socialist Club, the newly-founded DuBois Club and others, organized a Free Speech Movement support chapter. When Aptheker came to the UW to meet with FSM supporters, she also met with Provost Robin Flemming and others who claimed they wanted to understand the issues at Berkeley. Of course, the UW was not interested in meeting with the left on the UW campus, nor would it meet with the American Federation of Teachers local union. We staged a rally in support of the FSM, which turned out to be a huge success. Something was clearly stirring within the student body.[14]

But not enough, it turned out, to produce any identifiable actions. Students went home for the holidays.

Out of UW

In January 1965, my undergraduate career came to an abrupt, but successful halt one semester early. UW expelled me in October, claiming my two-and-half-years of graduate-level lab work were fake. However, after the intervention of Dr. Plaut and the chairs of the Botany and Zoology departments, the university allowed me to take a 12-credit exam in basic Biology. I passed — and suddenly gained a whole semester — becoming eligible to graduate with a degree in Zoology in January 1965.

Several consequences came of this saga. I learned that for every university rule there is an equal and opposite prevailing rule. But immediate graduation had its downsides, too. I was eligible to be drafted as soon as I left the UW, assuming I notified my draft board. Dolores and I would also be minus one paycheck since I was being paid to work in the lab. I would be unemployed as soon as my student status ended.

I graduated just in time to be available for a commitment to what became the anti-Vietnam war movement. But in mid-January 1965, Dolores and I were broke. I did not have a job and no plans to further my education. I did know that I wanted to do something about the escalating war. But I also knew this — 3,000 students times a wage increase of 50-cents-per-hour meant that each hour of student work cost the UW about $1500. Many of us worked a minimum of 10 hours per week. That came to $15,000 per week times the 18 week semester = $270,000 per semester.

They probably should have given me a scholarship.

1. My father's passing also removed a leading intellectual voice from the left and union movement. His last published piece "The Private Ownership of Public Property" Monthly Review, June 1962 vol. 14 number two pg. 96 is an illustration of the depth of his thinking. The article raised the issue that public monies financed R and D which was then turned over to the "private sector" The Internet is a current example.

2. The Front- a film by Woody Allen, 1976 attacking the blacklist.

3. Full tuition for out of state students in the 1961-62 school years was $362.50 per semester. It went up a bit in the next couple of years by the total for four years at that time was about $2100 since I graduated a semester early.

4. Nash,D.N; Plaut, Walter; "On the Presence of DNA in Larval Salivary Gland Nucleoli in Drosophila Melanogaster" *The Journal of Cell Biology*, 1965 vol. 27; no 3 pp 682-686; Emspak papers, WHS, Folder 3.385.

5. Leaflet "Hazard" Socialist Club, Madison Wisconsin March 1963; Emspak papers, WHS, Folder 3.378.

6. Gene Dennis was the son of Eugene Dennis, who had been the General Secretary of the CPUSA prior to his death in 1961.

7. Michael Eisenscher was the son of long time Wisconsin CP leader Sigmund Eisenscher. At this time he was organizing for the CP in Wisconsin.

8. Frank Emspak, Notes for Discussion-Socialist Club, spring 1963; Emspak papers, WHS, Folder 3.378.

9. Ibid.

10. Lockshin, Arnold, , "The Crisis in Vietnam: The Story of US Involvement" April? 1963. Published by the Socialist Club.

11. Free Speech Movement Short Histories available in Free Speech Movement Archives The only FSM website created & maintained by FSM vets source of original FSM documents and scholarship.

12. Bettina Aptheker was the daughter of Herbert Aptheker the leading theoretician of the CP and an accomplished scholar.

13. Free Speech Movement Short Histories available in Free Speech Movement Archives The only FSM website created & maintained by FSM vets source of original FSM documents and scholarship.

14. *The Daily Cardinal*, Vol LXXV no.63 December 12, 1964 pg. 2.

Chapter Three: What are We Fighting For?

On a hot August night in Washington, D.C., my friends and I stood in front of the White House, watching a handful of individual pacifists getting arrested for blocking the driveway. We had come to Washington to participate in the Congress of Unrepresented Peoples, determined to find a way to disrupt the escalating war in Vietnam. My friends and I, however, did not think individual actions alone, no matter how brave, were enough. We wanted to build a mass movement for peace and social justice strong enough to prevent President Lyndon Johnson from speaking anywhere in the U.S. in support of the war.

By late 1967, we had succeeded. It was almost impossible for President Johnson to speak anywhere outside of military installations or closed conferences without confronting citizens opposed to the war in Vietnam. Our journey to achieve this level of opposition to the war in Vietnam had started eight months earlier in January.

The year 1965 marked the emergence of a movement against the war in Vietnam. By June of 1965, Committees to End the War in Vietnam had sprung up throughout the U.S. and quickly became the organizational centers of the antiwar movement. One of the most robust committees grew in Madison, Wisconsin, building on the prior activities of the Socialist Club and the cultural network of the local left.

In early 1965, graduate students and faculty had taken the lead in opposition to the war, largely through lobbying and policy work. That changed by the end of 1965, when a wave of younger activists joined the antiwar movement, adopting a new strategy focused on direct action: The new generation of activists was breaking with the old. The teach-in movement was founded on the principle that the policy makers were ignorant of the real situation in Vietnam and if they and their fellow citizens really knew the facts, then the policy makers would see the errors of their ways and end the military intervention in Vietnam. In Madison, those of us who rejected the war entirely and refused to negotiate over its terms were not included in those teach-ins or attempted dialogues with administration spokespeople and pro-war think tank experts.

By mid-year 1965, we had organized the Madison Committee to End the War in Vietnam. Many of the Committees to End the War, like the Vietnam Day Committee in Berkeley (but unlike the more liberal antiwar organizations and commentators like the Committee for a SANE Nuclear Policy, or Miles McMillin of the Madison Capitol Times), did not believe that the war in Vietnam was a fluke, or a forgivable mistake, perpetrated by uninformed leaders. In late spring of 1965, we moved from debate to confrontation when so-called "truth teams"— really, representatives of the U.S. government on a public relations campaign — arrived on campus to tell students the "truth" about the war. We challenged the "truth sayers," and confronted them with our narrative. Unwilling to debate us, they left town.

In Madison, the antiwar leadership shifted to those of us who saw it would only be by direct action and the mobilization of thousands that the war could be brought to an end.

As in many universities, the Committee to End the War in Vietnam leadership in Madison was composed of student activists from a variety of left organizations, but was not dominated by any one of them. The Vietnam Day Committee in Berkeley, as well as certain other city-based committees, were also broadly based. Students for a Democratic Society (SDS) initiated resistance in many other universities, especially in the Ivy League.

Many of us in the student movement knew that we needed to find a way to come together in broader coalitions. Many of us recognized the leading role the Black-led civil rights movement, especially the Student Nonviolent Coordinating Committee, played as they connected the dots between the war, political rights for Black people and racism.

During the winter, spring and summer, I had been working at the University of Wisconsin Hospitals and clinics as a lab technician using skills I had learned as an undergrad. I was also helping to publish and edit *The Crisis*, the mimeographed paper of the Madison Committee.[1] In that capacity, I was in contact with leaders of most of the larger Committees to End the War in Vietnam all over the country, as well as with the various factions of our movement in Madison.

The Vietnam Day Committee (VDC) in Berkeley had a huge event in May called "Vietnam Day." At that time, they raised the idea of an international day of protest against the war in Vietnam. The VDC assumed that those of us who opposed the war were the majority, not a frightened, marginalized minority — and if so, we needed to get out there and show it via music, posters, speeches, marches and civil disobedience. As the VDC call for action said:

"Don't just petition for free speech, fight for it. And don't just complain about the war, get out and mobilize against it."

The Vietnam Day Committee brought together anyone who was opposed to the war in Vietnam, almost in a celebration of opposition. Within that context, specific slogans were not as important as the feeling and general demand that the U.S. should immediately get out of Vietnam. Jefferson Airplane played, then an unknown group. The VDC threw down the gauntlet of youth, exuberance and a clear desire to end the war in Vietnam.

Their vision and brio resonated with me. Almost immediately, I got in touch with them and actively began to organize support for the initiative. At the same time, as I was working as editor of *The Crisis,* I was in touch with many of the antiwar committees in the Midwest and East Coast and began to urge people to support the idea. Leaders in the SDS Vietnam summer project also began publicizing the call.

In July 1965, a group of progressives had begun meeting in Washington D.C. The leadership included Staughton Lynd of Yale University and education director of Mississippi Freedom Summer of 1964, as well as Bob Parris (Bob Moses) the visionary behind the Freedom Summer. [2]

The group called for a Congress of Unrepresented Peoples to declare Peace in Vietnam and to assemble in Washington DC on August 6th. That day was the anniversary of the day that the US dropped the atomic bomb on Hiroshima and was commemorated throughout the world by anti-nuclear activists.[3]

The call related the fight for democracy in the U.S. to opposition to the war — which, as they pointed out, "we did not declare ... we intend to have a government which truly represents us even if we have to create it ourselves."[4] The Congress call resonated with my thinking that only a movement which fought for real democracy could win against the war in Vietnam.

Organizers of the event did not think that something more concrete would come out of the Congress. When they sent out their initial invitations, they thought "maybe a time table on the various programs would emerge."[5] While it didn't start out that way, the Congress became a focal point for the organization and vigorous launch of the International Days of Protest.

August 1965: The National Coordinating Committee to End the War in Vietnam (NCC)

On the morning after our White House appearance, the Congress of Unrepresented People convened. We were the unrepresented people, but we would not be silent or unrepresented for long.

The five hundred or so Congress participants met out in the open on the Washington Mall. It was hot. The humidity was stifling. There was little shade — and no bathrooms. I was afraid half of us would get sunstroke. The leading pacifist organizations and many of the college-based Committees and civil rights activists from the South were present. [6] Because of the mobilizing efforts of SNCC, there was a significant number of Black students and community activists. Absent from the Congress was the liberal anti-communist wing of the anti-war movement, exemplified by the leadership of the Committee for a SANE nuclear policy.

Support for the Vietnam Day Committee's ideas of an International Days of Protest matured as the Congress went on. On Saturday, activists founded The National Coordinating Committee to End the War in Vietnam, which would become the national organizing node for that activity.

Participants wanted a national center which was not aligned with, or under the control, of any particular political group. Madison was chosen because it was seen as more or less politically independent and had an infrastructure due to the Madison Committee.

I was chosen chairman of the National Coordinating Committee to End the War in Vietnam (NCC) partially because I was known to many of individual activists due to the Crisis and my correspondence and partially due to my activities with the network of peace activists associated with the student committee for a SANE nuclear policy. I don't think anyone thought they were choosing a national leader. To govern the NCC, we set up a steering committee which included representatives from individual antiwar committees as well as from established groups like the Committee for Nonviolent Action.

The NCC was clear in its purpose. "Its objective is to strengthen local groups. We in no way look upon the National Committee as supplanting already established national political groups, but only to supplement their activities and involve other, heretofore isolated groups in national activity."[7] The existence of SNCC and their practice, commitment and vision were a major influence on the thinking and means of mobilization that the NCC attempted.[8]

I did not see the NCC as establishing "policy" for others or slogans to which antiwar organizations had to accept. We saw ourselves as an expression of the movement, a stimulator — and yes, as spokespeople for a movement. But not the defining leader or political director. Our framework was the war was immoral and wrong, and the U.S. had to get out as soon as possible.

The leadership of the Congress was overwhelmingly composed of people who had challenged the state via nonviolent direct action, so we thought it perfectly reasonable to go to our U.S. House of Representatives and declare peace:

"On August 9th workshop participants will be invited to join us in:
Walking towards the chamber of the House of Representatives to occupy the seats,
If we are stopped, to sitting down at the point where we are stopped;
Proclaiming ourselves a Congress of Unrepresented people;
Declaring peace in the form of statements by individuals

and community representatives; ... Persisting in this activity (if necessary) until all have been arrested."[9]

The next day, almost five hundred marchers and observers gathered near the Washington Monument and set out towards the House of Representatives. Bob Moses and Staughton Lynd led the march. Early on, someone threw red paint on the two, and both Bob and Staughton were arrested. As the newly minted chairman, I was asked to lead the marchers. We were accompanied by many of the SNCC national staff, and others experienced in dealing with the federal police, notably Donna Allen of Women Strike for Peace. After we had gone about seven or eight blocks, the police blocked the sidewalk and told us to stop.

Most of the marchers sat down. I informed the police that we had a right to walk on the sidewalk and proceed. The chief (I guess he was the chief, all I remember is that he had gold crowns) yelled something and the police began beating and arresting people. We began to sing as the police took all of us — about two hundred in all — to the old D.C. jail. No one had a chance to read statements or declare peace. The police made one big mistake from a public relations point of view. They started clubbing a reporter from *The New York Times* and that was the picture that many people saw on August 10th.

After being put in a holding pen with about twenty-five others, I was called before a judge and remanded back to the cells. No bail was offered — in contrast to almost everyone else, including Bob and Staughton.

It was now relatively late at night. I was sitting on the steps on some tier inside the D.C. jail with no food, no bathroom and no way to contact anyone. The D.C. jail, as all urban jails then (and now), was overcrowded primarily with people of color. In the midst of this, a large number of white activists were suddenly deposited.

After a while, one of the prisoners came up to me and told me not to worry. They knew what was going on and that he didn't expect any trouble. He was also concerned that I was just sitting on the stairs, unassigned.

At about midnight, the guards found me and told me I was free to go. I never did see a judge again. Then, as if in something out of a movie, the huge wooden 19th century double doors swung open, and I was told to walk across a wide cobblestone courtyard to the actual prison gates — also huge wooden doors. I had no idea what was going on.

But as I reached the second set of doors, they opened and outside, more or less completely surprised, were our Madison contingent. As I learned later, Women Strike for Peace leader Donna Allen and Russ Nixon, previously the D.C. lobbyist for the UE and then the Editor of the *National Guardian* had intervened with a federal judge to grant me bail and release. I think the charge was disorderly conduct. I have not been able to obtain any records.

On our way home, the car's transmission gave out on the Pennsylvania Turnpike at about 3 a.m. After awhile, someone identifying himself a "troubleshooter" pulled up alongside us. He said his job was to cruise up and down the turnpike looking for commercial vehicles that had broken down and then to contact the appropriate repair and tow service.

He wanted to know if we had anything to do with the arrests in D.C. We said "yes" — expecting the worst. However, after confiding in us that he thought the war was stupid, he took us to his house, gave us a place to stay, arranged for the car to be towed and repaired, and did so all at a price we could afford. This, because we had no money, was practically nothing. We took this as a harbinger of good things to come. If, in the middle of Pennsylvania, in the middle of the night, someone would stop and be helpful and make clear he supported what we were doing —then how could we be wrong in our estimate of the American people?

While the Pennsylvania experience gave us hope many people in the U.S. were willing to question the country's role in Vietnam or even reject it — this was not the opinion of a significant portion of Madison progressives. Miles McMillin, editor of *The Capital Times*, Madison's liberal newspaper, reflected the view of most, if not all "liberal" political commentators of the time.

"Emspak is an example of a very important element in this national debate," McMillin wrote. "It is the question of whether the Communists should identify themselves and the part they are playing in it. It makes a lot of difference whether one is hypocritically serving the nationalist aims of China or the Soviet Union in this struggle for peace." He used my refusal to accept his framework to justify his headline, "Commies Should Put Their Cards on the Table," and as he put it, "stop ducking the question."[10]

Although McMillin indicated he was opposed to the war, "which may turn out to be one of the most stupid ventures in our history," he dismissed our concerns with the war and its effect on American democracy.

McMillin went on to attack me, claiming I would hurt the movement. The whole tenor of his piece was focused on that issue. Although McMillin declared he was not like Joseph McCarthy, he was, in fact, fixated on whether or not I was a Communist. His rationale: "Those who want to discredit peace efforts are relying mainly on the fact that Communists are involved. Thus the whole movement is discredited."

He concluded that the "Peace Mongers" — the activists in the antiwar movement — come out and identify themselves as to whether they were Communists or not.

At almost the same time, the convention of the National Student Association (NSA) was being held in Madison. The NSA was by far the largest grouping of college student government organizations in the U.S. Vice-President Hubert Humphry gave a major speech addressing civil rights. But in the midst of this speech lauding peaceful civil rights protests, he went after the Congress of Unrepresented People. "We have been informed by some persons that they are 'unrepresented.' And we have been told that, therefore, they acquire the warrant to violate necessary laws relating to public assembly and safety.... it is incumbent upon those who demonstrate against our nation's policies in Southeast Asia to recognize that dissent is one thing, decision is another." [11]

While HHH spoke about responsibility and law and order, our office was subjected to illegality and disorder.

Unknown assailants attacked the office, smashing the windows and ransacking the place. We called the police, who said there was nothing they could do. Attacks continued nightly. After about the fourth time, I called the police again and informed them we would take direct physical action against the next person who broke into the office. (I really said "shoot him.") After that, there wasn't even any bubblegum left on the sidewalk outside. The incident caused me to believe in one of three things — the tooth fairy, coincidence or collusion. Or at least foreknowledge by the police about the attacks. I compare the actions of the Madison police to the actions of all police forces in the U.S. against the Black Panthers, who also said they would resist vandalism of their offices by force if necessary. Obviously, because we were white (mostly) we were not shot, arrested and incarcerated for defending our legitimate political rights.

The International Days of Protest: From Hue to Finland to Iowa

The new movement burst into the American consciousness with the International Days of Protest Against the War in Vietnam on October 15th and 16th. We published the call for the Days of Protest in early September 1965:

"America is at war…the soothing words of the president and his advisors cannot change or obscure the fact that many of those dead and maimed have been killed by Americans…

America is afraid. She is afraid of giving the vote to the people of South Vietnam. She is afraid to allow the people of Vietnam to decide their own destiny. The American government denies the South Vietnamese the vote just as surely as American Negroes have been suppressed for 300 years…..

So America bombs. Our country bombs, burns and tortures. Neither the cries of an orphaned child, nor the pain of a childless mother disturbs the present administration…

Not only the South Vietnamese and the American Negro have been disenfranchised, but all Americans have been disenfranchised. The last election has shown to be an echo, not a choice. As far as Vietnam was concerned the two nominees were but one.

Americans have been given no choice. Unless we leave the confines of the usual government channels, we shall not be heard…….Inaction is assent. …

We call for assemblies where all concerned, student and non-student, black and white, soldier and citizen will come together to show their opposition to the war in Vietnam.

We must show our government that the constituency of the great society stands behind peace in Vietnam. We must show that a Great Society does not include the war in Vietnam. We can prove, if we work together, that our government does not have the grassroots support it needs to carry out the war."[12]

The night before the announcement, our little staff had absolutely no clue as to what would happen next. [13] We had heard some rumors the Madison committee was mobilizing to demonstrate, and others were going to try and make a citizen's arrest on the base commander at the neighboring Truax Field Air National Guard Base. Activists from Berkeley and elsewhere sent positive vibes.

At about 6 a.m. on Friday October 15th, I received a phone call from a radio station in Rochester, New York. The station called me, they said, because I was the chairman of the National Co-Coordinating Committee to End the War in Vietnam. They wanted to know what was going on and told me that there was a demonstration in Rochester against the war that was part of International Days of Protest Against the War. I had never heard from anyone in Rochester before that moment. I knew that something important was happening.

When I got to our office a few blocks away, I discovered all the national TV and radio networks were camped out waiting for a statement. Our staff was as shocked and thrilled as I was. The call for the international days of protest had worked! We began receiving telegrams from all over the world — the National Students Union of Morocco, the President of the Student Government at Huê University in Vietnam, The National Women's Federation of the People's Republic of China, in addition to peace organizations in Finland, France and Italy. There were also demonstrations in many European cities, as well as in Japan.

In New York City, Eric Weinberger of the Fifth Avenue Peace Parade Committee, said the turnout was thirty to forty thousand protesters. "It was the biggest peace demonstration since the end of WWI. A weekend of great meaning."[14] Weinberger also mentioned one of the speakers was the person who wrote the "resist the draft" letter from McComb, Mississippi. Events occurred throughout the US — far beyond New York and San Francisco, most importantly.

The International Days of Protest also marked the first time there was a coordinated *international* response to a call for action against the War in Vietnam. This was a huge step forward — especially as it was not based on inter-party relationships. The antiwar movement went beyond that.

The International Days of Protest also marked the entry of public and widespread antiwar activity in the South. The Black freedom movement showed the relationship of the freedom movement in the South to the antiwar movement at large. But there was also activity amongst predominantly white students in Nashville, Louisville and Austin — and many other places. The IDP's success laid the basis for a Southern antiwar mobilization on February 12th.

Taken together, hundreds of demonstrations occurred throughout the U.S. Thousands participated in cities large and small. There was an amazing amount of international solidarity. Nothing like this had happened before.

The Days of Protest were so effective because everyone focused on ending the war, and expressed that determination in any way they saw fit in their local communities. We engaged people where they were politically — and had that message brought back to their neighbors.

We attacked the war instead of each other and released tremendous intellectual and organizational energy in the process. At the end of the day, it was clear the antiwar movement had shifted from more or less small and isolated groups — to a growing and self-consciousness movement. All portions of the activist antiwar movement responded, from SDS to pacifist organizations like the Committee for Nonviolent Action. Women's Strike for Peace and/or the Women's International League for Peace and Freedom were drivers, as were the Quakers.

Throughout the South, some who made up the heart and soul of SNCC and the Mississippi Freedom Summer were on the move, encouraged by organizations like the Highlander Center, which had trained many of the key activists. But in spite of the widespread support by community and campus organizations and the nonsectarian nature of the movement, the more anticommunist liberal organizations like the Committee for a SANE Nuclear policy, as well as many liberal Democrats who had begun to question the war, stood aside from the mobilizations.

Many individuals found that their lives changed as a result of the mobilization. For example, Mike Locker, who became a leader in SDS, was then at Earlham College — a small liberal arts school in Richmond, Indiana. He and his friends heard about the International Days of Protest. As he described it to me many years later, they decided to do something as a result and sat-in at the draft board. Arrested and charged, they fought the case in court. But as Locker put it, it was the beginning of a new way to see reality, and it propelled him into a period of activism that has lasted a lifetime.

Richard Wolff, who has become a noted economist and leader in the effort to organize worker owned co-ops, was a student in 1965. Wolff was tasked with going around the country and encouraging people to get involved in the antiwar effort. As he recounted it to me in June of 2018, he would go into some town after we (NCC) had contacted people, hold a meeting and go to the next town. What astounded him, he told me, was that in each small town people showed up. There were real meetings with real community people who were willing to take a stand.

The extensive media coverage was restricted to a cold war framework and sought to dismiss our motives and arguments, suggesting that we were draft-dodgers or worse — constantly raising the issue of communism and patriotism. In my hometown of Yonkers, *The Herald Statesman* trumpeted "Yonkers Youth Sparks Big Viet War Protest".[15] They quoted my mother: "No matter what differences they have in the means they use, they are all working for the same end, peace. Our family has always been dedicated to the idea of 'seeing to it that the greatest number of people can enjoy the greatest number of benefits that this country has to offer.'" A couple of days later, the paper printed a typical shallow attack. "Civic Leaders are asking, are the marchers just trying to get out of the draft? And if they are sincere are they being led by communists?"

Victor Riesel, a widely distributed commentator, was focused on the labor movement and known as an anti-communist and anti-mob person. His article was entitled "A Communist's Son."[16]

"It is not easy to do battle with a 22 year old, not even a 22 year old who has unleashed a movement to keep men from the security forces of this land...This chap is Frank Emspak, son of Julius, alias 'Comrade Juniper' now dead.......Frank Emspak should know why some forces inside the old CIO were called Communist by leaders in and out of the CIO. It is all so pertinent now. Julius Emspak a tough but subtle and wily Communist infighter was heavily responsible for making the old CIO vulnerable to charges of Communist infiltration"

One United Press International article distributed nationwide quoted Private James Sanford of Houston TX saying, "I don't feel like they should really be considered American citizens. They don't seem to have the patriotism that a true American should have."[17]

Other articles blamed us for putting American troops in danger. "Men of the US First Cavalry (airmobile) division launched and accomplished their mission Friday while some college students and others in the US, to Hanoi's delight, were launching their weekend of demonstrations against American participation in the war." [18]

I think that one of the most unsettling things to the powers-that-be was the nationwide, and in fact, worldwide level of mobilization. People in communities all over the country did something. They could not be dismissed as West Coast hippies or New Yorkers (a dog whistle meaning unpatriotic Jews). In that sense, the International Days of Protest were a success. They constituted a shot across the bow of the pro-war majority in the U.S.

government, at all levels. The Days also demonstrated that the movement against the war, while still small, had moved beyond the campus and small groups of students.

The Draft

I notified my draft board in August of 1965 that I was no longer working at my draft-exempt hospital job. On October 19th, after a week of national publicity including front page articles in the Yonkers local paper and appearances on national TV, [19] the Yonkers draft board changed my classification to 1-A and I was summoned for my pre-induction physical. The notification more or less coincided with my nationally broadcast comments about Robert S. McNamara, then U.S. Secretary of Defense. He was supposed to be a genius who had all of the facts and numbers. In contrast, we in the anti-war movement were characterized as communists, draft-dodgers and ignorant of facts.

However, prior to becoming Secretary of Defense, McNamara had been the head of the Ford Motor Company when it produced the Edsel, the biggest fiasco of an automobile ever. So, naturally, I inquired if the Edsel was an example of McNamara's acumen. The broadcast ended immediately thereafter. The draft notice arrived in a day or so.

Someone assaulted me (most likely not one of the draftees) at the pre-induction physical and took all my papers. But not to worry — at each physical evaluation station someone else would give me another piece of paper, so by the end of the line my folder was full. The physician evaluated the documents and declared me "4-F." This meant completely unfit for military service. My friends congratulated me. When I asked how this could be, the physician said, "You got a 4-F and you are complaining?"

On the way out the door, a Lt. Pinhiero detained me for what became an extensive interview. When he asked why I was in Wisconsin, I — thinking of the famous line from the movie

Casablanca — told him I had come to Wisconsin for the climate (it was about 25 degrees with a mixture of sleet and snow coming down). The conversation went downhill from there.

Meanwhile, the bus back to Madison was being held until my interrogation was over. My fellow draftees rocked the bus, broke the bus windows and demanded my release. Finally, they let me go — and back to Madison we went. But absent windows it was a chilly ride. A few months later, I was reclassified and the Army raised my eligibility from "4-F" to "1-Y" — meaning "not acceptable for induction under current standards."[20] I had to keep selective service informed as to my whereabouts until I was 40. I cannot in my heart of hearts know exactly what I would have done if I had been drafted, except I was firm on not going to Canada. America is my country.

The issue of my draft status came up constantly at any public events during the war and for many years afterwards when I ran for office in my union. In fact, even now, when I meet people more or less of equivalent age, the question always comes up — did you serve? When I made it clear that I was not hiding behind a student exemption or some other technicality — such as a bone spur — people, including most in the military, accepted that. Most of the antagonism came from fellow workers at the General Electric Company, who largely spent the war working draft-exempt jobs earning huge amounts of overtime. In comparison, returning veterans at GE generally supported me, as I had taken a principled position against the war. I was also a strong supporter of dealing with PTSD and the effects of Agent Orange. My father's original advice to register, not hide, served me in good stead.

First and Last National Conference of the NCC, November 1965

A month after the high of the Days of Protest, the NCC held its first (and last) national conference. Our goals for the conference were to consolidate the organization and plan for the next steps.

Our goals were as follows:

Educate: Hold a series of workshops, trainings and discussions about the war, its character and means of resistance;

Plan: Develop a plan of action for the next days of protest;

Unity: Exit the conference with a show of unity and direction, linking many different kinds of groups together in a common project: to end the war in Vietnam. We wanted to have a formal relationship with civil rights organizations, not only the SNCC, but groups like the Methodist Student Movement.

Build: Strengthen the NCC regards to financial resources and structure.

"Arnold? Is that you?"

Arnold Johnson was Peace Chairman of the Communist Party USA (CPUSA). In his youth, he had been a Methodist Minister. I was standing on the corner of 13th and R Street speaking with him when another busload of people pulled up looking for directions and the convention registration. It turns out they were a mostly Methodist congregation from Iowa. I was a bit nervous and was about to ask Arnold not to climb on the bus with me to greet the people, but he did it anyway. After introducing myself and before I could say much of anything else, a voice from the back of the bus called out — "Arnold, is this you?" The caller was a Methodist minister, one of the leaders of the delegation. He had been in the Methodist Seminary with Arnold in the 1930s. They hadn't seen each other in years. Of course, no one else on the bus had ever met a real member of the CPUSA — but he was received as an old friend by his fellow Iowans. It was really a great sight.

It is too bad we could not capture and nurture the same feelings during the rest of the conference.[21]

Assessment of NCC Conference

The NCC, which was really a coalition of local groups, failed to consolidate as an organization. At our formation, we had specifically stated that we were not a policy organization. The point of unity was opposition to the war in Vietnam. From the moment it convened, the Young Socialist Alliance (YSA) insisted that the NCC take the position of immediate withdrawal of US troops from Vietnam. While almost all members did so, many local groups as well as members of SDS and the CP did not believe that acceptance of that slogan as sort of an entry ticket was the way to organize a national movement.

While the NCC ideal was supported by many local committees and some national organizations, we were not able to put together a robust, nationally-respected leadership group that could defend that position and move beyond our then current level of organization. [22]

At the end of the weekend, the NCC had little to show except the decision to go forward with another round of Days of Protest, on March 25th and 25[th.] I stayed on as chairman. But plans to develop fundraising and expanded education services for local groups were never fully developed.

Several community groups — Black student organizations such as the Methodist Student Movement, in particular — were turned off by all the sectarian infighting and withdrew from active participation, as did SNCC. This was a huge blow and exposed a strategic weakness in the antiwar movement.

We could not overcome the mutual distrust portions of the pacifist movement had for some of the End the War committees, nor could we overcome the palpable, but unspoken distrust of people like me and some of our staff who were presumed close to the Communist Party.[23] Even though both pacifists and YSAers distrusted each other, they both were opposed to CP perceived influence.

Many people associated with SDS came to the conclusion that the way to go was to concentrate on building SDS and not spend political resources on building the coalition that the NCC embodied.

Organizing for the second International Days of Protest (IDP) was the focus of the NCC's activity in the spring of 1966, preceded by a southern Days of Protest in February 1966.

Our staff[24] had a positive overall assessment of the second Days of Protest. The number and size of demonstrations in the US had increased substantially, with big demonstrations in Japan where 600,000 were in the streets.[25] The number of active groups in the IDP was much larger than in October, perhaps 350 — considerably more than the 150 groups with ties to the NCC at the November Convention.[26] There was a huge turnout in New York with thousands marching down Fifth Ave.[27]

Coverage of the second IDP differed from October 1965, as well. There seemed to be less vituperation and a more straightforward reporting. At least the main demands of the participants were clearly stated and quoted.

But as a sign of the change in the NCC's political standing — NCC spokespeople were not asked to speak at any major event. My only speech was by phone to a huge demonstration in Italy, along with a few press interviews.

The center of gravity in the antiwar movement had begun to move away from the NCC immediately after the November meeting. In May, the Fifth Avenue Peace Parade called for a national mobilization to be held in New York in mid-October, 1966. They made their announcement without speaking with most of the local committees or bothering to work with us at the NCC office. While many local organizations were aggravated, the financial and political weight of that decision sunk the NCC. Obviously, the "Coordinating Committee" was not coordinating much of anything. At a meeting in Cleveland a few months later, many of the

NCC staff, key supporters, leaders, the New York mobilization committee, ("The Mobe") and pacifist leaders, effectively ended the NCC. Although it lasted a few more months.

The new mobilization committee did not pursue the idea of a research center, a well-developed education center, the ability to publish the Outline History of the War in Vietnam, or the creation of a true national paper like *Peace and Freedom News* — dedicated to local anti-war and civil rights activity reportage. The refusal to publish a newspaper explicitly linking civil rights and the war was a great loss, especially since our largest subscription base was in the South — Mississippi, more specifically.

A.J. Muste, who was the titular head of the mobilization, offered me the position of field secretary. He did this as a means of preserving some semblance of unity in our movement — and I accepted on that basis. For the next two months, I journeyed to Denver, Las Vegas, Portland, Eugene, Seattle, Spokane, Pullman, Albuquerque, Santa Fe, Phoenix and Tucson organizing for the upcoming autumn mobilization.

Assessment of the Impact of the NCC

No one in August of 1965 thought the NCC had the potential to actually launch a national movement, but indeed this is what happened. In 1966, it was clear the NCC project of coordinated national projection of local anti-war efforts had worked. One result was that various political organizations saw their influence diluted by being part of a national organization which had the ability to reach consensus and pose directions and emphasis — as opposed to imposing a specific political line. Political leadership in the pacifist and socialist organizations had no great desire to form an organization directed at organizing and resourcing local organizations that might not agree with their policies, and they didn't.

Results of the NCC's Collapse

The NCC was never duplicated. Our goal was to support the growth of local committees in whatever way we could. We envisioned our work as that of a national organizing committee rather than just a national mobilization committee. No nonsectarian, nationally situated peace organization, especially one that had either tactical or strategic coordination with the activists in the Black community, took its place. This lack of an organic relationship with Black and Hispanic communities weakened the movement to end the war in Vietnam and stunted the political development of many white antiwar activists.

The "peace movement" did not appreciate that the Black liberation struggle, especially in the South, was way ahead of most peace organizations when it came to understanding the war, its impact and its motivations. The strong draft resistance movement in Mississippi is but one example. MLK's Riverside Church speech in the autumn of 1967 is another.

But in fairness, the Mobe's strategy of organizing increasingly larger demonstrations in New York and Washington made it clear that millions opposed the war. Local groups could support the national actions. But it was a somewhat different focus than what we had at the NCC regarding the way in which a broad spectrum anti-war movement could be built.

There were lasting successes — vital communications had been developed with antiwar forces around the world and the cold war consensus had been challenged.

By 1967, there was political space for antiwar Democrats to challenge President Lyndon Johnson.

A Vet Stands Up for Democracy; Fraternities Scatter.

In the autumn of 1966, I spoke at the University of Arizona. Our group was heckled by pro-war people, mostly fraternity types. Local sponsors were intimidated and left the scene. All of a sudden, a person in uniform jumped up on stage — a Marine sergeant. "I'm finished," I thought. He asked about my draft status. Satisfied with the response, he then confronted the crowd, telling them he was just back from Vietnam; that what was going on there as described in the press was not true. It was his view that he fought there so that people here in the US could exercise their right to speak. It was clear from his comments that he had doubts about the war.

Noting there was a recruiting office a couple of blocks away, the Marine challenged the right wingers to accompany him (and I) to the nearby recruiting station since they obviously supported the war. The crowd disappeared. The soldier and I went out for a beer.

Endnotes For Chapter Three

1. On March 4, 1965 the committee launched a two page mimeographed newsletter called the "Crisis" with Tom Paine as the inspiration. The masthead read "These are times that try men's souls". Sue Reeves was the first editor. (Her Grandmother, Mother Bloor was a leader of the miners' union in the early 1900s). A few weeks later I became the second editor. We printed several hundred a week. Ultimately we had a circulation of close to 500.

2. Donna Allen WSP; Dagmar Wilson WSP; Carl Bloice, Walter M Tillow (Dubois Clubs; CP) Paul Lauter; Dave Dellinger;(leading peace activists) Eric Weinberger , Barbara Demming Bob Swann (Committee for Nonviolent Action) Bob Parris, Courtland Cox, Donna Richards, Jimmy Garrett (SNCC) Carl Ogelsby SDS from " A Call for a Congress of Unrepresented People to declare Peace in Vietnam on August 9,1965" see also letter from Paul Lauter (then of Goucher College to peace activist Dave Cohen WHS Emspak papers, folder 4.401,

3. Just to provide another example of the huge increase in the scale of those active against the war- in August of 1963 the Hiroshima day march in Madison had at most 50 people.

4. "Call for A Congress of Unrepresented People to Declare Peace in Vietnam on August 9, 1965" signed by leading pacifist, anti-Vietnam War, civil rights and WSP leaders. WHS, Emspak papers folder 4.401.

5. Letter from Paul Lauter, Goucher College to Dave Cohen; WHS, Emspak papers Box 4.401.

6. Organizations included American Friends Service Committee (Quakers), Women Strike for Peace, The Committee

for Nonviolent Action, The Dubois Clubs, SDS; and the anti HUAC movement.

7.WHS;Emspak papers Folder 4.401, *The Crisis* vol. 1 #24 Aug 20, 1965 pg. 1 National Coordinating Committee to End the War in Vietnam Formed in Washington".

8. WHS; Emspak papers; Folder 4.516 Report from John Perdew, December 22, 1963 to SNCC office regarding organizing practice in Southwest Georgia. File 4.31A .

9. "Call for A Congress of Unrepresented Peoples to Declare Peace in Vietnam on August 9, 1965" signed by 33 leading activists; the contact people were Eric Weinberger who was with the Committee for Nonviolent Action; and Bob Parris (Bob Moses) who was a leader of SNCC; Emspak papers, WHS, Folder 4.403.

10. McMillin, Miles "Hello Wisconsin", *Madison Capital Times*, August 1965 pg. 1; Emspak papers, WHS, Folder 4.403.

11. Hubert H. Humphrey, August 23,1965, National Student Association http://www2.mnhs.org/library/findaids/00442/ pdfa/00442-01668.pdf pages 13-16" I am also here to say frankly and critically that the behavior of some young Americans in recent months is not deserving of such attention. The right to dissent is a vital factor in maintaining the health of our democratic order. But there exists an equal obligation for those with responsibility to decide to act to choose among conflicting opinions and available options… We have been informed by some persons that they are "unrepresented." And we have been told that, therefore, they acquire the warrant to violate necessary laws relating to public assembly and safety. I must say that it is incumbent upon those who demonstrate against our nation's policies in Southeast Asia to recognize that dissent is one thing, decision is another. To those public officials who must decide -- who must choose among available options -- have

sought to fashion a policy which takes into account the facts of this terribly complex and tragic situation ....".

12. A Call for National Protest Against the War in Vietnam, October 15- and 16th" Published by the NCC, September 1965, Madison WI (Many variants but the same basic message).

13. The staff of the NCC consisted of me, Joan Levinson office manager and organizer, Duane Allen , Ray Robinson, on loan from SNCC; Alicia Kaplow bookkeeper and fundraiser and many volunteers who put together our mailings, mimeographed the leaflets \ answered inquiries and produced educational material.

14. Telegram Western Union, October 17, 1965 sent October 16, 1965 by Eric Weinberger Fifth Avenue Peace parade Committee. WHS, Emspak papers folder 4.506.

15. "Yonkers Youth Sparks Big Viet War Protest" *Herald Statesman* Friday October 15, 1965 pg. 1.

16. Riesel,:" Inside Labor" , *New York Journal American.* Monday October 25, 1965 page 10.

17. UPI, "Viet GIs Call Protest Great Disappointment", *Wisconsin State Journal,* vol. 206, No.17 Sunday October 17, 1965 page 1 WHS, Emspak papers folder 4.509.

18. Deutsch, Ronald I Associated Press writer "U.S. Troops Battle Cong to Save Helicopter, Crew"; *Wisconsin State Journal* ,vol. 206 No. 17, Sunday October 17,1965 page 1 WHS, Emspak papers 4.509.

19. National Archives, National Personnel records Center, Selective Service System records, Selective Service System Classification records. Numbers 362-390; sheet 13.

20. DD form 62, dated 10 Feb 1966 Statement of Acceptability Official records from Selective Service WHS, Emspak papers Folder 4.406.

21. **Food for Thought:** The WSP, The Women's Strike for Peace members and leaders had backed the formation of the NCC at the Congress of Unrepresented Peoples. Leaders lent their names to the International Days of Protest and NCC fundraising efforts. At our November conference, in DC, they tried to keep the focus on the issue of ending the war, not internecine battles. But they also did something else. Our staff did not have the resources or connections to arrange food for the conference participants. Most of us were broke anyway, and three or four days of eating out was a big expense. The WSP and their friends had the foresight to think of this. They provided a Thanksgiving dinner and much more for many of the hundreds of participants. Just think, the antiwar movement could have ground to a hungry and ill-tempered halt. Many did leave ill-tempered, but we had some great food in the meantime.

22. Adler, Renata. "The Price of Peace is Confusion"; *New Yorker*, December 11, 1965; WHS, Emspak papers folder 4.509.

23. The "we" by this time were the many groups that made up the "standing committee of the NCC" as well as the staff.

24. The staff mostly volunteer in the spring of 1966 consisted of Joan Levenson, Duane Allen, Judy Schoyer, Sue Goray, Ona Stonkus, Adam Schesch, Rena Leib , Doug Hull; John Goray, Bill Tabb, Steve Kreunen and Bob Schneider.

25. *Peace and Freedom News* #21-March 27 Special IDP issue; WHS, Emspak papers folder 4.504.

26. *Peace and Freedom News* #20, WHS, Emspak papers folder 4.504.

27. *New York Times* page 1 Sunday March 27, 1966 WHS, Emspak papers folder 4.509.

Chapter Four: Graduate School Successes and Detours

In early 1967, I was broke, depressed and totally unsure about my future. The NCC had fallen apart and my constant travels had removed me from active participation in the antiwar scene in Madison. I was more or less politically and socially isolated. I was unemployed and depended on Dolores' appointment as a Teaching Assistant in the French department.

I was persuaded to enter graduate school by two circumstances. What had seemed like a promising job prospect at the Hennepin Mill of the Jones and Laughlin Steel Company ultimately fell through. The Steelworkers district president, a progressive guy, had told the company that I was the in-plant Steelworkers organizer for the new local — and thus, I was hired by the company.

But it was not so long ago, the Steel Workers had been calling the UE and my father communists. So, when the Pittsburgh-based senior V.P. of the Steelworkers, Joseph Maloney, saw and recognized my name, he didn't take any chances. Cold warrior that he was — he told the company to fire me, which they did. This, of course, made sense from their point of view — the plant organizer almost always became the elected local union president.

Ultimately, I was probably better off not working at J and L— and so were the potential union members. Jones and Laughlin was isolated in the middle of the country with no longtime core of steel worker activists who could mentor me if they so chose. I was culturally and ideologically unprepared to lead or take on serious responsibilities in an environment like that.

At the same time, two of my father's closest allies, Carl Marzani[1] and Russ Nixon[2] urged me to go on to graduate school rather than taking the United Steelworkers job. Their reasoning went something like this:

1) I was still attached to the UW and young enough where I would not be disrupting my entire life by going to graduate school.

2) I had interest and knowledge.

3) A PhD would grant me employment mobility, either here or abroad.

As it turns out, they were correct. It took about 20 more years for the employment part to work out, but possession of the degree was a huge advantage as it gave me access to organizations (MIT) and federal agencies (Department of Defense), which probably would simply have dismissed me. In other words, signing requests for information as a PhD instead of machinist meant something. Many years later, the state of Massachusetts told me that I would not have even been considered for my position without the PhD.

Unlike some other radical historians, I was not so much interested in studying the history of the working class per se, nor becoming a certified professor of history. From the beginning, I was intellectually committed to using the graduate school opportunity to study my family's history, especially the history of the UE. I wanted to go beyond family lore and learn why the UE was the target of the federal government, and spurned by the labor federation of which it once was a part, the CIO. I wanted to understand my father's role in all of this.

Meanwhile, Dolores, who had been accepted to the graduate program in French, started her quest for a Masters and PhD in French literature in September 1964 — the same month we married. Dolores was a stellar student and an effective teaching assistant. However, in January of 1967, the chairman of the French department informed her she would not be coming back as a teaching assistant for another semester, and made it clear it was due to my antiwar activities.[3]

In response, the leading scholar of French literature on the campus, Germaine Brée approached Dolores with a job offer. Bréee, one of the few people in the modern language departments at UW to speak at the first teach-in against the war in Vietnam in April 1965, put it simply: "Your husband is a Marxist and that is why you were fired."

Detours on the Road to the PhD

I was moving from full-time antiwar activism to the study of history, but I could not quite leave the activism world behind. Three political developments intervened. First was the war at home — aka the Dow Riot; the second was a citywide referendum against the war in Vietnam. The third was the Black student strike. I was involved in the leadership of all three. Together, they illustrate the degree of unrest within a portion of the student body. But also the total hypocrisy of academia, which in theory, supported minority access to the University, the education of the UW for the pursuit of knowledge rather than the pursuit of war.

On October 18, 1967, students in Madison tried to block the Dow Chemical Company, a major producer of Napalm, from recruiting on campus.[4] Using clubs and tear gas, Madison police brutalized three-hundred people participating in the protest in broad daylight. In the end, about seventy people were admitted to the UW hospital, almost all of whom were students.

The Dow chemical strike became the center point for the 1979 film *The War at Home,* and emblematic of the type of student-led direct confrontation of the war machine. In the iconic photograph and poster of the attack by the police (poster on page 77), a cop is about to strike a student — me. The poster says, "Our foreign policy must always be an extension of this nation's domestic policy. Our safest guide to what we do abroad is a good look at what we are doing at home."[5]

Later that evening, Paul Soglin[6] and I, among others, helped pull together a student strike committee. Paul's successful candidacy for alderman was bolstered by his leadership in the Dow strike. In turn, this election launched his career as Madison's mayor.

The UW never altered its commitment to the Pentagon in regards to defense-related sponsored research, or its commitment to helping war related firms to recruit. But Dow marked the beginning of a stubborn, well-researched campaign to expose the UW's participation in the war effort, from research in biological warfare to targeting for ICBMs.

The upheaval lasted about a week, culminating in a large and peaceful march to the state capitol. It was the largest outpouring of student-led opposition to the war the UW had seen thus far. And while it involved a small proportion of students, the march formed the beginning of increasingly broad opposition to war and its many manifestations at UW and across Madison. One or two of the key organizers left the UW as a result of the demonstrations, but no one was expelled and there were no arrests. We did not, however, achieve the end of recruitments, either.

Madison Citizens for a Vote on Vietnam: The Referendum

Just prior to the Dow strike in August of 1967, Professor Maurice Zeitlin[7] began to assemble a group to launch a referendum campaign to demonstrate a majority of Madison citizens opposed the war in Vietnam.

Madison Citizens for a Vote on Vietnam argued the war was illegitimate and launched without the consent of the governed — the American people. The actual wording of the referendum was:

Poster of photograph from Dow chemical strike October, 1967
Poster courtesy Wisconsin Historical Society

"It is the policy of the people of the city of Madison that there be an immediate cease fire and the withdrawal of United States troops from Vietnam, so that the Vietnamese people can determine their own destiny." [8]

The five-member steering committee included three members from the progressive business community, Maurice Zeitlin and me. Maurice was the clear ideological and political leader. I was asked to join as the lead organizer responsible for the citywide campaign.

By design, the referendum campaign was not involved in the Democratic Party Presidential Primary of 1968.

A victory for this initiative was conceivable because a coalition of progressives had just won a court case allowing students living in Madison the right to vote. Our committee launched almost the same day as the Dow protests. Thoughtful (and nervous) people could see the contrast between direct action and a vote. I am sure we picked up some support because of that.

To get on the ballot, Madison Citizens had to collect notarized signatures from fifteen-percent of the gubernatorial vote in the elections of 1966 — about ten-thousand signatures. This was no small task. There was a window of about six weeks from November to mid-December to accomplish this.

On December 22, 1967, Madison Citizens for a Vote on Vietnam filed ninety-two-hundred certified signatures of qualified voters on the official "Petition for Referendum" forms stating the wording of the referendum and the desire for the city council to vote on it without alteration — and if not, to place it on the Spring 1968 ballot.

By the time of the April 1, 1968 citywide vote, we reached our canvass goal of about forty-percent of the residences in Madison. At least fifty-percent of all voters probably received a card from us asking for support. Building on the signature mobilization campaign, approximately three-hundred-seventy-five volunteers were active as canvassers, phone callers and leafleteers.

Opposition to the referendum solidified in a particularly shrewd attack. The Ad Hoc Committee to Defeat the War Referendum published a four-page newspaper type ad about a week before the vote. It quoted Senator Eugene McCarthy, the leading Democratic antiwar candidate, from a March 12, 1968 CBS interview declaring, "While immediate withdrawal would end the war, it would lose the peace." It also quoted RFK, who had not yet gotten into the race, saying, "I think it would be a major mistake to unilaterally withdraw."

Madison's labor unions voiced their opposition to the referendum and strong support for the war. The Dane County Committee on Political Education (COPE) of the Madison Federation of Labor (AFL-CIO), both opposed the referendum and refused to support any aldermanic candidate who supported the so-called "surrender referendum."[9]

But the nation's political environment changed between 1965 and April 1968. Increasingly large segments of society were questioning the war. Muhammad Ali had refused the draft.[10] Martin Luther King, Jr. had made a dramatic speech at the Riverside Church in New York City calling upon all decent people to end the war. American casualties were increasing. The Tet Offensive significantly changed the American public's perception of the war. If five-hundred-thousand troops in Vietnam could barely contain the "Viet Cong" — what would it take to win? When the Pentagon began talking about hundreds of thousands of more troops, it began to dawn on people that the war in Vietnam was not worth it. The draft was beginning to affect middle class people —college students, especially.

Things also changed in Madison. The *Capital Times*, still with Miles McMillin in charge, endorsed the referendum. No more attacks on commies. In mid-March, U.S. Representative Kastenmeier said if he lived in Madison he would vote yes. The most popular disc jockey in town endorsed the referendum, too. There was momentum.

On April 1, the referendum received 21,129 "Yes" votes out of 48,884 ballots cast — forty-three-percent. Contemporaneous reports said Lyndon Johnson withdrew from the race on March 31 because he did not want to lose the presidential primary, nor did he want a major city to endorse a more or less immediate withdrawal from Vietnam. [11]

Gene Parks was elected to the city council, becoming the first Black person in Madison to win an aldermanic seat. His campaign was aided by the general mobilization of people in his ward — and especially by the referendum campaign. The primarily Black precinct voted 49.7% for the referendum.

We were disappointed that we did not win the vote, and yet, we surpassed our goal of forty-percent. Even more importantly, we believed the growing strength of the movement against the war was one key factor in encouraging President Johnson to withdraw from the primary when he did.

The Madison effort demonstrated it was possible for progressives to build a community-based political campaign, that it was possible and effective to work outside of the two party system — and that a sizable portion of the population was ready to get out of Vietnam.

After the referendum detour, I decided it was time to take the graduate degree seriously— and by August I was awarded my MA in History.

The Black Student Strike of 1969

As the fight against racism intensified in the 1960s, the Communist Party increasingly focused its attention on combating racism. During this period of time the CPUSA had grown significantly, especially amongst a mobilized young Black leadership on the west coast. In Madison, the Party initiated the formation of

People against Racism (PAR), which included both campus and community people.

Our statement of principles began as follows: "Our function is not only to aid the Black students but to begin to raise consciousness against racism. The polices of the University in excluding virtually all poor people and especially nonwhites, have created an institution which is not in the best interests of any of us. Education is not a commodity to be bought or sold on the market...but a right."[12]

The racial climate at UW was one of indifference and sometimes hostility towards the civil rights movement and to those few Black students on campus — about two-percent of the student body. Most whites had no contact with Black students at all. Many students had no comprehension whatsoever of civil rights.

The topic of race shifted from discussion to action on November 21, 1968. On that day, ninety Black students at UW-Oshkosh sat-in at the UW-Oshkosh President's office and were expelled from the college. Several of the students re-enrolled and were accepted at UW-Madison. But in what PAR characterized as an extraordinary move, a committee composed of UW President Harrington, chancellors and regents, acting totally outside of the normal admissions process — overruled the admissions committee. The Black People's Alliance, the leading Black organization, demanded that there be a fair judicial process at UW-Oshkosh and that UW-Madison admit the accepted Oshkosh students.[13] Even prior to the expulsion of the Black students from Oshkosh, the Black People's Alliance had been raising demands to establish a Black Studies department and increase the admission of Black students to UW-Madison.

On Friday, February 7, 1969, in response to the UW Chancellor's refusal to meet, the Black students sat-in — and effectively seized — the sociology building.

The All University Conference — "The Black Revolution: To What Ends?" — became a flashpoint in the whole build up to the strike. Leading Black and white political activists, writers and poets came to the UW Madison for a series of lectures and seminars from February 3 to February 8. The conference was sponsored by many campus organizations, most of the campus ministries and other university entities, and featured prominent figures in the civil rights movement, including Jesse Jackson, Jonathan Kozol, and Dr. Alvin Poussaint.[14] I was part of a panel called "Racism in Madison," which focused on rampant housing segregation and other forms of discrimination practiced in Madison. Jews could only recently move into the neighboring wealthy suburbs of Maple Bluff and Monona — Blacks still could not.

The currents of protest and resistance also came together in the Black History Class, taught by Professor Robert Starobin,[15] a recognized scholar in the areas of race relations and Black history and an active member of Madison's progressive community. This was the first Black History class offered by the UW. Starobin hired Paul Richards and I as Teaching Assistants. We were supported by the Black students based on our work against racism on the campus.

It is hard to conceive of the viciousness of the UW's response to the student strike. The UW announced any TA that did not hold class would be fired. The governor of the state dispatched twenty-seven-hundred National Guard troops to the campus — some, we discovered, arrived with loaded weapons. During the strike, approximately thirty-five-hundred people were detained or charged with some infraction. Ultimately, I became head of the defense organization. The Black Student Center burned down — arson was suspected.

In a huge evolution of white consciousness, white students accepted the idea that the Black students would set the demands. On two occasions, thousands marched up State Street to the Madison State Capitol in a show of support.

Although I was part of the leadership committee, the Party was not recognized in the same way as Students for a Democratic

Society as ideological leaders. I attributed our lack of ideological leadership "in part [to]a failure to deal adequately with the concept of self-determination of people — the right of Black people to decide for themselves what kind of cultural, political and economic life they wish to participate in and the necessity for black-white unity in the fight for socialism."[16] However, in an attempt to derail the student movement, both the CP and I were publicly attacked as the strike began to take off.

The *Wisconsin State Journal* ran an above-the-fold, story that purported to be an account of the CP's leadership meeting of the day before, detailing my remarks (and identifying me) regarding the strike and the need to support it. Other strike leaders denounced the article and other similar attempts to split the leadership along either political or racial lines.

But in spite of our unified efforts, neither the left, nor the larger student movement was able to significantly alter the balance of power when it came to the issue of racism at UW.

The UW faculty sided with the administration, voting 524 to 518 not to admit the expelled Oshkosh students. The faculty and administration never saw them as equal partners in the negotiating process.[17] A majority of faculty also signed a petition supporting the actions of the chancellor in calling for National Guardsmen to restore order. But the magnitude of strike support induced the UW to settle.

The strike ended after about a week with a commitment by the UW to establish a Black Studies department; increase recruiting of Black students (but not at anything like the five-hundred demanded by the BPA), and rebuild the Black Student Center. The administration did not discipline strike leadership, Black or white. But that is not to say more covert repression was absent. As far as I can determine, no history grad student who was active in the leadership of the strike ever taught history at a University.

The History department was particularly hostile to the idea that students would have an important role in deciding who should be hired to teach and for what purpose. Many saw it as an abrogation of academic freedom. Starobin left at the end of the year for SUNY-Binghamton. He committed suicide two years later.

CODA: In 2019, the UW organized a series of seminars devoted to the Black strike. Participants were asked to share their reminiscences and assess the results. One aspect of the assessment stood out: The UW never came close to enrollment or faculty of color goals. In 2019, approximately one-hundred-and-ninety Black students were in a freshman class of about thirty-four-hundred. While the football team was about thirty-nine-percent Black, the student population at UW Madison was about one-percent Black. [18]

Our personal lives, meanwhile, turned in what would be a wonderful new direction that winter: Dolores became pregnant. We prepared for the great event throughout the spring. We embraced the natural childbirth movement. Both of us went to Lamaze classes. In 1969, very few men were involved in deliveries — for the most part, they were not involved at all. But on June 21 — my birthday — we had a party with lots of wine. Early the next day, Dolores went into labor and off we went to the hospital where our son, Jesse, was born. I was present at the birth — one of the first men to be in the delivery room at any Madison hospital. There was a huge crash during the birthing process when one of the medical students suddenly fainted and hit the deck. But all was well. Our obstetrician, Dr. Gloria Sardo, still wearing her golf shoes, came to the delivery room ready for anything that day.

Dolores was still working on her PhD in French literature and needed to travel to France to finish her research on the works of French poet and communist Louis Aragon. Earlier in the year, however, the U.S. State Department decided to block Dolores' Fulbright scholarship (on the grounds she could not/did not represent the people of the United States). But the Fulbright scholarship committee had already approved Dolores' award. Many of the commission members resigned in protest of this overt and public act of censorship. This included Germaine Brée — the committee chair and one of Dolores' professors. Luckily, Dolores was still able to travel to France with the help of a UW grant secured, in part, by Professor Brée.

I was working as a Project and Teaching Assistant that spring and summer as I finished up my course work for the history PhD. I was more than on track, having completed my MA the year before. I had done very well on my preliminary exams in November 1968, so from the UW's point of view, I was moving along at a very good pace. I decided to write about the break-up of the CIO, and the UW History department accepted my PhD thesis project.

Really, I was researching the history of our family. The United Electrical Workers (UE) was the largest of the left unions to leave the CIO — and my father was the key political target. I was a highly motivated researcher, but I also knew more or less what I was looking for in terms of basic source material. Given my research progress and standing on the prelim scale, I was eligible for a Ford fellowship, which I won, starting in January of 1970. The fellowship required that I do dissertation writing and research, but did not specify where I had to do it.

So, we immediately set off for Europe with our young son and an address for a rooming house in Paris. Later, with the assistance of acquaintances of Dolores' parents, we were able to rent an apartment at 76 Rue des Plantes in the 14th arrondissement. The sixth floor apartment overlooked Rue des Plantes and had two rooms, a kitchen, a water closet and shower (separate). The young woman who was the face of Clairol lived on the floor below. Patricia's face was all over Paris. I don't know how she could tolerate it.

Paris, for me, was great. No one in our neighborhood spoke English and there were no big food stores. So, the people at the bakery, the butcher, the vegetable market and the fish market all took it upon themselves to teach me the appropriate words for whatever they were selling. We had a babysitter for our son in the mornings, but each afternoon I took him to the park. I was the only man engaged in childcare. After the many mothers realized that I was going to be there every day they all decided I needed help — with juice, cookies, diapers, general child care and, of course, the appropriate translated words for child care.

In 1970, Paris had a large working class as the automobile plants had not yet closed. The political scene was characterized by the recent 1968 uprisings: There was a vibrant student move-ment and the CP still had neighborhood meetings. I spoke at both student and neighborhood meetings about the war and the U.S. student movement.

I was able to take notes from my historical research with me. The U.S. embassy also had a great library with transcripts from many House and Senate committee hearings. Without the distrac-tions of being a Madison activist, I was able to send chapters of my dissertation back home to the U.S. about every two weeks, receiv-ing comments and suggestions in return. By the time I arrived back in Madison in September 1970 I had a complete draft of the dis-sertation — approved chapter by chapter — ready for final editing.

The Paris Peace talks to end the war in Vietnam were in prog-ress while we were still in Paris. I was able to assist the National Liberation Front delegation in their interpretation of events in the U.S. One of the most memorable discussions concerned the bombing of Sterling Hall at the University of Wisconsin, which occurred on August 24, 1970. When it happened, I initially had a burst of elation — until I saw that a person had been killed. The Vietnamese on the other hand, immediately condemned the action saying it was a stupid piece of adventurism which would hurt the anti-war movement — in Wisconsin for sure, but also across the U.S. They were correct.

When we left Paris, we sublet the apartment to friends, were too broke to pay the city tax and gave it up the following year.

Our family returned to Madison from Paris in September of 1970. When we arrived in Madison we were dismayed to find the progressive movement in disarray. The Madison peace movement had been upended as a consequence of the bombing of Sterling Hall. The Black student movement was also in disarray. On the national scene, Angela Davis, a brilliant scholar, CP member and active in the defense of the Black Panthers, had been charged with conspiracy to murder. She was arrested in October. Dolores and I also became part of the leadership of the "Free Angela Davis" campaign.

The History department initially offered me a Teaching Assistant position in a subject I knew nothing about. I proposed they give the position to someone else and went to work at a higher paid job as a project assistant (essentially a lab technician) in the UW Hospital, where some friends and I initiated the Project Assistants Organizing committee and set out to organize a union for the project assistants.[19]

On a personal level, Dolores still had her project assistantship with Professor Germaine Brée, but it was becoming clear to her that she was no longer dedicated to becoming a scholar of French literature. We had also decided to have another child — and in August of 1971, Dolores gave birth to our daughter Freya. I think the almost tragic birth experience also helped propel her towards medicine.

History

One of the great things about studying history at the University of Wisconsin is the Wisconsin Historical Society (WHS), a state agency that seemed, at the time, designed to encourage the study of labor history. It houses one the largest collections of union newspapers in the country, as well as various documents from specific unions. It also housed the papers of the Americans for Democratic Action, and the rival Progressive Citizens of America. I was able to do a tremendous amount of my research just by going to the WHS. Luckily for me, the vast majority of the additional material I needed was in Washington, D.C., Wayne State University in Detroit, and the UE office in New York.

My dissertation focused on the reasons for the break-up of the CIO. It contradicted just about all the accepted narrative describing the labor movement of the late forties. I argued that the destruction of the political coalition which had built the CIO crippled the unions ideologically and organizationally — to the detriment of most workers. I demonstrated that the coalition of Communist Party members, class conscious workers along with strong union-conscious workers powered the constituent unions of the CIO into existence.

Without those class-conscious elements pushing for industrial unions, there probably would not have been the organization of the mass production industries. For me, the anti-communist attacks on leftists and left unions in the CIO was not a matter of expelling some undesirable and foreign element, but breaking up the family — in the most intimate sense of the word. I saw a type of breakup within the United Electrical Workers where families were turned against each other and lifelong friendships were destroyed. The ability of the union to represent its members was weakened, especially in firms like GE.

The presence of communists was an excuse and, in fact, had little to do with the motivations or the actual reasons for the expulsion of the eleven progressive unions and the extensive purges of staff and members that remained. I showed that the CIO abandoned political neutrality and became, for all practical purposes, a wing of the Democratic Party.

In spite of their militant rhetoric, I argued, the CIO accepted and used the Taft-Hartley Act as a means to go after the left — a strategy initiated by liberal forces led by Walter Reuther. I pointed out that, in effect, a government agency could control the internal politics of the union using non-communist oaths as the means. Union officers had to sign if their union was to use the National Labor Relations Board.

I showed that the biggest expenditure of funds and organizing talent by the CIO and constituent unions was to finance the raids by the International Union of Electrical Workers against the UE, not to organize the South as they were purportedly used for. In fact, multi-racial unions such as the Food and Tobacco Workers and the Mine Mill and Smelter workers (which had significant interracial southern membership) were attacked along with the strongly anti-racist Farm Equipment Workers.

In many ways, the offensive against the left in the CIO was a continuation of the increased tensions between the more conservative sections of the CIO and the Communist Party, as well as those allied with it. By 1940, those tensions were becoming more prominent, exacerbated by issues of foreign policy — specifically the CP's support of the Stalin-Hitler pact and opposition to getting involved in the war as a supporter of Britain. Within the UE, the issue became the defeat of James Carey, a leader of the right wing and member of the Association of Catholic Trade Unionists. He was defeated by AJ Fitzgerald of Local 201, Lynn, Massachusetts. Fitzgerald supported the Emspak-Matles wing of the union. In spite of charges by Carey that he was eliminated for political reasons, most scholars now agree that it was his incompetence that allowed him to be ousted. It also became clear that the initial success of McCarthyism in the labor movement led by the most "progressive" individuals, made possible the devastation of the professional and intellectual class later. But that was not the consensus in the sixties or seventies.

All of these conclusions were at variance with the received wisdom of the labor history profession and the UW Department of History. By June 1971, I was ready for the "pro forma" defense of the thesis. Each chapter of my manuscript had been accepted and, earlier in the year, I was authorized to prepare the final typed version for the library — an expensive and time-consuming project. The night before my thesis defense, my thesis advisor, Paul Glad, called and suggested I come over to his house for a drink. Dolores and I figured it would be a celebratory occasion.

Instead, when I got there I found two or three of the other members of the committee were also present. They informed me that my thesis would be rejected the next day. They offered no explanation, apology or anything else. "Too bad," they said after the police came (I don't remember if the cops actually came or not) — but I do remember I leapt over the couch with the intent to strangle my major professor. Others intervened — even the neighbors. After all, it was June and the windows were open.

I was shocked and angered. I went home and Dolores insisted I fight this — which I would not have done without her insistence.

I was never given a formal reason, neither in writing or verbally, for the rejection. I protested to the chairman of the department — who must have understood that it was not a good move on their part. I had moved rapidly through my coursework and prelims with a very high rank. I was a Ford Fellow. I had done extensive research. I acquired first-person testimony and contemporaneous documentation from original sources. All my individual chapters had been accepted and I was told to have the final version prepared for the library.

Given the potential to embarrass the department, I was assigned another professor — a conservative person whose specialty was 20th century diplomatic history. A decent scholar, Professor Cooper felt that the department was ill-served by their actions. He indicated that the body of work was fundamentally sound, but that I would have to rewrite it.

Cooper told me to get rid of the word "imperialism" and rejected my heavy reliance on internal union sources, especially oral history. His idea of "reliable sourcing" meant newspapers like *The New York Times*, which in my view could not give a full picture of the story. Much to their surprise, I'm sure, I acquiesced. Luckily, I had not quit my job at the UW Hospital. Even luckier was my friendship with Margaret Thorpe, a brilliant history student who had left the department because she could not stand the way she was treated.[20] She agreed to help me with the edits and five months later, I submitted another version. The chairman of the department, David Cronin, took over the management of the thesis defense. I was told everyone was in agreement and there would be no problem. I would defend my thesis in mid-December.

A few days before the pro forma thesis defense, the History Department added Jack Barbash, a professor in the Economics Department, to the committee. He had been a staffer with the AFL-CIO, and prior to that, a staff member for the Senate Internal Securities sub-committee chaired by Hubert Humphrey. One of the key targets of the committee was the United Electrical Workers — and among the individuals they focused on was my father. Ultimately, the legal issues went to the Supreme Court and in a landmark decision, [21] he and others similarly situated won the right to use the First Amendment, not just the Fifth, when being questioned about political beliefs.

Jack had been one of the university negotiators working against us when we tried to organize the Wisconsin Student Employees Association. He was also an opponent of the Teaching Assistants Association (TAA) — the first union to be recognized in the U.S.

representing graduate assistants — and like many anti-communist liberals, supported the war in Vietnam.

I protested of course, but was assured by the chairman the vote was going to be in my favor. The big day arrived. My hospital kidney research department prepared a little party for my triumphant return, and I went to the thesis defense.

At the time, all members of an official thesis defense review had to sign a warrant testifying to the fact they were there. If one person didn't sign, the meeting was invalid and could not grant a PhD.

After some preliminary remarks, the warrant was being passed around for signatures and got to Barbash.

He said he would not sign unless I answered the question, "Have you ever been or are you now a member of the Communist party?" Some of the faculty present urged Jack to stop fooling around — sign the document and allow the group to vote. Jack refused. I pointed out to Jack that he asked the same questions to my father and that I would not insult him or lower myself to answer such a question, which of course, had nothing to do with the contents of the thesis.

He refused to sign. At that point, the other professors left the room. No thesis defense. No PhD. Someone suggested I turn out the lights.[22]

Being a pessimist, I had already contacted William Gorham Rice, a distinguished law professor at the UW and head of the Wisconsin Civil Liberties Union. Although I did not know what was going to happen, the very appointment of Jack to the committee spelled danger. I asked Rice to try for a settlement, and in the event the settlement failed, to get an injunction against the university barring them from issuing any PhD at the January graduation ceremony unless I got mine. In mid-January, Rice called and gave me his word that the UW was going to issue the PhD. A few days later, I received the little red binder which held the degree.

Of course, no university would be crazy enough to hire me under these circumstances. I am not even sure I could have gotten a recommendation. But what I am sure of is that there were active attempts to ensure that I never worked in the field.

I have often thought about why I decided to fight for the degree. I didn't have a strong affinity for academia. Institutionally, the profession supported the war in Vietnam, could not, and would not, deal with racism or sexism and opposed unionization. While there might be a few Marxists around, the boundaries of intellectual expression were, and remain, pretty narrow. In spite of my alienation from the department and sense of hypocrisy embedded in the UW, I also think I was able to get an excellent education. But when it came to who would be moving society forward, I did not see the university in that role, nor did I see radicalized students in that capacity.

I was determined to get my degree because I wanted the value of my work recognized— and by implication, the value of my family and the left. Aside from that, I was stubborn. I had worked hard for the degree, jumped through the hoops and so I deserved the degree. I earned it, and I was not prepared to have it stolen.

Out of Madison

By December 1971, we had decided to move to Boston. I had been working as a Project Assistant in the Kidney transplant lab and had already given my notice. In part because of the prestige of the UW science establishment and strong letters of recommendations, I had been hired by the Harvard-associated Peter Bent Brigham Hospital as a senior lab technician. Boston was a center for hospital organizing and also a center for organizing within the electrical industry.

We loaded up the Volkswagen for the drive to Boston on January 3, 1972. We left Madison and never thought we would be back.

A vignette about life in Madison in the 1960s.

We initially lived in a great place — 1728 Van Hise Ave. Mr. Schley, the landlord, maintained the property. It was a good place to live for five years. But even more extraordinary, was the way Mr. Schley treated us. Tragically, Mr. Schley's son was killed in Vietnam. I, meanwhile, was a prominent member of the antiwar movement. You could not miss it; I was on the front pages of the papers. But never during our tenancy did Mr. Schley ever mention it or give us any trouble for it. I think that illustrates his basic decency and that of many people in Madison. Mr. Schley sold the house in May 1969.

Vignette: The Cold War in Labor Comes to a Symbolic End

In the summer of 1966, I went to Pittsburgh for a meeting of the Pittsburgh Committee to End the War in Vietnam. One of the main antagonists of the United Electrical Workers union was the Association of Catholic Trade Unionists, led by Father William Rice of Pittsburgh. A particular target was my father. But something had changed by 1966. Rice came to the meeting to ask, as he put it, for my forgiveness. He wanted to make amends for what he had done to build the anti-communist movement in the U.S. — especially relating to the United Electrical Workers. He knew his attacks had contributed to the stress that killed my father.

I was stunned. But I also felt something really important was happening. We had a civil conversation. I could only say how saddened I was and agreed it was time to make peace. Father Rice then left.

Maybe the most significant quality of this 1966 meeting with Father Rice was that it happened at all. It was essentially an example of Hubert Humphrey's worst fears: A pillar of the Cold War switching sides and going back to some of his roots. Here was a man who, more than most others helped bring down the left wing of the labor movement — making the labor movement a servant of the Democratic Party. Now, he was not only questioning what he had done, but actively working against it.

Rice was also an advisor to Mike Quill, president of the Transport Workers Union in New York City and also a former Communist. The monsignor urged Quill to come out against the war. Quill did so, just before he passed away a few months later, in the middle of the Transit Strike.

In 1977, Monsignor Rice and I were asked to present at a meeting of the Council of Humanities in Phoenix, Arizona. This was to be a retrospective of the left unions and the Cold War. Many of the leading cold warriors of the AFL-CIO were present. They expected Monsignor Rice and I would be at each other's throats. But instead, Rice made a stunning indictment of the Cold War and his attacks on the Communists and their supporters in the labor movement, who he argued were staunch trade unionists. He also said leading the anti-communist movement was the biggest mistake of his life.

Sidebar: The Great Newspaper Caper

During the summer of 1971 we house sat in the upscale Madison neighborhood of Nakoma. Our Wisconsin Nakoma neighbors were not used to having a bunch of young people — with a baby no less — living on the block, even as house-sitters. They were even less enamored because we often had people over, not all of whom were white.

In August of 1969, the UW published the registration edition of the *Daily Cardinal* — the campus newspaper. All 36,000 undergraduates had to get it, because it contained registration materials. However, the *Daily Cardinal* editorial staff was composed of progressive and radical students. In the lead editorial that week, they used the word "fuck." When the powers-that-be realized this word was in the paper, they moved to seize all copies. But by that time, the newspaper was already packed up in mail sacks at the post office.

So, intrepid defenders of free speech that we were — we rented a U-Haul, got down to the loading dock before the UW could and took the mail sacks. But what to do with them? The garage at the Emspak's Nakoma house seemed like an improbable hiding spot. Who would guess? So, that is what we did — closed the garage door and all was well. We parked the truck around the corner.

But when the neighbors spotted the truck they suspected "suspicious" activity and called the police. Apparently, they thought we were stealing the furniture. The police arrived and wanted to come in. Of course, there was no search warrant. But it was also obvious nothing was going on. We chatted. They leaned against the garage door and peered in the windows. Seeing the car where the owners had left it seven weeks earlier — and no evidence of anything else — they didn't push the subject. It being a warm evening, we invited officers into the house for coffee, hold the baby, look at the parrot — anything to make sure they were not interested in the garage. They did not offer to change the baby. The police left.

Meanwhile, negotiations with the university went on. The agreement was that *if* the offending word was blacked out, the paper could go out as if nothing happened. And so it was. A crew of students soon arrived with Magic Markers to cross out the offending word. The newspapers reappeared, repacked and brought back to the post office. Of course, since the offending word was blacked out with black ink, you could not miss it on a bet…but you couldn't read it either.

Endnotes For Chapter Four

1. Carl Marzani was an author, publisher, filmmaker and over-all genius. He wrote and edited the film *Dead Line for Action*, distributed by the UE in 1946. Among other things it showed the close relations of GE and Westinghouse enjoyed with the German and Japanese war machines respectively. In January 1947 Marzani was indicted for defrauding the government by receiving government pay while concealing CPUSA member-ship. He was convicted on 22 June 1947, but nine counts were overturned on appeal, while the Supreme Court split 4-4 on a rare rehearing of the last two charges. Marzani served all but four months of a thirty-six-month sentence. After he got out of jail he founded a progressive publishing house Marzani and Munsell. Carl was a friend and supporter of our efforts with the NCC and close to my father.

2. Russ Nixon had been the UE's legislative representative in Washington DC, and was then the Editor of the National Guardian, the nation's largest progressive weekly. He and Donna Allen had arranged for my release from the DC jail in August of 1965. He was a close friend of my father.

3. A few years later, the German Democratic Republic published a book "Who's Who in the CIA". The chairman of the UW French department among others was listed as a member. He did not deny the accusation when confronted with the leaflet that I had printed.

4. The Dow chemical company also manufactured napalm- a jellied gas that was used in bombs. It ignited on detonation, sticking to people and burning them to death- or wounding them grievously. Not so surprisingly during WWII it was used only in the Pacific theater, not in Europe. The practice of using this type of weapon against people of color continued with the war in Vietnam.

5. In October of 1967 I was a project assistant working for Maurice Zeitlin. On Dow day, I was crossing the street between the Sociology Building and the Commerce building with about a year's worth of data on what were called IBM cards on the way to the computer in Sterling hall. As I crossed the street I noticed the police gathering, and no-one between me and the police. Thinking fast I put the boxes of data underneath the radiator just as the police smashed thought the plate glass window facing the street to get at the students- and the police riot began. The poster has been featured in the Whitney museum in New York City.

6. Paul Soglin ultimately became the mayor of Madison, serving multiple terms (not all consecutive,) announcing his decision not to run again in July 2018.

7. Maurice Zeitlin was a professor in the Sociology Department. His was doing research on voting patterns in Chile; among other innovative research. He was an outspoken in opposition to the war in Vietnam; he spoke at the1965 Teach-in as well as in support of the Free Speech movement at UC Berkeley.

8. WHS Emspak papers folder 5.220.

9. The Ad-Hoc Committee to End the War in Vietnam WHS, Emspak papers folder 5.220.

10. Muhammad Ali- On April 28, 1967, with the United States at war in Vietnam, Ali refused to be inducted into the armed forces, saying "I ain't got no quarrel with those Vietcong." On June 20, 1967, Ali was convicted of draft evasion, sentenced to five years in prison, fined $10,000 and banned from boxing for three years. He stayed out of prison as his case was appealed and returned to the ring on October 26, 1970, knocking out Jerry Quarry in Atlanta in the third round. On March 8, 1971, Ali fought Joe Frazier in the "Fight of the Century" and lost after 15 rounds, the first loss of his professional boxing career. On June 28 of that same year, the U.S. Supreme Court overturned his conviction for evading the draft.

11. On March 30th 1968 the NBC correspondent in Madison told our committee that it was probable that the referendum would win, and that President Johnson was aware of that. He also told us that the possibility of a victory in a major city for a withdrawal vote was a factor that influenced Johnson to withdraw from the race.

12. People Against Racism, undated December 68 or January 69, mimeographed; Madison WI.

13 The BPA was the umbrella group of Black students which formulated the demands regarding Oshkosh students and later the strike in Madison.

14. Dr. Poussaint was my camp counselor when I was 13 at Camp Hurley, formerly Camp Juvenile.

15. Robert Starobin came from a left background. His father had been the foreign editor of the Daily Worker from 1945 to 1954. Starobin came to UW in 1968. He left in the summer of 1969 after teaching the Black History Class. He committed suicide in 1971.

16. Emspak, Frank "*The U.W. Strike*" Communist Viewpoint Supplementary Issue, Milwaukee, March 1969. original manuscript, 8 pages.

17. Emspak, Frank "*The U.W. Strike*" Communist Viewpoint Supplementary Issue, Milwaukee, March 1969. original manuscript, 8 pages.

18. University of Wisconsin, Office of the registrar, annual report, section "Enrollment" issued Annually; https://registrar.wisc.edu/enrollment-reports.

19. When I returned to Madison in 1991 I met Carol Weidel. She was hired as a PA in the hospital in 1972 and revived the or-

ganizing effort. In her basement were my original leaflets urging people to join the union.

20. I met fellow Margaret Thorpe whom I had been corresponding with for years as she was the secretary of the Los Angeles committee to End the War. She was a brilliant history student. Without her encouragement and assistance I never would have gotten through graduate school.

21. U.S. Supreme Court Emspak v. United States, 349 U.S. 190 (1955).

22. Ultimately a condensed version of the thesis was published. Emspak, Frank "*The Break-Up of the CIO*" Political Power and Social Theory; vol. 4 1984 pg. 101-138.

Chapter Five: Transitions-Medical School, the Communist Party and Joining the Working Class

The period between 1972 and 1975 was a time of great transitions in our lives.

Politically, we went from participating in a university-based student movement in a middle class city — to a working class movement in working class cities of Massachusetts. From our Dorchester Boston neighborhood — to the Ward Street neighborhood in Salem — and then to East Lynn.

Our student-based Communist Party in Madison, Wisconsin consisted of about ten members, six of whom were students and four of whom worked at jobs in the city so, we were not entirely divorced from the working class of the city. The North Shore of Boston (Salem, Lynn and Beverly) was an entirely different world. The CP had been destroyed in the 1950s through a combination of repression and the CP's decision to "mainstream." While there were a few sympathizers, the party had no local members. Our focus was entirely on working people and developing relationships with the Hispanic and Black communities.

As we were acclimating to our new life, Dolores made the monumental decision to become a physician, a project that consumed us for the next 10 years.

Raising two children in this tumultuous environment also brought us into the movement to provide affordable child care. No longer was this some sort of theoretical issue for us, but an absolutely fundamental need if we were to continue working and Dolores was to continue medical school and residency afterwards.

On January 3, 1972 we moved to an apartment in the middle of Dorchester, a working class neighborhood in Boston. We were aided in our housing efforts by two Communist Party comrades who lived at the end of the street. They also had a son named Timmy who was about Jesse's age.

Leaving lily white Madison for Dorchester was a total shock; we had moved into what amounted to a racial civil war.

The fight against school integration was at its height with school buses being stoned by mobs of white people. Our neighborhood was in the midst of blockbusting, fueled by racial prejudice and housing discrimination. Dorchester had been an all-white, ninety-percent Irish-Catholic working class neighborhood for generations. The properties for sale or rent were identified by parish. Just a few years prior, Blacks were forced to live in substandard and overcrowded housing located in the adjoining neighborhood of Roxbury. Thetford Avenue was about seventy-percent Black and thirty-percent white when we moved in. It was rapidly on the way to becoming an all-Black neighborhood.

My experience working in South Boston can provide a sense of the intense hatred swirling around. In 1976, I worked at the Grant Gear Company in South Boston, which employed about three-hundred workers from many ethnic backgrounds. The plant was roughly twenty-five-percent Black and located on the fringe of South Boston — the mobilized racist core of the city. Two blocks from the plant, neighborhood residents stoned school buses as they went up South Broadway to South Boston High School. There was one street Black workers could safely take from the subway at Broadway to the plant —and one awful diner.

One of our fellow workers, who was white, had just bought a new car and somehow negotiated with the company for a spot inside the fenced-in management parking lot. In a great show of generosity, he offered to take a bunch of us to the nearby bank to cash our checks. A carload of workers — Black and white — took off for the bank.

We never made it.

The car was stoned; someone tried to drop cement blocks on the car from buildings along the route (missing, thankfully). We were forced to turn back. The car was a wreck. Surprisingly, no one was hurt.

While Boston made the headlines, racial divisions and antagonisms were alive and well on the North Shore in Lynn and Salem where we lived. Lynn was famous for the huge number of fires in the low-income Hispanic and Black neighborhood as speculators burned down houses in the hopes of cashing in on urban renewal projects. Our Salem neighborhood of "Ward Street" had at one time been largely French Canadian, but was mostly Spanish-speaking.

It was a comfortable neighborhood for our young family. I harvested vegetables from my garden at the United Shoe Machine Company, which my Guatemalan neighbors across the street appreciated. They also appreciated the "Free Puerto Rico" sticker on my car. It turned out the head of that household worked in a foundry where I had a second job as a machinist — and, of course, we noticed each other.

Those kinds of warm relationships eventually led to the development of a class on Marxism with a group of Dominicans in the neighboring town of Peabody. Outside of our bubble, however, all seemed to stay the same. The United Shoe Machine Company was all white. Other major employers like GE were mostly so, with people of color well below the percentage in the employment area.

The Communist Party

"There was talk that I was a Communist. Just because my father was labeled a Communist, my mother was working for a Communist union, we had CP literature in the house and I went to a Party school. Well, that's how rumors get started." This was joke that long time Communist leader Gil Green often told but in my case it was certainly relevant.

Are you a Communist? I was asked this question constantly before I was a member of the CP. It was usually the first step in an attempt to discredit whatever issue I was raising. This was certainly the case with Miles McMillin of the Capital Times when he interviewed me about the Congress of Unrepresented Peoples in 1965. My answer was usually to ask why they wanted to know; although I could have answered: "No."

By the time I had joined the Party, I found that no one really wanted to know if I was a member. True, people who were trying to discredit me continued to ask, but not because they really were interested in joining the CP. When I was running for union office, supporters did not really want to know if I was a "real" CP member.

The union people just assumed I was a Communist. But without having to be confronted with definite knowledge, they could defend my positions vis-a-vis the union and company, and not have to defend the CP at the same time. This issue of the face of the Communist Party had plagued the group since the 1920s, resulting in its role and contribution to building the trade union movement never being clear.

I joined the Communist Party because I wanted to change our society. The Party of those years was based in the multi-racial and multi-ethnic working class and worked closely with Black communities and political leaders. The Party's work in this area provided a standard by which I could measure the mainstream liberal response to the challenges to America's racist past and present.

I was also attracted to the Party because I saw how they worked with other organizations in the antiwar movement. They tended to oppose the dogmatists and had an approach that focused on mobilizing a multi-racial coalition to demand the U.S. get out of Vietnam.

The Party engaged in serious educational efforts regarding Marxism, race and class. The discussions were much deeper than simple tactical discussions about immediate tasks. The Party clubs offered mutual support, which was extremely important given we were operating in a hostile environment.

By the early seventies, it was clear the Party would not achieve exponential growth like it once did in the1930s. But it was still a going concern with a significant number of people in community and labor organizing. Young people, especially Black people, made up the leadership in several areas. The arrest and prosecution of Angela Davis, along with her spirited defense initiated by the CP, thrust the organization into the forefront. In the Boston metro area, the Party was known as a principled and effective ally in the fight against racism.

The Communist Party in Madison included student activists, as well as those from industry and the community. While we did do practical work, including the referendum and participation in the Black student strike, we also spent a lot of time assessing such issues as the aristocracy of labor and its relationship to racism, unionization and other such matters. Due to our internal discussions on racism, the Party also made a significant contribution to the larger intellectual life of Madison. Two of us were also Teaching Assistants in the only Black Studies class offered at UW.

The North Shore of Boston was a different world. Until we moved into the area, the CP had been absent for at least fifteen years or so. Leading members had either been driven out of their jobs and left the area, or had been expelled or left the Party when they objected to the "mainstream" idea. Mainstream was the strategy the Party adopted in the mid-fifties as a means to protect the Party's influence in the union movement. In 1954, the Party had decided that the left unions were finished, and in order to influence the right wing unions especially those in the CIO, CP members were ordered to leave the left unions and join the right wing ones. On the North Shore that meant leaving the UE and joining the International Union of Electrical Workers. Members who did not do that were expelled. As far as influencing the union movement, or saving a functioning a Party led trade union nucleus, the strategy was a complete failure, with many people leaving the Party for good and others being absorbed into the dominant political culture of their new unions.

Starting in 1972 we began to rebuild the Party. Ultimately were able to build a membership which eventually totaled no more than ten people. We built the Party on the basis of developing a Farm Worker labor support committee, by working in a consistent and principled way at GE and with solidarity support work in Lynn. The Party was much diminished as compared to the late forties. Nor with a couple of exceptions, did we succeed in recruiting long time community residents

Partially because of geographical distance, but mostly because we did not feel really connected to the internal party discussions in Boston, we tended to distance ourselves from the inner Party debates- with one major exception- the perennial one of how open — or public — we should be. In a practical way, this debate surfaced when it came to the Party's insistence that members participate in getting signatures on nominating papers for Communist Party candidates. The signatures were public and widely circulated by the right wing opponents of the Party, thus endangering employment.

But they would also expose those who were not open Communists in ways that we felt endangered our political influence and relationships. This of course had been a discussion since the foundation of the CP and was recognition that even if the Party was "legal", in the minds of many it was a suspect and subversive organization.

In the end, it was our commitment to the people we served, as well as those who had elected us to union leadership positions, that led to our decision to leave the CP. When the Party endorsed the 1985 union contracts with GE, Party members at GE had been leading the opposition against it. Our group stuck with our commitments, both personal and political. In some ways, our decision resembled the mainstream issues of a generation prior. A top down decision was made, without the input from many of us on the ground and which, in our view, would cause us to destroy personal and political relationships. By that time, several of us had already been working at GE for nearly a decade and had built coalitions that elected us to union office or made us effective union stewards. At that point, there did not seem to be any benefit from being in the CP and most simply left it.

The end of the CP at GE was in large part driven by three factors.

The end of the CP at GE was in large part driven by three factors. The Party endorsed the 1985 IUE-GE contract with the General Electric Company. The procedural issue, as far as we were concerned, was the lack of any meaningful consultation with our group — arguably the largest shop club in the industry, as well as being within a strategic local. Our group and the local had been leading opposition to the contract. The substantive contractual issues dealt with the absence of meaningful protections against plant closures and the removal of work either overseas or to non- union manufacturers. This was not the first time a top-down scenario played out. The "mainstream" decisions were determined in much the same way.

Secondly, the Party failed to analyze the fundamental changes that were occurring in the basic unionized industrial landscape of the 1980s — and as a result, lacked a strategic plan to deal with them. The new technologies of the era had the potential to change the organization of work but the discussion of automation focused almost solely on the employment impact, which while important, was only a small portion of the challenge. There was no vision or meaningful discussion of the way that a socialist would conceive of the new workplace.

Finally, the internal political culture of the CPUSA seemed impervious to change. The idea of the all-knowing general secretary embodying all the thought of the central committee, giving long speeches covering the world view, something that the leaders in the USSR tended to do, was copied by the CPUSA and derided by many movement activists coming into the Party. The practice of real collective leadership seemed absent.

In thinking back to what seemed to be huge arguments about the worker aristocracy and other issues which roiled the CP in the late sixties and early seventies, it seems clear that as an organization we did not fully comprehend the ferocity of the attack by major corporations on the very structure of the trade union movement. Maybe no one could have foreseen the de-industrialization of the U.S., which was beginning to take place by 1975 or so, or that one of the main targets would be the labor aristocracy. But we were unable to bring the theoretical understandings down to the practical political level with sufficient clarity and commitment to build an effective movement against plant closures.

The theory of the labor aristocracy would suggest that while this segment of the working class had the organizational ability to do something about plant closings, the political will and understanding would not be there. When Lenin and others spoke of the labor aristocracy they meant those workers whose situation was marginally better because they benefitted from the fruits of imperialism or racism. I among others, found the term useless and off putting. In fact strictly defined the "labor aristocracy" was the white, organized section of the American working class.

The Party's language would be enough to turn off many — and terms like "labor aristocracy" or "dictatorship of the proletariat" were no exception. "Labor aristocracy" meant almost the entire membership of Local 201 could be considered "labor aristocrats" because we were benefiting directly from U.S. foreign policy. Of course, none of us felt like "labor aristocracy" and people would have laughed us out of the workplace if we spoke that language.

Maybe the chance at rebirth of a mass left was illusory despite the growth, excitement and intellectual activity of the sixties. While we could not be immune from the actions of the USSR, the issues that brought about the demise of the CP were much closer to home. They included how to work with and appreciate Black liberation, insurgents within the unions and the student movements. Some of the leaders of these movements were the children of Communist Party members — past or current. These organizations were engaged with the Party, but the Party was not sure how to react to this and was never able to integrate these movements into the Party.

Dolores: French Literature to Medical School, 1971-75

By the spring of 1971, while we were still at UW, Dolores was struggling with her commitment to French literature. Literary criticism was a large part of the field and was not as engaging to her as it had previously been. In 1972, when she had decided to pursue a career as a physician, she realized that the only way she would get into medical school was if she took classes at top-rated places that would stand out to any reviewer. Thus, she took inorganic chemistry, physics and biochemistry classes at Boston University, Harvard and MIT respectively. In April 1973, Connecticut College (for Women) notified Dolores of her acceptance to a special program which prepared minority women for medical school. At about the same time, I achieved seniority at the United Shoe Machine Company in Beverly, MA.

Attendance at Connecticut College was full time, which meant relocating to New London. We decided that I would move to the North Shore of Boston and commute to New London on the weekends and Dolores would keep the kids, then two and four-years-old. On Labor Day weekend 1973, we made the move. Dolores' parents, who had begun (after almost 10 years!) to accept our marriage, helped out with child care. The arrangement was a terrible strain: I do not know how Dolores did it.

The oil crisis saved us. For about six weeks from Christmas break until mid-February, the school was closed and we were able to live together with the kids in Salem, Massachusetts. By the time it reopened, we could see the mid-May end of the school year, and figured that if we lasted as long as we did, a few more months would be possible.

Then disaster struck. In 1973 and 1974, sexism and discrimination still ruled the roost in medicine. Today, the question posed to Dolores at her Yale University interview — "What type of birth control do you use?"— would be unacceptable. But in 1973, it was actually not unusual. In the end, Dolores was not accepted to any medical school. This was a huge blow. But with the encouragement of her mother, who was assistant commissioner for health in Westchester County, Dolores was accepted to New York Medical College in Valhalla, New York.

With the help of family, we were able to move from Salem in early 1975, and buy a three-decker house in Lynn, MA. These three-deckers houses were omnipresent throughout the Boston metro area, and the most prevalent type of housing for working people. Our three-family house needed extensive renovations, none of which we could really afford. My friends and I did almost all of them.

Lynn was no garden spot, however. A family of small-time criminals lived next door. Their specialty was petty theft of various kinds. There was a gambling spot at the end of the street as well.

Living in Lynn enabled the kids to participate in Project Children-Model Cities Day Care. Project Children was free to low-income workers. Even with a sliding scale for people who were employed like Dolores and I, it was still far less expensive and of better quality than anything we could have afforded. But there was more. The center was also multi-racial and multi-ethnic. Many of the staffers and kids spoke Spanish. Our kids loved it, and 50 years later, still remember it fondly.

Model Cities Day Care was our lifeline. After a while, Dolores was elected chairman of the Community Advisory Committee — the organization that actually ran Project Children. This arrangement, however, was continually being undermined by the mayor who controlled the Lynn Community Development Department, which could award the contract for managing the center to anyone — with or without the agreement of the parents.[1]

In the spring of 1975, the city began maneuvers with North Shore Community College to take control of the center and give it to the college to train new teachers. Dolores and other enraged parents organized themselves to fight the takeover, and prepared a detailed grant application to the appropriate agencies to fund the center.

In September of 1975, when Dolores left for medical school, the parents elected me to be president of the Parents Board.

In late 1975, the city did not forward the money to the Advisory Board needed to run Project Children. In early 1977, after fruitless efforts to resolve the issue, parents decided to take the kids and sit in at the mayor's office until we received the needed funds. Although the newspaper article doesn't mention it, the city closed the bathrooms, leaving the toddlers with nowhere to go. I suggested the potted plants in the mayor's office. We stayed in the office for about two to three hours, until the mayor and his chief poverty officer came and agreed to pay the arrears. Our multi-ethnic, multi-racial and multilingual parents group kept the day care center open — and the city and North Shore Community college at bay — for almost 3 years.

The mayor responded a few weeks later. I had applied for city subsidized housing repairs. Our house met all the qualifications. But when the housing inspector came, he condemned the house and ordered everyone out in 24 hours. (The usual gift of an envelope or a bottle left strategically did not work). Luckily for me, my local union, IUE Local 201, was the largest organization in town and supportive of us. The president of the local had some beef with the mayor and told him I was the union's representative on the committee to allocate fuel oil. A couple of days later the condemnation order was forgotten. Over the next 5 years, I regularly applied for "fix-up and repaint" assistance. As the head of that agency said to me directly, in the hearing range of others, "you are first on the list… and you will never get approved." And indeed we never got a cent.

Being a Single Parent

In September 1975, Dolores had started school at New York Medical College in Valhalla, NY, while I worked the third shift at USM in Beverley and took care of the kids. By that time, Jesse was in the nearby Brickett elementary school. Parent's night was an all-female affair and when I showed up without a wife, it caused a stir. When I was asked about my family situation, I told the truth: my wife was in medical school. The principal simply didn't believe it, and began talking about instituting a "children in need of service" procedure, which meant the city would oversee the family. A few days later, I showed up to meet with her, decked out in a sports jacket, professorial attire, and a haircut. I explained that I was doing a participant observer study of community pathology in East Lynn. My wife was in school — and since that tended to fit the stereotype of a professional, not some third-shift foundry worker, it worked. No more concerns from the Brickett School about the kids.

I can't adequately describe the tension and feelings of confusion the kids must have felt. Jesse goes off to school with his grandmother, but when he comes home he finds his mother is gone. He acted out by refusing to go to after school activities or day care, and came home every afternoon instead. It took me a couple of years before I could get him to go to some after school stuff. Eight years later, Jesse graduated eighth grade at more or less the same time Dolores finished her residency at Tufts.

During this time, many of the people we knew with kids were in tough financial straits. Jesse and Freya's closest Lynn friends were from single-parent families. Usually —almost every Saturday, but many evenings too — there would be five kids at dinner or breakfast. Dolores and I, in spite of the commuting, had a much more stable family arrangement than many and the resources to be able to feed everyone. We also had food stamps.

Although the kids seem to look back on this time without much hostility, I look back on it with much resentment, seeing the intransigence of employers, especially GE.

There was a two-week shutdown at GE every summer. Low-seniority workers (like me at that time) were given the opportunity to work. We had no vacation time. In theory, it was not obligatory. That being the case, in the summer of 1977, I made the decision to take the time off to be with the kids. But as I was leaving on the Friday before the shutdown, the company informed me I would be required to be at work on Monday. I could not find appropriate child care for the whole day for Jesse. Freya was just finishing up with Model Cities Day Care. So, with some trepidation, I left Jesse alone for the morning and told him to stay inside until a babysitter got there at about Noon.

But he had just gotten a new bike for his birthday — so, of course, he went outside to ride it.

It was stolen a couple of hours later as he rode it along the beach. I still remember this yellow bike. I was furious. As it turned out, GE did not want me to do my usual skilled job, but count electronic components. There was absolutely no reason for this and when I protested upon arrival, I was told I would be suspended if I left.

In 1979, I was elected to represent my fellow workers at the GE-Wilmington plant. I was, for all practical purposes, still a single parent trying to juggle child care needs and, now, a job which required attention twenty-four-hours-a-day. The expectations were that when the union and company were in negotiations they would continue through dinner time. While this might work for single men or men whose wives took care of the kids, it did not work with me, or with the women who had been elected shop stewards and who were on our team. In our house, we had dinner at 6 p.m. — no matter where anyone was or what they were doing. It was our way of bringing stability to the family. Jesse and Freya expected it. So, as 6 p.m. approached, I told the company we were taking a recess and I would be back later. They demurred. At that point, I announced from then on, any negotiations going on in the afternoon would end at 5 p.m. so the team could have dinner with their families. We would return, if child care issues were dealt with, at 7:30 p.m. Just saying this and following through was a shock to GE, and it meant at least one barrier to union participation was lowered. More than half of the workers at the Wilmington plant I represented were women — so making it possible for them to participate was important.

The years between 1975 and 1983, when Dolores were in medical school and residency, was a tense period. It would simply have not been possible for me to maintain my level of activity, or for Dolores to concentrate as she did, without the support of our friends from the neighborhood and the United Shoe Machine. We lived in working class Lynn. Our upstairs tenants, often times flight attendants, helped take care of the kids when they were sick, or when I was called to the plant. One day, our babysitter dropped off Freya, then about seven, on a snowbank in front of her friend's house. An alert neighbor brought her in, called GE and made them find me so I could get home and pick her up.

There were always kids around with somebody's parent just next door or across the street. The expectation was the kids, both Jesse and Freya, would be out on their own running around after school until it was time to come in and do their homework or eat dinner. Ultimately, we had the ability to hire a great provider for after school care — but that was late in the game — about 1981. We still have the chocolate chip recipe in the NYT cookbook from Lula. Lula's husband also worked at GE in the Heat Treat department and was a committed union person.

After two years at New York Medical College, Dolores was able to transfer to Tufts University School of Medicine in Boston for her last two years of medical school. Even though she had to be at the hospital nightly and on many other occasions, her ability to live at home was a godsend.

But one thing we were never able to accomplish was building the type of progressive teaching and support network for the kids that we had in metro New York during the late fifties. My children learned about unions and organizing because they were living it between the ages of about four to eighteen. As my daughter said many years later, she remembers people coming to the house for meetings, all wearing big boots or work shoes. But immersed as we were, that did not mean our progeny had the chance to talk with their peers about the philosophy of what we were up to or why we were doing it.

From UW to PBB to USM

Before leaving Madison, I decided to participate in the new industrial concentration of hospital organizing. I had been hired as a laboratory technician at Peter Bent Brigham (PBB) Hospital, one of the key organizing targets of Local 1199, which ultimately became the healthcare division of the SEIU.[2] The union was open to working with or hiring progressive organizers, including former and current Communist Party members and organizers who had some vision of class consciousness.

Organizing in the Hospital

The Boston Communist Party developed a detailed analysis of the medical establishment including who was actually in control of the hospitals and ideas to develop community resistance to hospital expansion, which destroyed low-income housing with no thought of replacement.[3]

The PBB facility was divided into two worlds, with the doctors on top and everyone else left scrambling on the bottom. The divisions were reinforced by clear racial divides between job classifications. Almost all the ward clerks were white and the cleaning staff was almost entirely Black and Haitian; the kitchen was mostly Black. The technical services, including respiratory therapists, were increasingly integrating, however. I was a senior research lab technician, most of whom were white or Asian. We wore white coats. The white coat was like a badge that allowed me to go anywhere in the hospital, a huge advantage as far as union organizing was concerned. I also spoke French —poorly, but passably — so, it was possible to speak with Haitian workers.

In mid-July 1972, differences within the organizing committee suddenly blew up. The unionization drive was crushed when Bill Rogers, one of the committed union activists, drew "Join 1199" on a bathroom wall in red lipstick. An informer told management and Bill was fired. [4] Almost immediately, a group of militant workers mobilized and staged a sit-in inside the administration office. The workers involved in the sit-in were told to leave or be fired — and most were fired on the spot. Union supporters like me who were known to management, were immobilized. Management got the word out as to what would happen to union people caught engaging in union activity. Key union supporters ended their willingness to participate. Some saw the union as foolhardy and engaging in an action that endangered them without even discussing it. People no longer trusted the organizing committee. The momentum for the drive was lost and the drive sputtered to a halt.

Shortly thereafter, the director of our lab announced the lab would be closing by March 1, 1973 — and the three of us working there would lose our jobs. Dolores and I could barely make it given child care expenses, so I was contemplating taking another part-time job. I decided to make my leap into the industrial working class. In a way, I was not risking much — I still had my lab job.

At this point, Dolores was working days and going to Boston University taking pre-med courses at night. I had a full-time day job and a 4 p.m. to midnight "second" job at the Cambion Company. Luckily, the hours were slowly diminishing at the lab. We kept this up for months, although I don't know how.

CAMBION to United Shoe Machine

Cambion, a maker of electronic components and a target of the United Electrical Workers, employed about 200 people, mostly low-wage earners who made and assembled electronic components for other higher-end hi-tech firms. I applied after discussing it with my comrades, especially the UE. Of course, any person in human resources who could breathe could figure I was not some unemployed tech worker or machinist. But they were desperate. My job interview, among other things, required me to place round pegs in the appropriate round hole, thus demonstrating dexterity. I truthfully filled out an application form noting I was a high school graduate.

The company was known for nickel-and-diming its workers to death. Thus, even before I said anything, it was clear people were thinking about a union. I reported this to the UE organizer and thought it was ripe for organization. The UE agreed, and as I was leaving, another person was encouraged to work at Cambion. Eventually, the UE won a certification election, but after a long strike lost a recertification election.

In October 1972, Don Tormey, the leading UE staff person in New England, told me the United Shoe Machine Plant in Beverly was hiring and urged me to apply.

Endnotes For Chapter Five

1. WHS; Emspak Papers, Folders 6.600-6.655 "Model City Day Care Proposals, supporting documents and evaluations".

2. In the late 1950s, the druggist-based union launched large-scale organizing drives at voluntary hospitals in New York, mobilizing a heavily African-American and Puerto Rican-American workforce in the first flush of the postwar Civil Rights Movement. Martin Luther King, Jr. famously described 1199 as "my favorite union". Coretta Scott King became the honorary chair of 1199's organizing campaigns as it sought to expand outside of New York City beginning the late 1960s. The union's first campaign outside of New York City was the formation of District 1199B in Columbia, South Carolina in 1969. The union led a strike there that never led to a contract, but had success in creating new 1199 districts in Upstate New York, Philadelphia (and later other parts of Pennsylvania), Connecticut, Rhode Island, West Virginia, Kentucky, Ohio, and elsewhere.(Wikipedia) It is now the basis of the healthcare division of the Service Employees International union ion the east coast.

3. WHS; Emspak papers File Folder 6.200Notes and reports re: Organizing Boston Hospitals.

4. In 1975 Bill Rogers won the Boston marathon- the first of four victories. He was a graduate of Wesleyan and committed to progressive causes. In the summer of 1972 after he was fired I saw him after running around Jamaica Pond in Boston and asked if he was worried about being fired. He said "no" so that he could concentrate on his running. I thought that weird- and continued on my bike to work at the hospital. Of course 3 years later he won the Boston marathon and became one of the most proficient runners of the time- and established his running shoe company.

Chapter Six: The World Gone By-
The United Shoe Machine Company and UE local 271

Late in October 1972, I stared at a complicated blueprint of a cam, the guts of the machine I had been hired to operate at United Shoe Machine, then the largest and most profitable manufacturer of shoe machines in the world. The hiring officer there was interested in my ability to read blueprints, not my level of education. I thank my 8th grade shop teacher for teaching us to read blueprints and do mechanical drawing—the first skills required of me in my new job.[1]

United Shoe workers joined the United Electrical Workers Union—UE—in 1940. In 1972, the local had become one of the largest and most stable locals in UE District Two, with about 600 people in the bargaining unit. Don Tormey, the leading UE staff person, was interested in having younger progressive people join the local to ensure that the progressive union ideals of his generation would survive. Between October 1972, when I was hired at the United Shoe Machine Corporation (USM), and November 1975, when I was laid off, I became a competent skilled worker and union activist.

United Shoe's main factory was located north of Boston, in Beverly, MA. It was within commuting distance from the city but could have been hours away given the cultural differences between

Boston and the factory. Whole neighborhoods were built around the plant, with foremen and administrative staff in single-family housing on one side of the plant, and triple-decker apartments on the other side, near the railroad tracks for the immigrant work-force. Two ponds to cool the turbines in the powerhouse sat on the property, giving it an almost rural character. There were several acres of land for employee vegetable gardens that were tilled by the company. While the ethnic composition of the neighborhoods had changed, the neighborhoods were still divided by class and race. No one in their right mind would have predicted that in 10 years the Shoe would be in rapid decline.

To say the Shoe was provincial was an understatement: The work-force was all male until 1973, when a female sweeper was hired. A few months later, additional women were hired on the special Mossberg [2] contract job, but at a lower laborers' rate. Unlike almost any other place at that time, a majority of workers in the foundry were first and second generation Italians, and there were no Black people in the shop. As far as I could tell the only Jewish worker in the shop was someone who ran the stockroom and, despite my objections, myself. The union's business agent, Jerry Steinberg, was also Jewish. Up until the mid-sixties, less than a decade before I was hired, Catholics could not become foremen, only Protestants. A good number of the workers lived in Beverly and many had graduated from Beverly High School. The last Beverly high school apprentice class had graduated from the Shoe in about 1968.

Factories and their culture, like those of United Shoe, are long gone, along with most of us who worked in them. But they were the center of people's lives for generations. The people in a plant like United Shoe lived in a self-contained but parallel world to the one outside. To an extent, it was the union that connected the workforce to the outside world.

After my interview, I was taken to the automatic screw machine department. [3] To the foreman's shock, I had been hired. The foreman, Bob, introduced me to the lead man in the small screw machine area, who showed me the machine I was to set up and operate, as well as the cams, the tools that I needed to properly place in the machine, and the print of the part I was going to make. He pointed out the tool room, the inspectors' spot, the bathroom, and where to punch in and out. When he came back a few minutes later he realized that it was going to be a long time before I would be proficient: I had no idea where to start.

Piece Work [4]

Union members were paid piecework, the system codified by Frederick W Taylor.[5] Taylorism sought to identify the time it took for each action of the worker, and thus to control each action of the worker, with the objective of maximizing production and profit. The labor theory of value is really the basis for Taylorism: Taylor recognized that value flowed from labor, and he believed that workers were always trying to "steal" time and work inefficiently.

In fact, experienced workers in the machine trades were constantly looking for ways to do the work more efficiently in order to reduce the excessive work pace which characterized piecework. In most shops the official "method sheet," which illustrated the company's operating instructions for each position, was prominently displayed for every job on every machine. The real method, meanwhile, could be found in a little notebook that most of us kept and would share with others who might get that job.[6] With the support of an alert union, workers also tried to make sure that the burden of running the shop was placed appropriately on management. For instance, if tools were not ready, if blueprints were late, if a crane was not available or any of a myriad of items that could go wrong did, management would pay and the time would not count against one's piecework production. This area was a source of intense conflict.

The piecework system magnified one cultural shock—the value of the spoken word. In graduate school, you could talk your way through a problem and get your solution accepted. For instance, one could have a disagreement about a source or some historical incident, and after some debate the professor might accept your point of view. But not at United Shoe. You could talk all you wanted, but if the part did not meet the dimensions specified in the blue print, it was junk. Your day was a waste, and even if the parts could be salvaged, you were not going to get credit for them.

You could try to "make the rate" via physical production, or you could learn how to use a pencil and figure out the best mixture of production, set up time, and "rest and delay" (for example, waiting for tools, or time to go to the restroom) to meet management's demands and your own. The most skilled and adept people were experts in both areas. Experienced foremen, many of whom had been skilled workers, knew exactly what was going on. Thus, in most well-run locations, a social norm of production was established. This norm allowed for flexibility on the job: If there was some emergency, the foreman would ask people to "help him out" with a particular job, with the understanding that things would go back to normal when the emergency was over.

A couple of days after I started my job at the Shoe, I was approached by another more or less younger worker, Charlie P. Charlie introduced himself and told me that I was going to have trouble.

"With what?" I inquired. "The beard," he said. He told me that along with him, I was about the only other person in the building with a beard. "People didn't like that," he said. In the early seventies, beards signaled "hippies" or ne'er do wells to my fellow workers. He also told me that his father had been one of the few people to testify against the UE in the various anti-red attacks in the fifties, but all that was in the past, and aside from the beard, Charlie himself was accepted in the shop. Charlie became a solid, militant leader of the local as the Shoe began its decline a few years later. He mentioned that just about the entire workforce knew that my father had been the Secretary-Treasurer of the UE and was curious as to what I was doing in the shop when I obviously had limited machine skills. Over the next few weeks people came by to introduce themselves, usually along some axis of loyalty to the UE.

Meanwhile, I struggled to learn the job.

A Word About Skill

Within any group of workers trying to accomplish something, some are more knowledgeable than others. Those are the people most valuable to the company, but also to their coworkers. They understand the tasks to be performed and have the knowledge needed and know the sequence of steps needed to get something done. Within a union, these workers are the key to almost any victory, not just because they can control the actual flow of work, but because they are usually respected and appreciated by their peers.

In a machine shop like USM, skill meant a combination of abilities and tasks. You had to be able to read and interpret blueprints; do the math necessary to calculate both your pay and certain tolerances; be able to use hand held measuring equipment. Additionally, a skilled machinist knew which tools would cut the metal, their limits in terms of cutting speeds and rate of feeding the tool to the metal. The most skilled people had a real understanding of the overall job, how everything fit together and the function of the product being produced. Taken together, this combination of skills and abilities is defined as "tacit" knowledge. The people with this kind of tacit knowledge could offer solid advice to people like me who knew little.

Management always wanted to take control of this work, either through a system like Taylorism, or by replacing many parts of the skilled job with Computer Aided or Computer Numerically Controlled machine tools.

As I became more skilled, it was possible for me to really appreciate the talent and ingenuity of my fellow workers. The

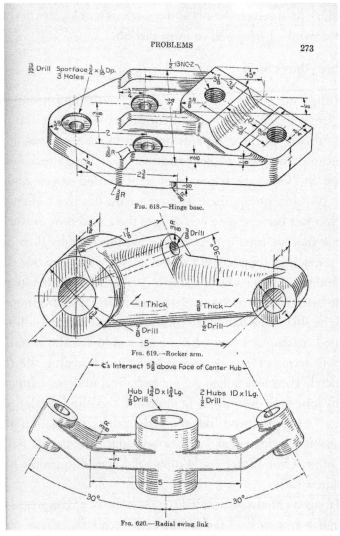

Working Drawing (or instructions) that a machinist would see as he or she prepared to produce the part.

understanding of skill and its importance became my intellectual foundation for the next 25 years of attempts to control the design and implementation of the new computer aided manufacturing.

In 1973, computer-aided machine tools were in their infancy, but a revolution in the apportionment of skill and control of the workplace was about to take place. By 1990, many of the machines I had worked on were in museums. Management succeeded in many, but not in all places, implementing production systems that reduced meaningful use of the tacit knowledge of the shop floor and thus undermined a source of working class strength.

Learning to Survive

A first survival lesson was provided by Charlie S., who became a lifelong friend. "Stay out of the foreman's line of sight," Charlie told me, early on. "The less he sees of you, the better."

After a while, I began to have lunch with the guys who worked across the aisle from me. We had a 30 minute unpaid lunch—enough time for some to go out to the bar down the street, or set up the card game or sit around and talk. Initially, the group was aghast at the fact that I lived in Dorchester. It wasn't the commute; some people drove from New Hampshire. It was "Boston," meaning Black people. As we discussed the matter, it turned out that of the group only a couple of people had been to Boston once or twice to go to a Red Sox game.

Given their biases, I thought that having a Free Angela button on my jacket would cause alarm among my coworkers. It didn't—but mostly because no one knew who Angela Davis was and that she had been falsely accused of conspiracy to commit murder. My beard outweighed any questions about the button.

There was a social hierarchy in the shop, and as a new person I was at the bottom. People intuited that I had an education, and they thought I was basically stupid for being in the machine shop at the Shoe. Once it became clear that I wasn't a jerk, people began to think that the UE had sent me to work to learn about the local and then take over as Business Agent. Nothing I said changed that perception.

What did change my status was Whitey's shoe. Whitey was a lunch mate and an extremely volatile person—a misogynist and a racist. He was also an excellent machinist and very smart, and was, for the most part, tolerated by his peers. He came to work each day in a pair of military-style steel toed shoes, so polished you could practically see your reflection in them.

We were talking one day and he made some particularly bigoted, nasty remark. Generally, we ignored those comments— which could have been the case this time too. Not that day. I was cleaning my teeth, and spit on the floor right next to one of these impeccable shoes. Dead silence. People thought I was about to get murdered, but I held my ground, said nothing and went on with the toothpick.

Somehow, everyone heard about this and by midafternoon my social stock went up.

Another big revelation about the sociology of the plant came at Christmas. At about 9:00 AM on the morning before our Christmas day off, people stopped work and began to circulate throughout the factory. Workers stopped at each machine station, shook hands, wished each other Merry Christmas and had a drink. It took about two hours to go through our wing. I was cordially received, and met all kinds of new people. Many people went for lunch and did not come back, and by about 3:00 PM, the word went out that everyone who was still there could leave an hour early. The tradition of visiting had been going on for years and would continue until the place closed. This friendship was nothing like my experiences in the University world, where there was little sense of community.

By January of 1973, I realized I had been accepted by the rest of my department. Peace and civil rights organizations had scheduled a march against racism and war for Inauguration Day on Saturday, January 20. I told my shop mates that I was going to DC for the anti-war march, which might not have been surprising; they knew I opposed the war. But no one in my department had ever met a "real" anti-war protester, and of course there was lots of debate about what I was going to do.

To my utter surprise, Felix, the inspector, went around and took up a collection to help defray the costs of my trip, and maybe even to hire a lawyer if I needed one. Everyone expressed concern for my well-being – generally in the form of a comment: "Don't get clubbed."

This contradicted accounts in the press of white working class disapproval, and even hatred for anti-war demonstrators.

Organization through Gardening

One of the few benefits available to me at the plant was a 40 by 60 foot garden plot on the USM property. The plots were assigned on the basis of seniority and with the understanding that you would actually take care of yours. People who didn't take care of their plots did not get a second chance. I applied and in due time, was assigned my own plot in the "lower" gardens. The food that I raised was an important part of our household, and I grew enough vegetables to feed the neighborhood. I was also being judged by the rest of the gardeners, whose plots were weeded, symmetrical and well maintained.

Getting the garden plot was a great opportunity for another reason, too: I had a way, other than politics, of relating to people. I learned about vegetables, but also about the Italian community. Unlike the other gardeners, I grew flowers, a fact that caused some controversy. The older gardeners, many of whom came from Sicily, thought that every square inch should be used for food. Flowers were a waste of time, and they told me so. However, their wives had a different view, as I gave away bunches of flowers for the gardeners to take home. During my second year of gardening, the Italians began to grow flowers. By my third year, I was moved up to one of the most desirable plots in the "upper" gardens, which I maintained until 1983—several years after I was laid off.

When I ran for union office in 1974 I found that the gardeners had made their judgement. They told our fellow union members that I was a solid contributor, and while I was also being attacked as a troublemaker, outsider, and communist, their endorsements meant that I had friends in many places.

The Union

By 1972, the people who had founded the new unions of the 1930s were disappearing but not yet completely gone. Anthony Arthur Petkovitch was one of the last industrial blacksmiths of the old era. Petkovitch did the same type of work as my grandfather, who had been an industrial blacksmith at GE prior to his death. Petkovitch's job was to make parts for machines that broke down, many of which were forged and shaped by hand. He was also a participant in efforts to organize the Ford motor company in Chicago in 1937-38. Ford had viciously attacked these workers, and many were hurt, but the company was eventually forced to give in. Petkovich always talked about this to his fellow workers at the much more conservative Shoe, and they thought that he was a little eccentric. But as time went on, and some of my contemporaries became more involved in renewing the union, they tended to listen more to what he had to say.

There was also a group of highly skilled and more or less public members of the Communist Party at United Shoe. In 1920 the workers at United Shoe went on strike. The company reacted with ferocity, discharging almost the entire work force and breaking the strike. At the time—the twenties and thirties—about 2,000 workers were employed at the Shoe and it was a target for radical organizers. The most dedicated were members of the Communist Party. Within the Italian working class community radicalism was an accepted part of the political environment. They became an important part of the original core organizers of the UE local.

In 1972 those workers were still mostly employed at the Shoe. I went to see them one day and was warmly welcomed. We talked about the union, their families, their history and how far they had come socially and economically. They attributed their situation to the strength of the union, and were concerned about the union's future health. Neither I nor they were concerned about the future of the company. They were looking forward to retirement from a stable company with an adequate pension. There was no hint of imminent collapse. Tony Di Vincenzo, one of the early leaders of the union, introduced me to all the people in the highly skilled tool and die department[7] and told people to be supportive. Tony was not interested in discussing the Party, in terms of joining it or being involved, but he did not attack it either and recognized its positive effect on the development of the union. A few months later he retired. He was the last link with that generation of radicals in the plant and the current workforce.

From November 1972 through March 1973, I had no time for political work as I continued to work at the hospital until the lab shut down in March. I was also trying to figure out how to be a communist and a unionist—what did it mean and exactly how was one supposed to act?

My first attempt to involve the local in the outside world occurred on September 11th, 1973, during the Chilean coup. My friend Adam Schesch, a graduate student doing research in Chile, was arrested and held in Chile's National Stadium with his wife and young son and thousands of others who had, for one reason or another, been identified as enemies of Pinochet's new authoritarian state. [8]

The US was complicit in the coup and was not interested in helping American leftists who had gone to Chile to support the socialist government. Luckily, we found a connection with Beverly and Local 271—Nuns from the La Salette [9] order who had a retreat in nearby Rowley had also been arrested and were being held.

At my request, and after some thought and discussion, UE local 271 officially contacted the progressive and antiwar Congressman Michael Harrington and urged him to intervene with the State Department on behalf of both. He did so, and by all accounts it was helpful—Schesch and his family were released and returned home. An unknown number of Chileans were executed in that stadium, which is now notorious for torture and extrajudicial killings. Some foreign activists, including American citizens, were also killed.

The actual intervention of our local in something beyond the sphere of labor law was a new thing, especially considering our status as a conservative local of the left-leaning UE. Local 271 represented only United Shoe in Beverly, so the culture of insularity had a real physical basis. Because the company had a monopoly position, the firm's profits were steady. Wages were indexed according to the Bureau of Labor Statistics cost of living announcement each year. From time to time, the company would agree to increase the base. Likewise, benefits equaled, but in general did not surpass GE—the area leader. Internally, the local was frugal and honest. In a sense, there was no reason for membership mobilization as long as things went along this somewhat placid path. Other unions had, on numerous occasions, attempted to raid the local in Beverly, but none, apparently, came close.

The union structure itself encouraged low internal activity. Officers and stewards had super seniority, which meant that if you were a steward you automatically became the most senior in your department. If you were an Executive Board member or negotiating committee member you had plant-wide seniority. As a result, workers often elected the most senior person as steward, whether or not he was interested in the union. This was the case in the screw machine department where I worked. Thus younger, low seniority workers like me, were generally not elected.

By 1972, when the union agreed to a lower pay rate on a contract to produce shot gun firing chambers for the Mossberg arms company, the system had begun to fray around the edges.[10] The pension was underfunded and there was a growing understanding that pensions needed to be protected in some way.[11] There was also some concern as the contract negotiations approached in 1974, but generally, complacency was still the rule. UE local 271 was a competent and well-managed union, but "don't rock the boat" was the mantra of the day. Although at a national level, the UE took a stand in favor of civil rights (the UE was the first international union to invite MLK in the mid-fifties) and for other progressive causes, locals like 271 essentially ignored those positions. Locals were autonomous as far as resolutions like this were concerned. Thus when I began to raise issues of labor solidarity, pension reform, and membership involvement by making the newsletter more interesting, there was considerable resistance.

Although conservative in some ways, the local functioned with a strong commitment to unionism as they understood it. UE members at local 271 refused to do work bound for struck GE plants during the 1969 GE strike. The union had a clause in their contract allowing workers to refuse to produce work bound for a struck plant—which was in and of itself an extraordinarily uncommon clause. When the GE strike began, workers refused to pack up and load work for struck GE plants, or produce new parts. When the company suspended the workers in question, the entire plant

133

walked out. The walkout lasted for a couple of days. Eventually, the company got an injunction against the local and people were forced back to work; workers who were suspended were reinstated, but the work remained undone. This was a tremendous and rare show of solidarity at that time.

And while a competent, well organized but self-contained unit could do well by its members in the controlled environment of 1946-1970, an organization characterized by this type of culture was completely at sea when confronted with the wholesale deindustrialization soon to come. No individual local could survive the wave of capital mobility on its own. As has become painfully clear, perhaps a real nationally coordinated and progressive movement might have slowed or stopped the forced march of decapitalization of industry, but nothing like that existed. The successful extirpation of well-established working class communists meant that people were gone who had a vision shared nationally. This absence of people with a class perspective was central to the inability of organized labor to assess the growing deindustrialization and find ways to counter it.

Labor Solidarity at USM

In December 1974, Local 271 invited a representative of the Farm Workers to the local meeting to report on their strike and ask for support, which was granted in the form of a resolution and small financial contribution.

In the wider world of the North Shore, there was an active community based pro-farmworker committee and one of the targets was Lynnway Liquor- a popular liquor store across the street from the GE River Works plant in Lynn. The United Farmworkers had been on strike against the Gallo wine company for some months with growing popular support especially from organized labor. As a consequence Lynnway Liquors across the street from the GE Lynn plant with about 6,000 union members agreed to stop displaying Gallo wines. But Lynnway Liquors reneged on the agreement and Local 201, in support of the national boycott of Gallo wines, endorsed a picket line. Community members as well as local 201 members participated.

One Saturday in March 1975, pickets were attacked by unknown assailants, who were rumored to be associated with organized crime. After some fighting the assailants left and the picket resumed. At about noon, Peter Hodes, a comrade from Lynn who worked at GE, and I joined the picket line. I had been keeping local 271 informed, as by then I was a member of the Executive Board of the local. However, the local had not formally endorsed my participation. A few minutes after we arrived, the pickets were attacked again and a brawl broke out. Just as one of the attackers raised his club to hit Peter, his jacket rode up and revealed the Lynn police belt underneath. The police had taken off their badges and identification and attacked us.

Naturally, we were all arrested. The police charged us with a felony—assault and battery on a police officer. If convicted there would be a one year mandatory year in jail. When I went to the local and asked if there was legal assistance available, they pointed out that I had not been authorized officially to participate as a board member, never mind getting arrested.

In one of the many bizarre twists in the labor movement, I asked IUE local 201 if I could be included in their legal defense of Peter. They referred me to their law firm of Angoff and Goldman. Sam Angoff had been one of the lawyers who led the legal charge against the UE and helped establish the IUE displacing the UE from Lynn GE.

I was somewhat surprised when Angoff would see me personally. When we met, Sam told me about his support of the IUE, which he said was a mistake. (A little late, but still a surprise to me).

Then he offered his firm's resources pro bono and told me not to worry so much. His associate Al Goldman was assigned to the case.

At the trial, as if reading from a script, the police testified that we had attacked them, that they had identified themselves and that we were the problem. We testified that all of what the police said was essentially nonsense. The idea that we had constitutional rights, let alone the right to picket peacefully, did not come up. We did point out that we were partially on state land when we were arrested and the Lynn police did not have jurisdiction, but that was deemed irrelevant.

All looked grim. The bailiff approached us and asked if we had anything to say. An envelope changed hands.

The envelope was discussed with the judge, who summoned the police to the bench. All sat down.

The judge asked again if there was anything anyone wanted to add.

And then a miracle: The police testified again and now said they were not sure who was who, or who hit who. The judge pronounced the sentence. "No picketing, one year probation and if repeated, the charges would be reinstated." And as a special bonus, after about 10 years, the record would be expunged, so there would be no record of the arrest and conviction.[12] The farmworker organizer who had been arrested with us was told to leave town.

A couple of years later, when I was a member of local 201, the perennial discussion of legal fees came up. Someone had been questioning an undefined $1500 legal expense, dating from the spring of 1975. It appeared to be costs connected with the Farmworkers picket.

By September of 1973 I had been in discussions with Jerry Steinberg as to how to improve the union's newspaper- *The Blue Sheet.* [13] I also been befriended by union President Ray McClory, a progressive minded person who wanted the union to be more involved in the world, but who also sensed that something was amiss as regards how the union was operating Vis a Vis the company. The chief steward, Harry Ball, was a very conservative business minded unionist and formerly a popular football player from Beverly High School. He did not like grievances, or people who questioned him. The Stewards Council was composed of many of his supporters, but there was also a strong group of traditional UE people; many from the foundry, who did not like the way things were proceeding. In this mix, because of my education and abilities to organize I could be an important asset to the progressive wing and thus not a favorite of Harry.

The Pension Committee

In the shop the feeling was that since I went to college I ought to be able to understand the pension plan in all its complexities. After some discussion with the business agent I proposed that we establish a USM local 271 Pension Committee whose purpose was to inform the membership about the issues regarding the pension, make sure the local's ideas were understood and supported by Senator Kennedy and Representative Harrington and assist in the mobilization for the upcoming 1974 contract.

At the national level, the UE supported a comprehensive approach to the issue including adequate funding; vesting, insurance, protection against fraud and portability.[14]

As structured in 1973 USM controlled the pension in all aspects. There was no union member on the governing board of the pension. There was no federal legislation insuring pensions, or protecting workers against the loss of their pension. Onerous vesting rights were the rule. Companies like USM or GE continually told the workers that they were stable and there was no need for any government interference. And, for workers in some firms, like

USM, their words made sense. USM had "always" been there. Thus dealing with the pension involved several interrelated issues.

First, there was an ideological issue- we were challenging the company's honesty and word. Second there were the actual complex issues of funding, vesting, and payouts.

Third, there was a need to mobilize. People weren't used to it. A contract mobilization might have some resonance, but a political mobilization was something else. We asked people to sign post-cards, petitions and letters and thus publicly declare themselves for the union position.

Fourth, the establishment and functioning of a committee like the Pension Committee was a potential source of power and upset the internal political status quo.

From a class conscious perspective, I saw the pension as an issue that raised class issues, and moved beyond just the individual grievance world. Mobilization around this type of issue exposed the weakness of the company's refusal to guarantee the pension. It raised some questions about the relationship between the union and company and put various people who apologized for USM on the spot.

Our attitude was straightforward. "Pensions are a right not a privilege. Because we work for the company and produce a profit we are entitled to at least some role in the funds that ensure our future".[15] We demanded a guarantee by the company of the pension, for its corporate life- should Beverley close. No one thought that the corporate life of USM was in jeopardy but still…. [16]

We challenged the USM bargaining strategy of playing off the younger workers against the older workers with fear as the main tool. We successfully brought the issue to the membership via the Blue Sheet and with membership mobilization the union won some improvements to the plan in the 1974 negotiations, but not enough overall to overcome weaknesses in the federal law. USM had agreed to put in one million dollars to help bridge the gap, but as Jerry Steinberg pointed out, "should employment at the Shoe fall off considerably, a problem may arise."[17]

The Blue Sheet

Increased communication via the union's newsletter was one way to put class consciousness into action so I proposed a plan to revitalize the paper which was accepted by the Business Agent Jerry Steinberg.[18] However with his retirement we were not able to continue. Unlike the GE local which had a large number of young radical people, many of whom were already putting out leaflets and distributing newspapers, USM had none of that. The intellectual infrastructure was not there to really push and support such an initiative.

The UE and Me

Local 271's president Ray McClory and BA Steinberg believed that in time the UE would be happy to have me as a staff person as I would have a combination of practical experience plus knowledge of how the union actually worked both internally and Vis a Vis the company.

I often joked that I was the only progeny of a UE officer that was never hired by the UE, not that I expected or wanted a staff job. As far as I was concerned, I was doing what my parents had said about becoming an activist. "Go to work in the industry, become a competent worker and thus gain respect of your fellow workers as a contributor, not just a talker, and run for office on some principled basis". I believed it was advantageous for the union movement to add to its arsenal a person with shop experience, a communist with class consciousness and an education. As strange as such a person might be at first to their fellow workers, the people I worked with saw my education and perspective as an advantage and an equalizer in relationship to the management.

In the spring of 1974 UE organizing director Hugh Harley asked me to meet with him at the UE office in Boston. When I left the plant that day, one of the foremen congratulated me thinking I was about to get a nice union job. I think everyone in the plant had the same idea.

Much to my surprise, Hugh Harley told me in no uncertain terms that I was rocking the boat in a trusted, secure local. The International had been receiving anonymous letters complaining about me. I reacted to Harley's accusations by attacking him, and I suggested what he could do with the anonymous letters. [19] For me, the UE was family and this was an extremely painful and upsetting discussion. A few months later it was repeated in New York City when I met with Jim Matles, the secretary treasurer of the UE, a close family friend and someone whom I knew my whole life. Jim and I disagreed along the same lines as Hugh Harley and I. We argued as I would not agree to leave the Shoe and become unemployed.

There were some tensions in the UE in 1962 when my father passed away; probably over how to renew the union movement and the UE's role in it. My father's friends saw the agents for change as class conscious workers, maybe CP members, legitimized by being elected at the local level at least initially.

I suspect, but could never confirm that the CP's mainstream decisions in the mid-fifties were at the root of the problem with the UE and me.[20] So while the UE wanted class conscious as well as union conscious people on their staff and in leadership, they preferred to choose those people themselves. I am sure based on their prior experience they were concerned about the loyalty of individuals to the UE.

In the shop, and this was always the case, everyone seemed to know what happened before I returned the next day. Opinion was divided. The President and BA were disappointed, but not shocked.

My personal stock went up. I was not the chosen son of a union leader who was simply passing time at the Shoe. I think it became clear to some at that point that I could be a real agent for change in the local.

The conservative supporters of the Chief Shop Steward Harry Ball who probably initiated the letters were disappointed that instead of resigning or being intimidated I was staying at the Shoe. They began to realize that I was a real life independent, radical and trade union person.

USM and in all probability some in the union saw me as a real danger and when they had the opportunity, they acted on that belief. Later that summer I had been laid off from my higher skilled lathe job moved to the aforementioned Mossberg job at lower pay, and second shift. This department was unique in that most of the employees were young people in their twenties including several women as well as older workers who had been bumped from some other job and so were generally unhappy. The rate of production was very high. Several hundred Mossberg shotgun firing chambers were produced each shift. In deference to the reality of younger people, the firm looked the other way after the dinner break and thus I was able to bring in my radio. The department decided between music (and what kind) and the ball game.

Sometime in July right after the shutdown, the company attempted to fire me for assaulting the foreman. I had said to the foreman that he looked awful and that he should take care of himself before he dropped dead on the job. The senior management, over the foreman's objections, decided to interpret that remark as a threat. As in so many cases like this, the entire plant knew about it before me. I found out that I was about to be fired, because when I came to work my friends on the first shift were preparing to walk out in protest. When I went upstairs to my Mossberg department it was sort of like being the angel of death. Everyone disappeared.

Even the shop steward. The foreman stopped me and said we had to go see the second shift manager.

Since I was charged with a discharge offense (assault), the chief steward Harry Ball was there as well. It became obvious that he was really not interested in helping me keep my job. Nothing like a termination happened at USM without chief steward Harry Ball agreeing to it.

Three things then ensued:

1) The Mossberg workers, about 30 or so, stopped work and so now the company and union were faced with an illegal work stoppage;

2) A senior member of management showed up at the meeting and said the same thing to the foreman as I had said "Louie-you look lousy and should be in the hospital". (And in fact he had an ulcer and did go to the hospital).

3) UE local 271 President McClory arrived.

Now there was a problem. There was a work stoppage. The officers of the union clearly disagreed but the president supported me. And there was no basis for the assault charge in the first place. They solved the problem with the senior manager saying that the whole thing was foolish and rescinded the termination in progress.

The meeting was over and the political shift within the local began. President McClory appointed me steward. A few months later my fellow workers elected me to the local's Executive Board resulting in super seniority and a jurisdiction of the second shift for the entire plant. The lesson was clear too- direct action, a work stoppage by my fellow workers is what made the company look for a way out. It also demonstrated that the chief steward was no longer 100% in charge.

Challenges in the Workplace

United Shoe illustrated both the ingenuity of the workforce as well as the more brutal and out of this world character of the working class in this era. Two examples will suffice.

During much of 1974 until the spring of 1975 I worked on the third shift, did my union business in the afternoons and early evening and went to work. The third shift at USM comprised about 25 workers in this vast plant. You would look around in the darkness and see a pool of light somewhere far away. There was the shop cat- who always seemed to materialize when one least expected it. Traffic on the main street of Beverly died away after about 2:00 AM and did not pick up again until 5:00 in the morning.

But not to be deterred by the small numbers and a vast plant, people found each other and cooked chicken.

The foundry had an annealing room - about the size of a small house. It was usually at about 350 to 400 degrees. Perfect for roast chicken. A little odd to see a chicken in a small roasting pan on a railway flatcar in the middle of a huge oven.

The brutal edge of the place was best illustrated towards the end of the spring of 1975. I was back on the second shift as orders and employment began to decline. "Dave" had been laid off from his highly skilled job and agreed to take the Mossberg job because he thought he would be called back, but if not, he only had a short time to go before retirement. He was a big guy. He didn't like the union, he didn't like "hippies" and he particularly didn't like me telling him not to break the rate and not to disable the safety lever on his "climb" milling machine. It was there so that when you put the parts to be milled into the fixture, you had to use two hands to start the machine, thus making it impossible to lose one. Dave knew better. One evening just before Memorial Day we were all working away and we could hear it...here in the middle of the huge racket of machines something wasn't right- just for a second.

But we all knew.

I ran over just as Dave collapsed. We called the ambulance- but I could see his fingers still on the machine. I picked them up, put them in my pocket, told the foreman I was going to the hospital (about 5 minutes away) and maybe we could save the fingers.

When I got to the hospital I ran into the emergency room pulled the fingers out of my pocket, put them on the counter and said that someone at the Shoe had been hurt and said to the startled and probably frightened nurse "Put these in saline-maybe they could be saved".

This did not go over well. From the nurses or receptionists perspective, someone had run to the emergency room, blood running down his shirt and generally covered with grease and metal chips and was giving orders. They told me to get out. I pleaded with them. They threatened to call the police. (In 1983, Dolores, by then a physician, started work at that hospital).

Meanwhile the ambulance could not get into the plant because the emergency back gate was locked. By the time they reached Dave, got him to the operating room and began work, the opportunity to save most of his hand and reattach the fingers was long gone.

A couple of days later, when he was able to talk, the union (myself, the BA and the President); the company and their insurance lawyer were at the bedside. The company offered Dave a job for life, said he could come back and would have his higher rate of pay restored if ONLY he did not file a grievance, demand workman's comp or insist on his rights. Being the company man he was, after some nasty remarks to the union he agreed. Three years later (at most) his department was abolished and he was out in the street as an unemployed one handed machinist.

Meanwhile back at the Mossberg department, the company had just announced that we should all go back to work. People were shaken and upset. I announced that everyone was going home and would be paid until the end of the shift. After some discussion the company agreed. I suggested that since it was the Memorial Day weekend and Mossberg was losing production that everyone is given the opportunity to work Memorial Day. People were paid time and a half plus the holiday pay. It was the only OT I ever worked in 15 years. I never believed in overtime because I thought that the company should hire more workers and I also wanted to be home with the kids.

Just as an aside as to what the culture was in May of 1975 on our street in Lynn: As I drove up at about 8:00 PM on a beautiful spring night people came into the street off their porches and Dolores ran out of the house to greet me. There would be no reason to be home at the "wrong" time unless one was laid off or there was an accident. Not as dramatic as the scene in *"How Green was My Valley"* when the mine whistles blew and people knew there was a cave in, but still, Lynn was a GE town, people worked specific times and a significant number of people on the street had been or were working at GE.

At about this time June 1975 it was becoming obvious that something was amiss at United Shoe. The Xerox work was gone- and not replaced. The Mossberg job would end June 30. A big experimental machine that used a shoe machine (the "clicker") redesigned to be computer controlled and to insert components for printed circuit boards was unused, and unsold as Chrysler, which had declared bankruptcy, refused to take possession. And the new large machining bay was having trouble. Rumor was that the firm was up for sale.

Significant layoffs seemed to be on the horizon. Given that I had super seniority due to my E-Board position I could not be laid off until I was out of office. However the only job left was the foundry. The foundry offered the possibility of being called back to a higher paying skilled job but also keeping the health and dental benefits. So I took it.

In the short period of time from January 1972 to July of 1975 I had moved from PhD student to senior lab technician to machinist to laborer. But I did not anticipate moving to the 19th century.

The Foundry

The USM foundry was a modern foundry as the coal fired furnaces had been replaced by two electric kettles, cooled by a water jacket, lined with fireproof brick, and each holding about 10 tons of molten steel. The steel and other chemicals or minerals were dumped into the kettles, by hand through two chutes-one for each kettle, located above the kettle, on the third floor. The idea was to throw in about 1000 pounds each time one opened the chute- for about 10 times per chute per evening shift. After we charged the furnaces, we reloaded material for the next night- in other words two people each moved about 18 tons of material each night.

We started at 10:00 PM and we finished loading the furnaces by about 2:00 AM and the rest of the work by about 5. We could go home when we finished- after taking a shower. We were paid for 8 hours.

The heat was impressive- in July almost impossible. There had been a 36" hole in the roof for the old chimney, which was now papered over. There was the door to another part of the roof, where we went out for air. Along a wall was the air intake and hot air out-flow from the computer controls. The air was awful- you could not see to the end of the building.

What made the foundry "modern" were the computer controlled electric furnaces. As will become evident shortly, having an air intake in a heavily polluted environment was not too bright.

As an E-Board member, shop steward and someone with a general idea of health and safety I was appalled. When our little group of two plus the furnace tender complained about the heat and dust we got the usual story-"It has been this way forever. We did it, so can you". There was no recognition that the working conditions might lead to an early death.

After arguing about the need for a fan for a few days, and in my case taking it to the E-Board of the union, we took action. A new strain of flu broke out- and we became ill and unable to come to work to charge the furnaces for the next day's pour. Suddenly foundry management found a 36" fan, and installed it. Miraculously we recovered in time to save the next day's work.

Our little group had other adventures. One night at about 3:00 AM we went out for pizza. However, when we came back we discovered that one of the ceramic plugs in a kettle had failed, and molten steel was pouring on the floor. Clearly a disaster. The furnace tender was able to staunch the flow, but now we still had a large pancake of steel slowly cooling. If it remained the foundry would be closed as the pancake of steel was oozing into the rail tracks which carried the ladles of steel.

What to do? My college education came to the rescue. I knew that if we put cold water on the steel the exploding water seeping under the pancake would probably free it enough so we could pick it up with a pay loader. We turned on the firehose; the steel pancake was freed from the floor as the water exploded underneath it. Using a pay loader we dumped the pancake out the back door on the scrap heap.

Foundry saved! We were heroes. We went home before anyone came in but left a note saying there had been a problem.

Not long after I hit the sack the company called and asked me, as the senior man and union representative, to come back to the plant and explain exactly what happened. We explained that the furnace sprung a leak. We showed how the furnace tender fixed the leak and I explained how we got the steel out the door. They wanted to know why the foreman's office, a good portion of the back wall of the foundry and several lockers were destroyed. I explained that the pancake of steel could not fit out the door or down the aisle and so we did the right thing- we saved the foundry- albeit with some casualties. They bought it. But we **did** make the right decision. I neglected to mention the pizza.

Another incident I believe helped seal the ultimate fate of the foundry. Other similarly designed foundries had exploded when cooling water leaking through the ill maintained kettle walls and firebrick reached the molten steel. Our crew was sensitive to this and hence when the alarm went off we didn't hang around to assess the problem. From the third floor, I remember jumping to the second floor landing and running down the stairs and out the door. We were followed by the power house crew, the cat, and anyone else around. Even the guards wanted to move back from the gate.

We saw the whole power house begin to shake itself apart and tiles come off the roof, as the turbines which generated the electricity for the electric kettles went from fully loaded to zero instantaneously and thus began spinning at impossible speeds.

As it turned out the filters for the incoming air had clogged, located as they were in an environment which could not get more polluted. Hence, no air and the controls overheated and turned off-instantaneously cutting the demand for electricity, which reduced the load on the turbines from 100% to zero.

This course of events was a real disaster. First there was 20 tons of steel slowly cooling. If it was not tapped or kept warm the foundry would be finished. Secondly, the turbines also generated electricity for the factory itself- and now there was no power.

In this emergency situation Mass electric was able to reroute power within a day or so. While it took a couple of days to get production back to normal the foundry was saved.

However, it also became clear that the USM was on shaky ground. After a week or so the company announced that the foundry would be on a four day week. In addition they announced layoffs in the various machining departments. They also told us that negotiations were in progress to sell the firm to Emhart- a smaller firm.

While we did not fully comprehend it, the beginning of the end for USM was in process.

By this time in October, union elections were coming up.

I had super seniority as I was on the Executive Board. If I campaigned to keep my position I probably would win, but I did not feel comfortable campaigning to keep my job as others who had more seniority were losing theirs. In fact almost half of the shop was in the process of being laid off and much of it was on a 4 day week-including the foundry. But I was automatically on the ballot. I lost gaining more votes than when I won the year before, but still came in seventh out of six.

The next day the company sent me a telegram (!) laying me off at the end of the week.

My game plan had been to become an elected union leader in a meaningful location so as to be able to build a more class conscious union movement. On the North Shore of Boston only USM (UE) and GE (local 201 of the IUE) made sense in terms of building a political base within the union movement. That strategy seemed dead in the water in mid-October 1975.

The eventual demise of USM took another couple of years. The factory itself was gone by the early 1980s. I left the Shoe with the experience, not just the theory, that a union needed to be an effective and honest organization dealing with day to day issues, but that every once in a while direct action was needed to ensure fair treatment.

1. All these skills are obsolete or obscure to most readers. Thomas E French, *A Manual of Engineering Drawing for Students and Draftsmen;* (McGraw-Hill Book Company Inc., New York and London 1941). This book was the bible of blueprint and mechanical drawing curricula from about 1920 to 1960. It belonged originally to my uncle Leonard Abrams who had graduated from the CCC as an engineering associate. First printing 1911.

2. "The Mossberg Job" A special manufacturing line was established to manufacture firing chambers for the inexpensive Mossberg Shotgun. About 70 people worked there over three shifts. It was lower skilled, lower paid and both an entry point and a place where more skilled workers on layoff could work.

3. Automatic screw machines, now mostly long gone, were a type of lathe whose tools were directed by a set of cams. The machine could run without the machinist moving each cutting tool into position- hence "automatic". These machines could make parts out of round stock- screws; wheels, gear blanks, nuts, bolts etc. Numerically controlled machines replaced mechanically controlled machines – that is cam controlled machines- automatic screw machines by about 1995.

4. The musical *The Pajama Game* describes piecework with the song "seven and a half cents".

5. Robert Kanigel, *The One best Way: Frederick Winslow Taylor and the Enigma of Efficiency*, (Viking The Penguin Group-Penguin Books USA NY, NY. 1997) an exhaustive biography of Taylor.

6. Examples of method sheets for parts to be machined. The part is a firing chamber for a Mossberg shotgun, circa 1975. Wisconsin Historical Society, Emspak papers, Folder 6.7000 USM.

7. This department consisted mostly of tool and die makers who were given a task, but neither the tools nor the methods to do it- their job was to figure out how to make the part and thus these people were the most skilled in the plant.

8. "Missing" a film directed by Costa Garvis and starring Jack Lemmon is a more or less historically accurate account of the killing of an American progressive, much like our friend Adam.

9. Inspired by the apparition of the beautiful Virgin Mary in La Salette, France in 1846, the Missionaries of La Salette today promote reconciliation, living and working around the world alongside the poorest of the poor. (website: LaSalette America)

10. The O.F Mossberg and Sons Company, a manufacturer of firearms. They were not in the top end in 1974. Their slogan is "Arm Yourself".

11. Edwin Neuman "Pensions: The Broken Promise" Broadcast 9/12/1972 by NBC Video Documentary [Long Form Specials/ Datelines, etc.] copyright NBC Universal.

12. In Wisconsin a corporate officer must disclose all prior convictions when organizing a corporation as I did with Diversified Media Enterprises. Our attorney contacted Lynn, and found there was no record of any arrests, so it appears Lynn did live up to their agreement.

13. Typewritten proposals for the Blue Sheet-written late 1973. Wisconsin Historical Society-Emspak Papers, Folder 6.704.

14. Ibid.

15.Draft of Notes by pension committee to BA and negotiating committee. December 1973 Wisconsin Historical Society, Emspak Papers, Folder 6.705.

16. UE Local 271 –Blue Sheet December 1973, mimeographed, Wisconsin Historical Society Emspak Papers, folder 16.705 .

17. UE Local 271 Blue Sheet, December 1973, mimeographed WHS, Emspak papers folder 16.705.

18. Frank Emspak, Newsletter Proposal to Local 271 officers and Business agent May? 1974. WHS, Emspak papers. Folder 6.706.

19. Letter from Frank Emspak to Tom Wright, spring 1977; reviews issues with USM. Wisconsin Historical Society Emspak Papers, Folder 6.708.

20. "Mainstream" was the decision of the CP to order its members to leave the progressive unions which had survived the CIO's attacks and to join the more conservative ones in their industry. In the UE's case this meant leaving the UE and joining the IUE.

Chapter Seven: Building the Union at GE Wilmington Local 201

On a warm night in June 1984, my coworkers and I stood around waiting for the final union membership vote on GE's vision for manufacturing — the "Factory of the Future." The Factory of the Future was a new manufacturing plant for aircraft parts, to be located in West Lynn at the site of the soon-to-be-shuttered West Lynn GE factory. GE touted the investment as a vote of confidence in an old unionized location, while at the same time threatening to place the investment elsewhere if the union local did not comply with its vision.

GE's Factory of the Future, with its twelve-hour-days and seven-day weeks required a change in the definition of the standard work day, defined in the national contract as eight hours and the standard work week of five days. The new schedule required by the company meant that one was not paid overtime after eight hours. The new work schedule would also change the way vacation and holidays were calculated.

The company had the enthusiastic support of the International Union (IUE), the District and most of the local leadership in implementing the new vision for the plant. Local media and all the politicians supported GE and suggested those of us who opposed the company's retrograde vision were putting the very existence of the Lynn plant in jeopardy. Anyone paying attention, however, heard the company's thinly-veiled threat: accept the proposals without significant alterations or there will never be investment in Lynn. In many ways, GE's stance reflected their longstanding bargaining position that the first offer was the only offer, and except for some cosmetic changes, workers could take it or leave it.

People sensed the autonomy of the machinists would end as the work became more machine-paced and monitored much more closely with a new computer system. The membership questioned the design of the overall system and the skill level of the new jobs.

Today, workers are raising the same issues about autonomy at work. By 2021, computer-paced work has moved from the factory to the office and even to the healthcare system. Epic Medical Information Systems, for instance, tracks the number of patients each physician sees in an hour. Many institutions such as the UW Medical Foundation specify the time a physician should spend with a patient and their compensation is influenced by their ability to meet those measurements. This kind of surveillance has consistently intensified across all manner of jobs. As a consequence, workers from coffee shops to Silicon Valley, from hospitals to the app-based gig jobs, have begun to push back, raising the same kinds of issues that we did at GE.

Excessive and unpredictable scheduling; company driven efforts to eliminate affordable medical care, undermining job security and pensions are still with us because the interests of working people and our communities have not had the strength to insist that our interests become part of the design of the technologies powering our economy. Management's designs has remained fixed on increasing shareholder value, by increasing productivity and thus maximizing profits, whatever the ancillary costs.

There were several factors that pushed a significant portion of the IUE Local 201 membership to challenge GE and our national union on such a fundamental issue as investment in the Lynn operation. Fundamental to the effort was the rebuilding of a militant union-conscious organization within Local 201. This was aided by the effective use of union committees by progressive people to serve as organizing centers within the local.

The Culture

The educational and organizational work of these committees took place within a determined fight to expand the democratic space within the local. Fundamental to all of this was the fact that a portion of the membership already had a strong union culture.

The culture that underlay the militancy of the local was a multi-generational organism. Despite both union and company efforts to purge leaders associated with the Communist Party or the United Electrical Workers, when I was hired in 1976 there was still a large group of workers who had a strong sense of what a union could be. Senior leaders in the IUE were always nervous that somehow that spirit of a union would reassert itself, stoked by the influx of a new generation of class conscious troublemakers.

The most dominant aspect of our local's culture was a deep distrust of the company. Certainly almost any worker at "The GE" knew it was among the best-paying plants in the area and had some of the best benefits. But few trusted the company. Many felt they always had to maneuver to get paid properly on piecework, or that the company was always trying to chisel them regarding benefits. There was arrogance in the way the company acted that was insulting, and aside from contributing to bad blood, also sent a message of its power. Foremen were required to wear ties at work, thus ensuring a visual reminder of who was who. Workers were always addressed by their first names. The language the company used to describe the work force — not as machinists, but machine operators — devalued skills and ability. The result was sort of a love/hate relationship.

Even though the company expanded employment in the late seventies and eighties, a substantial number of workers still remembered and had participated in a one-hundred- and-one-day strike in 1969. On one level or another, many understood benefits and wages were a result of that strike. Some believed it would be foolish to engage the company again, while others drew inspiration from the strike's memory.

GE never accepted the union. The national negotiating strategy called *Boulwarism*[1] was essentially a take-it-or-leave-it strategy. The company was an "open shop" until 1986. In other words, workers at the plant were not required to join the union. The company had a strong ideological disposition against so-called "third parties" — unions as well as arbitrators. Thus, large parts of the GE contract were not subject to arbitration, but after going through a grievance procedure, workers had the right to strike during the life of the contract. Most contracts do not include provisions allowing workers to have a legal means to strike during the life of the contract. In GE's case, any unit of a local, from a department to a whole division, in any location, could vote to strike — and often did so. Aspects of the national contract subject to arbitration were discharges, and if a local union had negotiated supplements to the national contract, proper employee placements in case of layoffs and opportunities for upgrades.

This attitude on the part of the company fed into a sense of union solidarity, as most members understood that on almost any issue the company would reject the union's position. At the local level, this came down to never agreeing with the union when we grieved that the rate of a specific job should be increased. One result was a series of small strikes in specific departments or job classifications over the rates of pay for specific jobs, most of which were unsuccessful.

Lynn was also known in labor relations circles as a "personality driven location." In other words, labor relations were as much due to the personality of the leading players, rather than company policy dictating the relationship. One of the senior labor strategists for corporate GE was Ray Holland, the chief labor relations person in Lynn. Holland set policy for the five businesses that made up GE in Lynn: Small and Medium Turbine, Aircraft Engine, the Gear Plant, West Lynn and the Aircraft Instruments and Aerospace Instrument Division (Wilmington). Thanks to Holland, GE-Lynn was a national laboratory for the implementation of new technology.

In some respects, the analysis of labor relations as a function of personality was accurate. But personalizing the relationship between the workers and management, especially by the union, obscured the class nature of the disputes and hindered understanding of the company's longer term strategies. Thus "solving" problems came to mean only challenging or replacing some specific personnel.

Building a base –The Aircraft Instrument Division- Wilmington MA.

The Lynn GE local had been one of the founding locals of the UE in 1937. However, the UE lost certification elections there in 1950, and again in 1960. The Lynn local, always somewhat conservative within the UE, was one of the original supporters of the International Union of Electrical Workers (IUE), which had been launched by the CIO to replace the UE. Almost all of the leadership — the stewards and Executive Board members within the Wilmington plant — had been pro-IUE partisans in the election of 1960.

I was hired at the General Electric Company's Aircraft Instrument Division located in Wilmington, MA in November

1976, the third generation of my family to work at GE, following my grandparents, father and uncles.[2] Because my father had been secretary-treasurer of the UE, a substantial minority of the workers knew our name and had opinions about my family

Because my father had been secretary-treasurer of the UE, a substantial minority of the workers knew our name and had opinions about my family.

The Union as a Tribe

When I was elected to the Executive Board of IUE Local 201 in 1979, six out of thirteen full-time officers were either participants in the destruction of the UE and the establishment of the IUE or their sons.[3] Two were sons of UE supporters. In 1979, we remained on the same sides of the political divide as our forebears.

The Wilmington plant of GE was part of the Aircraft Instrument Division and had been spun off from the West Lynn plant, which was soon scheduled for closure. Almost all the workers in Wilmington were from Lynn. As a result, there was a huge web of wives, sisters, in-laws and political allegiances between the Wilmington plant and the rest of Local 201. In the time I was at GE, employment rose from about six-thousand union members to about eight-thousand. The Wilmington workforce grew from about six-hundred union-eligible workers to very close to one-thousand.

Because of the influx of many young people, the political situation was becoming more open, especially in Wilmington where new Portuguese and Central American hires were coming from the neighboring towns of Lawrence and Lowell — some bringing militant trade union experience with them. Throughout the local, there were large numbers of younger people who had never experienced the political disputes within the union or the long 1969 strike against GE. For younger workers, good healthcare, including pregnancy leaves, was a higher priority than pension benefits.

That influx of a new generation contributed to unprecedented upheaval in Local 201. Between 1976 and 1987, there were eighteen plant-wide votes — a huge number.

In 1976, IUE Local 201 was the largest industrial union local in Massachusetts. 201 was a target for any organization wishing to influence the electrical industry. In this sense, the importance of GE was no different than in the 1930s — the overall union strength of the electrical industry depended on a strong and militant union presence at GE. If unions did not successfully take on GE, eventually they would become unable to effectively represent workers in the industry at large.

My Life at GE:

In October 1976, as I walked through the Wilmington GE machine shop with the foreman for an interview, workers who had been laid-off from the United Shoe Machine company greeted me and confirmed to the foreman that I really did know how to do the job. Although I did not know this at the time, the foreman hired me because he felt he had a family obligation dating from his time in the UE. [4]

The union was complicit in the blacklist against progressives and fiercely opposed my hire. I never would have survived at Wilmington without the timely intervention of the shop steward who made sure I was moved immediately to the third shift and did not sign my IUE Local 201 union card until the day my probation was over. My steward felt, correctly, that the card would alert the union leadership to my presence and they would want the company to fire me before the probation period was up.[5] In March 1977, on the first day after probation, I signed a union card.

Why was there such an interest in me by both GE management and especially by the union?

It stemmed from a political decision by the Congress of Industrial Organizations to establish the IUE as the anti-Communist alternative to the UE. Failing in their attempts to eliminate the elected left leadership of the UE, they set up a rival union and triggered a civil war within the electrical industry. In representation elections that followed, the IUE did not win overwhelming support from GE workers within two of the largest plants —Schenectady, NY and Erie, PA voting for the UE. Lynn voted for the IUE in a very close vote, amidst threats by leading politicians that a UE victory would mean the end of defense work.

Both GE and the leadership of the IUE feared that somehow a new generation of class conscious workers might emerge, threatening the status quo. They were especially concerned with Lynn because of its strategic position within the GE manufacturing system and its centrality to the politics of the IUE. Some locals were more influential and politically active than others and GE Lynn-Local 201 was precisely that type of place.

Every class conscious left political organization, especially the Communist Party, understood the importance of GE-Lynn and Local 201, and attempted, with varying degrees of success, to encourage their members to get hired at GE.

I was exactly the type of person the company most feared, even if they didn't know me personally. I was a decently-skilled worker. I had organizational experience. I had name recognition, and almost anyone with any seniority at GE knew about the UE and many believed it was the better union. The company was convinced, as was the union, that I was a member of the Communist Party.

Almost immediately after I signed my union card, the River Works management asked Wilmington labor relations to fire me, but it was too late. My probation was over and discharges could be arbitrated. The company solved the problem by firing the personnel manager who had approved my original hire. GE was particularly aggravated because they had successfully prevented my hire at the GE locations associated with the Lynn River Works.[6]

Going to GE was a family-inspired duty: GE was the corporation the union had to conquer to be effective. For me, GE was the completion of a journey reconnecting with my family's roots. I was at peace with myself and I think that inner sense of completion was sensed by my fellow workers. They, in the main, accepted me as part of the GE family — maybe a bit strange after all, but there were a lot of unconventional people in the Wilmington plant. For example, a significant number of my fellow workers were gay or lesbian and out. Some of them were the smartest unionists, the ones who out-maneuvered the company and gave leadership — and that wasn't lost on their coworkers who, for the most part, respected their contributions.

Most people saw me as a "Red," an underground supporter of the UE and someone with an education. I was not Catholic, and when asked, I said I was a non-believer. But somehow, all of this was overlooked by a majority of my coworkers. Despite historical and ongoing tensions within the local, there was still a shared culture. In this case, the culture revolved around the love/hate relationship with GE and the understanding that there had to be a union.

Building a Movement at Wilmington

When one thinks of the industrial workforce of the 1970s from the vantage point of 2021, young, active and militant are not the images that come to mind. But in 1976, the Wilmington plant had a cohort of militant young workers, many of who worked in the Thermocouple department,[7] where in the summer of 1977, I was assigned while waiting for a new job.

An air conditioning duct ran through our workroom. On one particularly sweltering day, the temperature was a chilly fifty degrees. The duct had a massive hole in it and thus the cold air blasted into our little room and nowhere else. At this point, we had experienced several days of really awful heat with more forecast.

The rest of the floor was complaining about the heat and humidity, but nothing was done.

Our little group of three decided to take action. I informed the company the room was too cold to work and therefore we were not going to continue. In other words, on the hottest day of the year we had a work stoppage because it was too cold. Within a few minutes, the whole department was slowing down, talking about how crazy we were. Soon, of course, the rumor was all over the first shift.

Within a few hours, the system was repaired and the rest of the floor was bearable. We were celebrated, and given the popularity of the action, no one was disciplined.

Not soon thereafter, I came to work wearing a T-shirt from Dolores's medical school. The T-shirt was the cross section of a penis, although it looked like a flower. It was an inside joke for the medical students.

After people in the department understood it, I could not get enough of them to give away. The company could not make everybody stop wearing a T-shirt of a flower. Meanwhile, the idea of me having a wife in medical school seemed a lot less threatening.

Friday night dinners for the second shift machine shop and flowmeter departments were an example of the ingenuity and high level of organization that was possible when people were truly motivated. We were motivated for sure, since there was no cafeteria and we didn't have enough time to go out and get anything. Lunch was just eighteen minutes, since we were a twenty-four-hour a day operation.

In order to have a decent meal, we had to devise a means of preparing it ourselves. That meant finding a place to boil water or using equipment like the special ovens built to test the heat tolerance of instruments. All the preparations had to be done before the official break, so that we could sit down and actually enjoy our meal. Friday dinner was usually spaghetti & meatballs, cheese, Italian bread, and dessert. The trick was being able to sit down just as the lunch break began. As long as we were through eating and had everything cleaned up by 7:45 p.m. there was no problem. From time to time, someone brought dinner over to the foreman. If a senior member of management was somehow on the premises or coming into the building, the guard (who also got dinner) let us know.

Our biggest challenge was St. Patrick's Day, when the smell of corned beef and cabbage wafted throughout the facility. On days like that we had to make extra to satisfy other supervisors and friends in other parts of the building.

Base-Building at the Wilmington Plant

As far as many in Local 201 were concerned, the Wilmington plant was a backwater, but secure source of votes for the leadership, isolated as it was from Lynn. From my point of view, Wilmington could be a strategic asset for the left — if we could win it. It could become a source of political influence within the leadership of the local and a source of political support for progressives elsewhere in the local. The conservative leadership of the local had a rather disparaging view of Wilmington, based in large part on their sexism, as about half of the workers were women. They held this view of Wilmington until a few days before the union election of 1979.

In late March 1977, I received a call from the union office in Lynn. They informed me a foreman was removing parts from a department that was on strike at the Wilmington plant and taking it to an outside contractor. The union wanted me to intervene. I said I would check.

Indeed, from my vantage point behind some big scrap barrels, I could see the foreman loading material. I could also see the plant security hidden in another spot, so if I had intervened I would have probably been fired on some basis or another. After I called the union to confirm a foreman was moving strike work, the union did nothing. A few days later, my foreman suggested that I look a bit busier during my shift.

By mid-1977, I had been appointed to the Health and Safety Committee and had begun to look at chemical hazards, as well as the issue of toxic metals, such as Beryllium, which was used in some welding department applications. I was getting a reputation as someone who actually used his college education on behalf of others.

Successfully challenging the intellectual dominance of the company in ways our fellow workers could see, was probably the most important thing we did.

OSHA had initiated "New Directions" grants to unions or non-profits for the express purpose of hiring professionals to carry out workplace education, inspections and, if necessary, file complaints. The Health and Safety Committee under the chairmanship of Ron Malloy,[8] taking note of my "professional" experience, put me in charge of writing the grant. To our great pleasure, we received the money and went about hiring two industrial hygienists.[9] They became a presence on the shop floor and were skillful advocates assisting the stewards and officers in pursuing health and safety issues. I think we were the only local union in the country with a full-time staff of two hygienists.[10]

We encouraged groups of workers to raise issues, thus building an identifiable base of people who would be willing to fight for better working conditions. Two years later, this direct action paid off when the government funding ended and our committee had to go to the membership and ask for a dues increase to maintain the staff. After a hard-fought campaign, with most of the union top leadership opposed, we won a referendum to raise the dues. This victory for a progressive coalition indicated that the balance of power in the local was shifting.

By mid-1978, I was appointed steward on the second shift, which enabled me to meet both first and third-shifters. Often, several people would be waiting for me to come in at 3 p.m. so we could discuss the contract. Just meeting people and having these discussions was a challenge to the union leadership.

On October 25, 1978, I announced my decision to run for a position on the Executive Board in the Wilmington plant.[11, 12] The board member was the face of the union, a combination of chief shop steward, union organizer, negotiator and a member of the policy board of the local. It was a full-time position, meaning that although I would remain on the company payroll, my actual salary was paid by the union. It was equal to what I would earn on the job, with no overtime. The primary role of the thirteen-member Executive Board was to process grievances — that is, to decide which ones would go to the third step and potential arbitration — as well as authorize work stoppages and ratify agreements if any came as a result of those stoppages. My election would mean there would be a union militant, spirit-of-the-UE, class conscious person on the IUE Local 201 executive board for the first time since about 1950.

My initial supporters were the group of militant workers in the Thermocouple department. Many were young people, but had been at GE for five to ten years by that point.

The political culture overall at the Wilmington plant was broadened by the hire of at least five progressive women in skilled jobs in the machine shop and in the electronic test area. They were strong advocates regarding the issues of sex bias and union rights, and as time went on, became active members of the women's legislative and health and safety committees. They, too, supported my run for office.

The basis of my campaign was "rates, respect and a straight answer." Wilmington wage rates were lower than equivalent jobs in Lynn, and the Willington bargaining unit did not have contact supplements for shift preference, layoff and transfer or job posting. The company did not respect the union or the stewards. I made it clear that I wanted the company to treat our stewards as equals and not as supplicants when it came to interactions with the company.

I won the support of the women in Instrument Assembly because I addressed their concerns about wage rates and overall treatment. Several of them had been the initial grievants in the successful sex bias suit by the United Electrical Workers in 1944. The War Labor Board, which acted as an arbitrator in wage disputes like this, decided in favor of the women, ordering GE to pay women the same rate of pay as men if they were doing the same work. GE ignored the findings and with the demise of the War Labor Board and subsequent destruction of the UE, nothing changed. That 1944 War Labor Board settlement became the basis for establishing the bounds of our sex bias settlement in 1983.

The red-baiting soon kicked into high gear. The union leadership put out leaflets, and reprinted materials from the 1950s which characterized the UE, and my family in particular, as Communist agents out to destroy America. Since almost any progressive idea could be attacked as Communist-inspired, it was impossible for anyone labeled as a Communist to deny the charge, and at the same time advocate for change. This, of course, was the idea.

I countered the red baiting directly, writing:

"The Fake Issue at Wilmington: Communism.
No one has ever won a pay raise by dredging up the past. Nobody has ever won a rate increase by yelling "Communism."
My father Julius Emspak was secretary-treasurer of the United Electrical Workers (UE) from 1937 until he died in 1962. His dream, and the dream of many GE employees of his generation were to bring solid, honest unionism to GE. For a time, this dream was realized…"

Dredging up the past, slandering the dead is a disgrace. We don't need Watergate tactics here in Wilmington. We must learn from the past — not desecrate it."[12]

My opponent, a longtime IUE stalwart, ran on the basis of her commitment and militancy, evidenced by the fact that she had filed more grievances than almost anyone else. As she put it in her leaflet, "She may not have a PhD in philosophy from a Midwestern college, nor is she a union politician…what she does have is the knowledge that comes from earning a living as a worker in the shop."[13]

Leaflets passed out by the union leadership on her behalf were reprints of the material from the original attacks by the IUE on the UE, complete with an unflattering picture of my father, "identified as a top communist leader." The headline of the leaflet was "UE Leads Red Parade."[14] But this time, times had changed.

One group of people in the machine shop set a pile of these on fire. I won about 70% of the vote. The reelection campaigns in 1981, 1983 and 1985 were tame by comparison— most of the time I did not have an opponent — and when I did, my percentage increased.

Ethnicity and religion were a visible aspect of Wilmington culture. Well over seventy-five-percent of the workforces were practicing Catholics of one ethnic group or another. A good number went to church in nearby Lawrence where I had worked with the Catholic Church regarding refugees from the civil war in El Salvador. The priest there was a progressive-minded person.[15]

In April 1978, I went to a congress of the World Federation of Trade Unions in Prague, not yet having decided to run for election in 1979. Before I went, I had collected money from fellow workers to buy a set of micrometers for the Vietnamese delegation to the WFTU as a sign of peace. The event was widely known and commented upon. The WFTU was composed of Communist-led unions around the globe, including the largest unions in France and Italy, as well unions in the so-called Third World who opposed neocolonialism. The AFL-CIO backed the rival International Confederation of Free Trade Unions. On Easter Sunday, just as I arrived to take pictures of the beautiful Gothic cathedral, the big doors opened and the bishop stepped out. I took a photo.

I passed the pictures around when I returned. One of the women in the assembly area told me she was struck by the pictures of the church, and especially the Bishop. She took the photos to her church in Lawrence and had them blessed by the priest. She told me I couldn't be a bad person if I had pictures like this. Of course, many people heard of this and agreed with her. The steward in the area, who I will refer to as DR, was the lead local red-baiter and attacked me as a Communist — the usual. But after the pictures were seemingly blessed by the church, he looked like a jerk with his continuous attacks on my trip. In our world of Wilmington, this was the first time in years he had been challenged and exposed for the fool he was.

In a way, DR was illustrative of a type of male union steward typical in departments which were mostly women. He was the lead hand. He disrespected women. He insulted the foreman (behind the foreman's back), but never really challenged the foreman or the company when it came to fundamental issues like wage rates or the treatment of others. He was known by the company to disappear for considerable periods of time and thus, was vulnerable to being pressured by the firm. But he was a valuable campaigner for the administration. He worked by intimidation.

The entire complement of union officers supported my opponent and dominated the election committee. My supporters, convinced the vote would be stolen once it became clear I might win it, insisted on riding along in the car carrying the ballots to the union hall eleven miles away. Upon arrival at the hall, my witnesses literally sat on the ballot boxes until all the votes were counted. It was a pretty tense evening, and it took both President Al Hamilton and Business Agent Peter Teel some time before they congratulated me. More senior union leadership from District Two said nothing.[16]

New to the Board

My personal notes reflect the disillusionment I felt as I began my tenure on the Executive Board. "On the board there was no discussion of GE except as it related to a specific grievance...no overall assessment is made...or what we should be negotiating for...The policy board meetings we have had so far have to do with the building...." [17]

My assessment of the grievance landscape was that "as far as Wilmington grievances are concerned no [wage] rate case seems to have been won by the union...only the EEOC has awarded rate increases; secondly, most stewards do not function as stewards and have little idea how to function, thirdly some stewards actively speak against the people they are supposed to represent. Our problem [meaning progressives and myself] was that when we won office we didn't expect it and hence were not prepared to run a slate of stewards, committeemen etc. to take on the company".[18]

Progressives faced the following challenges:

1) The need to build a union organization from the ground up, identifying and recruiting strong union people to be stewards and committee people.

2) Organizing the fight for a national contract which would expire on June 30 1979.

3) Winning the respect of the company for the union and our stewards. I needed to make sure that the company dealt with me as the face of the union in the Wilmington plant, not with others either within the facility or outside of it. The company was used to dealing directly with the Assistant Business agent based in Lynn.

4) Effectively confronting the discriminatory practices in Wilm-

ington. This took on more urgency as the company was expanding and placing lower seniority and often less skilled men on higher rated jobs while refusing to offer them to more skilled and senior women.

The first time after the election that I went to the plant with the Assistant Business Agent, he remarked that there was a palpable change in the atmosphere. What he sensed was that the members understood — even if not all supported it — that a coalition of militant and union conscious workers was capable of challenging the company in three areas.

These areas were:

A) Opposition to the IUE-GE national contract.[19]

B) Equity; the discriminatory job classification system, sex-defined upgrade paths and lower wages for all "women's" job classifications.

C) Respect; especially an issue in Wilmington. GE foremen and labor relations simply did not treat union workers and officers as equals. I was rankled by the way in which the company addressed my fellow workers, union officers and stewards. It was always by our first names. It was fake informality to suggest good will and equality.

On one of my first days as an elected officer we met with the company. The Union Relations Manager introduced himself.

"Hello Frank, I am Bob." I said nothing. After a couple of minutes, I asked if we had been formally introduced. Of course, we had not. I pointed out that we were not friends and had not been formally introduced, and so, in that case, I expected to be addressed formally, as was acceptable in civilized society. Until I agreed to be addressed informally, I insisted on my formal title — Dr. Emspak. As I said "Hi, I'm Dr. Emspak. Are you Mr. Fraser?" The company was astonished and my fellow stewards were thrilled. Somehow, without anyone ever leaving the room, the entire plant heard about this. The company threatened an unfair labor practice charge because I was refusing to meet — but I pointed out we were meeting and would even call Bob Fraser "Mr. Fraser" if he wanted. After the company asked if they could call me Frank, I agreed — having made the point. I also suggested when they meet a new steward for the first time, they address the person properly.

Forcing the company to respect the union on the shop floor was amongst our most important objectives. Shortly after my election, the company refused to let me speak to a member while she was at work in accordance with the practice of notifying the foreman without disrupting production. When the foreman tried to eject me, I refused to leave until (or if) I was dragged out by the police. The company backed down. Of course, it was due in part to more and more people stopping work to watch the confrontation. It was clear to me — and to the company — that people would support the union.

Theater is one thing, and it was important to establish a new relationship with GE. But delivering on promises to deal effectively with the discriminatory wage, job posting and upgrading and job classification issues was another. There were several aspects to the discriminatory wage structure at all GE facilities with a significant female workforce. They included more or less identical job functions which were given different titles. For example, "dispatcher" for men and "supervisory aid" for women were the same job — but "supervisory aids" earned less. Some of the jobs were the gateway to higher level jobs — but women were never allowed to be upgraded to these gateway jobs. Vague or nonexistent pathways for advancement encourage favoritism and magnify racial and sex discrimination biases. Systems like this characterize nonunion workplaces and are a major source of wage and sex discrimination and employee dissatisfaction today, especially in the newer hi-tech industries.[20] In our case, the union could only grieve that the "senior, qualified candidate" get a particular job. Needless to say, without any supporting language as to what constituted "qualified," the union lost many of these cases.

However, there was one important aspect of the GE contracts that potentially gave workers some leverage. GE was hostile to all forms of outside interference. They opposed arbitration because arbitrators were outside third parties and, theoretically, independent. In the absence of specific contract language mandating arbitration of grievances, members had the right to strike in pursuit of a grievance settlement — after following a three-step negotiating procedure. The exceptions were discharges and written procedures for lay-offs, transfers and job posting and upgrading. Wilmington had no agreements regarding the latter.

In a union local of seven thousand, or even a location like Wilmington with up to nine-hundred members, there were, of course, many departments with unsettled grievances and the right to strike. But for practical reasons, these rights were rarely exercised. One couldn't strike over every issue — a fact well known by both management and the workforce — so these grievances were eventually tabled.

Local 201's Executive Board decided which grievances would be pursued and ultimately which departments would be authorized to strike over a grievance. This decision was intensely political as giving the local board member a strike number helped protect them politically; they were seen doing something, even though in most cases there was no real attempt to organize a strike and, hence, the grievance died.

In the union political world of the seventies and eighties, the prior generation of union radicals had either retired or been driven out of the unions, and there were few who had the skill or political commitment to organize. As a result of no leadership, or leadership committed to a passive membership, such a system could actually be quite stable.

Cases were already progressing toward direct action when I took office, but without an expectation that it would lead to much. As a new board member having won unexpectedly on a platform that explicitly challenged the status quo I needed to deliver on substance. People elected me to get change-and they expected it. GE's refusal to upgrade the senior qualified person to the dispatcher's job in the Thermocouple department became the grievance we chose to mobilize around. After a tense negotiation session with the company our team of stewards, witnesses vice president of the local and myself rejected the company's final offer. We had demanded the firm fill two new dispatch jobs with the senior qualified applicants, one of whom was a woman who had been temporarily on the job. The firm refused and assigned two senior men to the position.

The Friday before Labor Day 1979, one-hundred-sixty people on two shifts in the thermocouple department walked out in protest of the plant's sexist hiring practices.[21] This was the first organized strike on this issue in memory. Again, the dispatch job was the "men's job," heretofore unavailable to women, and higher paying than the "supervisory aid" job — its equivalent offered only to women. It was clear we were challenging the system, not just trying to win a job for one person.

The strike lasted a month. In the settlement, GE offered three jobs — the two filled by the men and one "shortly" to be filled by the grievant. In a late-night negotiating session with GE-Wilmington, and over my objections and the objections of our witnesses, the Assistant Business Agent accepted the company's offer to upgrade two men and consider our grievant for a third position later.

On the way back to Lynn we stopped at the President's house to brief him, but when I attempted to leave, I was prevented from doing so for several hours in order to undercut my efforts to mobilize opposition to the settlement. However, the member witnesses and stewards who had organized for the strike in the first place had begun to reach out to their fellow members and by the time of the membership meeting two days later there was a solid majority to oppose the settlement.

The next day, the Executive Board voted to accept the agreement, expunging my "no" vote. Pursuant to the local's constitution, the striking members had the right to ratify or reject the proposed settlement. Almost the entire department attended the settlement ratification meeting and when the president announced the results of the board meeting he said the vote was unanimous. When asked, I said I didn't vote for it. The assembled members got the picture. The President called for the members to stand and give the leadership a vote of confidence and support for the settlement. One person reluctantly stood up to vote "yes" and was immediately urged to sit down. The rejection was unanimous. No-one was going to go to work.

It was both inspiring and exciting. In the emergency board meeting which followed, I reiterated the senior qualified person would get the job and after that the company could fill as many positions as they wanted — but now, instead of three, we wanted five.

It took a week, which really was GE's punishment for impertinence, but the company ultimately settled with us for three immediate jobs, plus two to be established shortly thereafter, and the senior qualified people would get the job. For the first time in the history of the plant, women would now be eligible for and selected for the formerly, men's "dispatch job." This was a huge breakthrough.

As the Assistant Business Agent observed from October 1979 on, the Wilmington management would be dealing with me. The backroom deals, private discussions and phone calls between the Business Agents and the company were all over. Our strike in Wilmington challenged the relationships between the company and business agents of the union relying on a passive membership.

The stewards, membership and I had taken the fight against discrimination out of the legalistic morass and put it in the hands of workers in the Thermocouple department, and by implication, workers throughout the local. In truth, Wilmington was not the center of the union as far as GE or the union leadership was concerned, so our movement did not (yet) directly threaten the overall status quo with the remainder of the GE complex. But still, the Wilmington management could not expect to be bailed out by union officers from Lynn. Within Wilmington, during the month-long strike, stewards and supporters of the administration were confronted and forced to stop undermining the strike and union. Some stewards, confronted with members who expected them to act like a union person resigned and were replaced by more union and class conscious individuals.

Taken together, these victories changed the balance of forces at least within the Wilmington plant, in part within the local, and also within the left in local 201(and to an extent within the CP). The local union leadership also understood I would not succumb to their machinations and that my loyalties were to the people who elected me. It set the basis for continued mobilization around our sex bias suit, and showed that a strike could be won. Thus, by the end of 1979 company officials respected me and our stewards, and the membership increasingly saw that I was dedicated to them. We had also established a progressive base in the local which could give encouragement to others in the main plant and advocate for actions as a member of the Executive Board of the local.

Endnotes For Chapter Seven

1. This bargaining method was named after GE's vice president of union and community relations Lemuel Boulware. It consisted of offering the union one basic offer, refusing to move off that offer in any meaningful way and subjecting the workforce to a huge public relations campaign to convince them to accept the offer.

2. My father Julius graduated from the apprentice program in GE Schenectady and then went to Union College on a partial GE scholarship. My uncle Frank worked at GE Schenectady from the time he was about 20 until he retired on disability in 1960 or so. My uncle Vic worked at GE his whole working life retiring in 1965. My grandfather Frank was an industrial blacksmith at GE until his untimely death. My grandmother Theresa was a cleaning woman at GE. The husband of my Aunt Annie worked at another GE wholly owned subsidiary for his entire working life.

3. In 1979 the full time officers of Executive Board of Local 201 contained three IUE partisans and 2 UE partisans. Jim Sweeney, Fred Merchant; Leo McCarthy; -IUE and UE Frank Emspak, Ron Malloy.

4. John White began work at GE West Lynn prior to WWII. He had been a UE stalwart but could not countenance the IUE. He became a foreman in 1950 when the IUE beat the UE in the representation election. His family notified me at the time of John's passing to relate the story of my hire. (Emspak, personal notes).

5. The steward, John McDonnel, went on to say he couldn't understand how the front office hired me, but probably they did not recognize the name as Terri was young and probably had no idea of the history of the union. However he recognized

the name as did every worker in the department over age 40. He also told me that he made a big mistake in 1950 voting the UE out, and didn't want to make another mistake and thus would do what he could to keep me out of sight. (Emspak, personal notes).

6. Several years later when I was in negotiations with GE and during a recess, Joe Pickering, an HR staff person confirmed the blacklist and how thorough they were. (Emspak, personal notes).

7. The department produced heat sensors for jet engines and gas turbines, a crucial component. There were about 160 workers on two shifts.

8. Ron Malloy worked in the River works turbine division. His father Ray Malloy was a former Business Agent of the local, forced to resign due to his independent frame of mind, being physically thrown out of the union hall in 1960. Ron's mother worked in Wilmington. When I saw her in 2019 when she was 101 she was still a committed socialist and trade unionist .Ultimately Ron was elected Business Agent of local 201 in 1985. After his defeat he became a labor side lawyer with a practice in Lynn.

9. IUE Local 201 hired Jim Weeks and Richard Youngstown. Both went on to have distinguished careers in the trade union movement, Weeks became health and safety Director of the UMW.

10. IUE Local 201 had to file unfair labor practice charges in order to enable the hygienists to enter the GE premises.

11. WHS, Emspak papers, Folder 8.906 Typed contemporary note regarding election, my chances and upcoming contract mobilization.

12. WHS Emspak papers, Folder 8.906Leaflet-typed original version *"The real issues at Wilmington GE"*.

13. WHS, Emspak papers, Folder 8.906 Leaflet *Mary Meguer-Wilmington Executive Board.*

14. WHS, Emspak papers, Folder 8.906 Leaflet *"UE leads Red Parade".*

15. Just how important the church was to many of the members in our plant was illustrated a few years later. A large Portuguese family suffered a death in the family. When I brought the bible over the night before the funeral, I was told immediate relatives were given permission to go to the funeral. But others were not. I asked GE to excuse all family members for the funeral. The GE refused and threatened to suspend anyone who left. I was appalled. I called the church and asked if I could bring some friends to the funeral mass and received an affirmative answer telling the priest I was bringing the first shift of the Wilmington GE plant. About 200 people actually came to the mass. This constituted an unauthorized and illegal work stoppage. All returned after mass. After some discussion the local management agreed to tell senior management that there had been a power outage.

16. 1979 WHS, Emspak papers, Folder 8.905 *"Fun and Games in The Shop"* diary March 1979-mid August 1979.

17. After a disabling internal fight, IUE Local 201 decided to build a union hall including a bar. The issues regarding construction, maintenance, repair and the bar took up huge amounts of time and were extremely divisive. These issues lasted for the entire 8 years that I was a member of the leadership of the local.

18. WHS Emspak papers Folder 8.905 *"Fun and Games in The Shop"* diary March 1979-mid August 1979.

19. WHS; Emspak papers Folder 8.905 *"Our Rock Bottom Contract for 1979"* for a detailed critique, unsigned but written by the membership and officers opposed to the contract.

20. The University of Wisconsin is an example of what a job classification system looks like in a nonunion employer. In 2021 there were 1300 job titles for about 4,000 individuals, no rules for advancement, and huge pay differences within each job title, a fertile field for favoritism.

21. Later in the afternoon the Business Agent criticized me for "letting "the people go on strike as they would lose the Labor Day holiday pay. Justice was in the minds of the people, not holiday pay.

Chapter Eight: Local 201 Confronts the Future: Technology and the Workforce

In the early 80s, the left in Local 201 consisted of people from various socialist groups, including the CP, as well as union militants who did not see themselves as socialist, but rather as opponents of GE. The left militant union coalition was represented throughout the plant, but especially in the health and safety committee, the women's committee and the new technology committee — groups that believed in and tried to implement membership-driven actions for health and safety and against sex bias and the challenges of new technology.

In many ways, IUE Local 201 was insulated from the attacks on other private sector unions. GE-Lynn was essentially a defense plant, and much of its business came from the Department of Defense, which contracted GE-Lynn to produce military jet engines. The general view held by almost everyone was one of optimism; that it was possible to gain something from the contracts, strikes, and legal suits. Mobilizations could pay off. Unlike the steel workers, Greyhound bus drivers, and auto workers — our union was not yet being forced into pay concessions or being forced to give up the defined benefit pension plan. And compared to the Professional

Air Traffic Controllers, whose union had been brutally crushed in 1981 by President Ronald Reagan himself, we found ourselves in a position of relative power.

Although the loss of work in the marine gear division was troubling and decisions to reduce the production of steam turbines could have a potentially large impact on the local, the general attitude (at least through 1985) was that increases in the Aircraft Department would take up the slack.

The national contract between the IUE and GE expired on June 30, 1979. By April, national contract negotiations between GE and the union's coordinated bargaining team were beginning. Issues included inadequate pay increases, the need to improve the pension, language requested by the union to limit plant closings — and the need, if such closings occurred, for increased unemployment benefits. As the months went by, there was no indication GE was willing to move on the union's key issues. There was an absence of leadership from the top and no serious planning for a strike.

Concern about the lack of apparent progress triggered a membership-led mobilization for a decent national contract. We used the March 1979 local union election campaigns to focus attention on the need for contract changes and to launch a worker-led campaign against a substandard national contract. Over the next three months, "We" (meaning class conscious leftists), built a strong movement called, "WAGE — Win Against General Electric" — to defeat the contract.

Progressives organized a petition drive for a newspaper ad exposing the contract for what it was. We felt the wage increase was inadequate and the pension provisions scrooge-like. The proposed contract would further undermine the health plan and included no meaningful protection against job loss due to plant closures. GE had made moves to open new, nonunion plants, which would further erode the power of unionized GE workers. As membership opposition increased, most of the local leadership began to oppose the contract, including Business Agent Peter Teel, a leading member of the national negotiating team.

In late June, the national IUE and UE conference boards[1] accepted the tentative agreement. Up until that time, the Communist Party's *Weekly Worker* had been opposing the contract as inadequate. Since by then the local leadership was also opposed to the contract, the leadership was having a tough time attacking the left or myself as Communists and disruptors. But the CP changed its position, taking their lead from the progressive UE, which had determined a strike was not possible. The morning the CP endorsed the contract one of the right-wingers couldn't wait. He ran into the union hall with a *Weekly Worker*,[2] dropped it on my desk, and said something to the effect of "Now what are you going to do?" I asked him for more money for our left caucus-sponsored newspaper ad opposing the contract. Ultimately, the local voted against the contract. In contrast to past history, the Wilmington location also had a significant anti-contract majority.

When we — the CP members in GE — continued our opposition to the contract, the Wilmington membership and committed unionists in the River Works recognized my loyalty was to our members and progressive trade unionists — and not the international union or the CP. A few weeks later, in a conversation with me, Teel made a couple of observations. First, he said he would be willing to work with anyone who was willing to put time into building the union. Secondly, Teel said he had wondered what I was going to do when the CP supported the contract. When I stuck with our position and continued to organize against the contract, he said he realized I was an independent person and dedicated to the membership. As he observed, that made me a real danger to the status quo. In the following years, I did my best to live up to his expectations. For the next three years, we were able to work together (if not always in complete agreement) to push forward the sex bias suit and to at least begin to discuss the issues of automation and computerization. Teel also stopped undermining me in Wilmington and put an end to his sporadic efforts to keep my column out of the union newspaper.

The Fight for Equity

In 1977, the IUE international had settled a nationwide sex bias suit with GE. The settlement did not address some of the most important issues in Wilmington and West Lynn. Specifically, most wage rates were left untouched — especially the lowest production wage rate in the shop, which was significantly below the lowest rate at the River Works. Job posting and upgrading, as well as layoff and transfer supplements to the national contact, were also left out of the agreement. Both of these supplements strengthened seniority and laid out specific pathways for upgrades or layoffs.

In response to these objections and in an attempt to support the incumbent board member, the local leadership voted to reject the settlement. Rejection allowed local 201 to pursue legal action independently. It looked like the union was doing something.

But now in 1979 the political balance of power in the local was shifting and what had been a legal battle contesting the settlement became a political movement within the local inspired and led in part by the Women's Committee and now aided by my election to the Executive Board representing the jurisdiction most affected by any settlement. The victorious Thermocouple strike was one example of willingness of the members to take on the company's sex bias. The Prep to Braze strike in the Aircraft division of the River Works where the members sought an increase in the rate of the job commensurate with the skills needed to perform it, was another.

In an original move, the Women's Committee secured their own counsel[3] to represent the class – women. At this point, the pursuit of the sex bias suit was no longer just an activity of Local 201, but also of independent counsel representing the class of women.

In the River Works plant, the Women's Committee pressured the leadership via petitions, newspaper articles, leaflets, and an effective use of the grievance procedure. An inconclusive strike in a small department over wage rates also served to encourage some of the Lynn-based leadership to support legal action. In Wilmington, aside from the Thermocouple strike, we organized various work actions to make it clear to the company women were not going to accept second-class status.

Sex bias was a defining factor of the GE wage system. A large percentage of GE's national workforce was women. While in the Lynn River Works about 85% of the local's membership was men, in Wilmington and West Lynn, the ratio was about 70-30, with women predominating.

Our suit demanded jobs be re-evaluated on the basis of "comparable worth," a doctrine that said if a job requires substantially the same skill, care and effort needed to accomplish it, then it should be paid the same. This is distinct from "equal pay for equal work" which looks at the same job and compares the wage rates of men and women. Thus the 1944 War Labor Board case compared male workers to female workers in the West Lynn plant performing the same work.

Comparable worth was a huge opportunity to revalue the jobs held by women. In addition, we demanded Wilmington and West Lynn employees be covered by contract supplements relating to job posting and upgrading, layoff and transfer, and shift preference — rights which the union had won for the predominantly male plants of the rest of the local.

Wage discrimination extended to the piece work system. At least until the late sixties, if not later, piecework payment vouchers were labeled "M" or "F" — with the "F" being paid less per piece than the "M." Aside from the discriminatory payments per piece themselves, the piecework system itself in West Lynn and Wilmington was inferior to the system in the River Works. The Wilmington system was called the "Bedeaux" system and paid on a sliding scale — not the same price per piece produced. Essentially, as your production rose, the price per piece fell. It was awful.

Women were also ill-served by GE's seniority system. Women were forced to break service if they left work upon the birth of a child. Pregnancy was treated as a sign of good health, not like any other illness, so medical insurance did not cover it, and it was not considered medical leave. If women were hired back, their seniority would start at zero. The seniority system governed the amount of a pension and access to higher rated jobs and the order of layoffs.

In 1978, the IUE had won a lawsuit that forced the company to treat pregnancy like any other illness, and victory made women eligible for medical insurance coverage and sick leave. But in practice, the company was not implementing this — so, as part of the sex bias settlement a specific agreement was necessary.[4] The company's attitude was shaped by their long-standing commitment to the inferiority of women. This breakthrough pregnancy settlement allowed mothers time with their newborns without breaking service. My wife Dolores, who was by then practicing obstetrics and gynecology, had a significant number of patients from GE, and her persistent letters of support and complaints helped the members considerably.[5]

In accordance with a court order responding to our issues in the 1977 suit, and in an effort to force settlement, the court ordered GE, local 201 and the Women's Committee to engage in settlement discussions. We were in negotiations with GE from mid-1979 until early 1982. The Women's Committee was represented by attorney

Nancy Gertner. The union's team usually consisted of Business Agent Peter Teel and myself, but sometimes other officers, too, depending on the topic. The legal costs and investment of staff time were immense.

A considerable minority within the local opposed financial and personnel resources being devoted to this. Others were very upset with the activities of the Women's Committee, as it was also a basis for political opposition to some of the board members or other officers. This group also saw the case as direct assistance for me as the Wilmington troublemaker and Communist. But to his credit, the business agent was pretty consistent: too reserved for some, but still committed to the case.

In the event our lawsuit succeeded, the company might have to cover our legal fees. But by 1980, we sorely needed help in covering our representation costs. Political relations between the local and the International made that prospect seem unlikely, however.

In 1980, the IUE had just undergone a divisive election for International President. Our progressive group supported David Fitzmaurice publicly, if not particularly strongly. Fitzmaurice campaigned against corruption and appeared willing to take on GE. Peter Teel enthusiastically supported John Shambo, who was the head of the IUE bargaining team and had just negotiated a contract that our progressive group opposed. In his enthusiasm for his candidate, Business Agent Teel had signed a leaflet calling candidate David Fitzmaurice a pervert. David won the 1980 election.

In this atmosphere, we went down to union headquarters in D.C. to meet President Fitzmaurice to get financial support for the suit. Fitzmaurice refused to see Teel, but he did agree to meet me in the ballroom of the Shoreham Hotel. President Fitzmaurice said he wanted to meet me because in 1948, when he was president of UE local 707 in Cleveland,[6] my father had come there and dressed him down in front of the membership.

Fitzmaurice explained he had never forgiven my father for that — and wanted me to know it, as he was going to make sure we didn't get a dime — never mind the $250,000 we were looking for. I pointed out that I was five-years-old at the time of his confrontation with my father. Fitzmaurice relented a bit, and as he was about to turn away, I handed him a copy of his grievance, explaining it was one of the original grievances that was the basis of UE's claims against the GE. He then called out to where Peter Teel was standing and said he would give the local the money — but that Peter was still a no good bastard. Fitzmaurice made good on his word and we got the money necessary to continue.

By early 1982, we began to make progress on all aspects of the agreement. To define the class of women impacted by the settlement, the company was insisting we accept a cut off date of 1977, which was when Local 201 rejected the national settlement. We rejected that idea and sought for a means to expand the class of women covered by the suit.

Here is where a PhD in history became of great value as I had studied the work of the War Labor Board and the UE during WWII. In 1944, the War Labor Board had found GE guilty of sex discrimination using a comparable worth standard. The War Labor Board ordered the company to pay women the same as men for comparable jobs. GE ignored the order. Three of the named grievants worked in West Lynn in 1944 and were still employed at the Wilmington plant in 1982.

I eventually located the original complaint of Lillian Dzedziak in a National Archives depository in the basement of a government building in Suitland, Maryland. Later that evening when we met with the company, I pulled out Lilian Dziedziak's grievance from 1944. I explained that she wanted to know about her grievance including back pay and other issues. When we met with Lillian she was thrilled we had found the original case. The case allowed the class of women represented by Nancy Gertner and the union to establish the boundaries of the class as all of the thousands of women who had worked at any Lynn-related location from 1944 when the case was originally settled — onward until the current date.

Since the company had destroyed most of the piecework documents from the period in question, we had no real way of determining what each of the many women were owed for back pension payments.[7] But we came up with a figure, and shortly before Christmas 1983, a large number of women received a five-figure check.

The final settlement meant the Wilmington location now had contract supplements equal in content and application to the rest of the local. Wage rates were raised by an average of two rates, and a significant number of women who had been improperly refused upgrades were now eligible for upgrade to higher rated jobs, as well as back pay.

This caused great theater. Many of the women, who were in their fifties or early sixties, were not interested in taking a new job. But they were interested in making a point. The company was doing its best to do nothing in the shop publicly. We insisted the human resource manager come out to the floor and offer the grievants their rightful job. Under some pressure, this was done. And to the great glee of the members, many of the women refused the job, had their say with the manager, and took their backpay.

The militant pursuit of the sex bias suit[8] against GE was an example of progressives taking the mantle of leadership from a reluctant union and moving forward. While we had some momentum in Wilmington because of the successful thermocouple strike, it was the strong and militant Women's Committee organized in the River Works that made it possible to go ahead.

In 2021, when analysts ask about the attitude of working class whites, I think comparing what is clearly a sense of grievance and despair to the attitude of these women, who won something — not money, but respect and recognition for the work they had done — may help explain why there is such disillusionment.

Sidebar/Vignette

Another vignette demonstrates the otherworldliness of my time in GE. One pay day, GE Wilmington had my check delivered to the guard shack at GE River Works where Dolores would pick it up. Shortly before she arrived, Ray Holland, devout Catholic, father of twelve children; leader of the GE Union Relations team — informed the union team that he wanted to meet Dolores and show her that the GE management was not a bunch of horrible people. He led GE's fierce resistance to pregnancy leave, and up until six months prior, had his staff question all leaves of absences for pregnancy or pregnancy-related matters — especially letters from Dolores.

Ray explained to Dolores (Dr. Emspak! Really!) that the company wanted to know what she thought of the plant hospital and medical service. The union was grieving this issue with OSHA and was about to try to sue the company. He asked her to go on a tour, look at the plant hospital and then report back. We would all wait. "All" by that point, were the senior five or six HR management and five or six of our negotiating committee. When the touring party returned about an hour-and-half later, Dolores explained how inadequate the facility was and that it was actually dangerous given the type of injuries we could have in that place.

Ray thanked her and after some pleasantries had her escorted from the plant, retrieve her car (which they had allowed her to drive onto the property, unlike me), and we resumed normal warfare. A few weeks later, however, the company actually took Dolores' suggestions to heart.

The successful outcome of the sex bias suit was due in large part to the efforts of the Women's Committee and our strong support in Wilmington. The victory increased my stature in the local. The success laid a basis for the left to contest for plant-wide leadership. That opportunity arose the next year when the five progressive officers on the board put me forward as the candidate for Assistant Business Agent.

The sex bias victory also increased our ability to challenge national IUE leadership at the conference board — the organization made up of leaders from all GE locals.[9]

At an annual meeting of the Conference Board, I was invited to a party that some of the delegates had thrown.

As I walked in the door, I quickly found out the object of the party was me. After a short conversation, I was assaulted and knocked to the floor. As I was laying there about to be clobbered with a chair, someone[10] came in as if in the movies and said, "That's enough. I think he got the message." The person peered over and said in a friendly tone, "How are you? I knew your father. I just wanted to say hello...and make sure you understand that you will not be speaking tomorrow."

He helped me up, told the people to give me a drink and asked if I understood. I foolishly said, "No." But they, in fact, were done for the night.

The next morning, looking worse for wear, I arrived at the meeting. I went up to the chairperson, John Shambo, and told him I intended to speak. In the spring of 1981, the big issue was GE's efforts to impose a two-tier wage proposal Local 201 adamantly opposed. I needed to speak on behalf of my coworkers.

John Shambo looked at me and said, "I last saw you when you were about ten. What happened to you?" Of course he knew — but I was from one of the largest locals in the union, and Local 201 did not support an assault on their delegates. I spoke to oppose

GE's efforts to initiate the two-tier wage system. Our local helped lead the successful campaign against that and Shambo went along reluctantly. Once I established I would not be intimidated, I was not bothered for the next six years.[11]

New Manufacturing Comes to GE

The effort by the membership to control the implementation of new technology in manufacturing, scheduling and surveillance was another flashpoint. Starting in 1979, a broad group of class-conscious activists and dedicated union members began to develop the capacity to pose alternatives to GE's top-down, dumbed-down and high surveillance vision of the new workplace. We were strong enough to force a vote on the company's proposals — a unique event in the labor movement. We got to that point because of a consistent vision that emphasized our members should benefit from the technology — not lose jobs, skills and autonomy.

Utilizing tools to shape and form metal are central to the work of machinists. The machine tools used in most U.S. machine shops functioned pretty much the same way since their introduction in the 19th century through the mid-seventies. But even as technology changed, the relation between capital and labor stayed the same. And the battle lines as to design, implementation and distribution of the increased productivity due to new technology became even more intense.

My thoughts about technology and the centrality of work emanated from my family. Some of my father's tools from his apprentice days were still in our basement and I fooled around with them, curious as to what they measured.[12] Skilled work and skilled workers were part of the dialogue in the family. As a teenager, I was given a book to read about modern machining discussing the first semi-automatic machines for making automobile engine blocks. My father talked and wrote about automation. So, I was primed to think that it was important as I became more politically involved.

Marxism and the Party's emphasis on work and the working class was another factor in my thinking about the value of labor and skill. I reasoned that if wealth was created by labor then, clearly, the tools used were crucial to the production of wealth. My training as a scientist also gave me some understanding about the new technologies.

But the most important factor contributing to my assessments of the new technology came from my experience actually working with conventional machining at the United Shoe Machine Company. In the traditional production context, my skill lay in my knowledge of the tools and the sequence of operations needed to make a piece — the tacit knowledge of any skilled machinist.

In the new systems, management sought to replace this human-based, tacit knowledge with computer-based control systems. Today, there are sophisticated systems that allow remote control, accurate measurements and, thus, feedback and correction. But in the early eighties, the systems were still in development and serious productivity problems emerged as soon as the new machines were put to work.

If the new tech could be implemented successfully, management reasoned it could potentially eliminate a large section of its most skilled workforce. In so doing, management would capture the real design and control of production, given the remaining employees — engineers doing the programming — were mostly non-union.[13]

This is not a question of employment levels, but an issue of control. Judging from how much effort and money the company put into designing technologies that excluded the worker — one can only conclude that control of the workplace was the real objective. GE never supported any research into alternative designs that favored flexibility or designs allowing workers to maintain control of their work. In fact, when we in Wilmington, working with MIT, came up with a way of programming machines to make complex parts starting from an analog principle, the company refused to investigate it —even though costs and design time were significantly improved as compared with GE's completely digital systems.

General Electric-Lynn was ground zero for the implementation of the new computer-based production. In this early period (1969-78), GE in Lynn had one of the largest deployments of numerically-controlled (NC) machine tools in the country. Initially, most of the new machines did not achieve productivity gains. There were simply too many problems of proper programming and tooling for the new machines to produce high quality aircraft parts efficiently. To address the problem, GE established the Pilot Program in the Aircraft Engine Division of the Lynn River Works. Within the framework of GE, the pilot program was extraordinarily innovative. It was in part the brain child of Ray Holland and focused on solving production problems in Lynn, but was widely seen as a possible model for other locations.

GE and IUE Local 201 negotiated a special contract supplement that allowed a group of machinists, paid at a higher rate, to work with engineers to get the equipment running. In the new systems, an engineer would give the machinists the program, which could not be altered by the machinists. When something went wrong, the engineer had to be enlisted to fix it — and the system engendered huge delays.

In older systems, the machinist could address the problem. In the new systems control was removed from the workplace. So, the issue — the real conflict — arose over the question of how much latitude the machinists should have. Would the machinist's scope of control be elevated to include the programming of the new equipment? Would the tacit knowledge of the machinist be allowed to play a part in a production system that included the machinist in real decision-making — or would the systems be designed to circumvent the machinist and eventually turn the job into something that GE had always wanted — machine operators instead of machinists?

The conflict between management and worker control of the shop floor was as old as the formalization of Taylorism in the early twentieth century. Defining each movement of the worker and paying only for that is the heart of the Tayloristic concept. In theory, except for the most skilled work, setting up a complicated machine that is the proper placement of each tool, the setting of the speeds and feeds, can be codified. As discussed earlier, the skill of the metalworker lay in the ability of the worker to figure out better ways to do the job. By the mid-century, as efforts by companies to expand their real control of the workplace via the use of computerization, workers began to raise issues initially focused on the fear of job loss.

The MIT Program in Science Technology and Society

In 1977, MIT Professor David Noble was studying the introduction of Numerically Controlled (NC) equipment, especially its design features.[14] Noble was part of a small group of historians, engineers and union leaders exploring the design of the new technology with an eye towards worker control. Noble, among others, understood that control is a social issue, not a technological one.

At that time, I was working on what was then new NC equipment in Wilmington. Peter Teel and I had been in contact about the issues involved in computer-aided machining, and he decided it would be a good idea for me to talk with David. In spite of the business agent's conservative practice and proclivities, he understood the new machines would have a significant impact on the workforce, and was trying to find ways to have a proper rate of pay for the machinists. The company thought since the "brains" were now in the machine and not the operator — they could pay less.[15]

David arranged for my appointment as the first scholar to the MIT Program in Science Technology and Society for the year 1980-81, and thus I was both a newly-elected union officer and on the staff at MIT.[16] No one, including me, knew exactly what to make of this. But it did get the attention of the River Works management team, and it did validate much of the analysis the newly formed IUE 201 technology committee produced. At MIT, my focus was to research other software design ideas that would favor worker control — the computer-aided craftsman, as we called it a few years later.

Shop stewards in Great Britain, metalworkers in Germany and their cohorts in Scandinavia, through their unions, began agitating for new job descriptions that expanded scope of control. Some English, and especially German and Scandinavian research institutes, began to organize programs to investigate new methods of work organization. These efforts, often pushed by the unions, resulted in an identifiable group of engineers who began to collaborate. This collaboration, in turn, resulted in the formation of the Social Effects of Automation Technical Committee of the International Federation of Automatic Controls.[17] Eventually, I became the vice-chair of that committee. But at this early stage, the relationships were between the Committee, David Noble at MIT, and the project, in part led by David on science, technology and society.

With the support of the MIT Program on Science, Technology and Society, and as a result of the practical work within Local 201, I was asked to participate in various international meetings with engineers and other union leaders. Through the MIT connection, I was introduced to the broader world of union participation in the design and conception of new technologies, then rapidly developing in Germany and Scandinavia (or in the U.S. and the UAW stance at the Ford Motor Company, for example).[18]

The accomplishments of the Scandinavian and German unions became part of the bargaining demands by our local vis-a-vis GE. At this early stage of industrial transformation, I was still optimistic that it might still be possible for the labor movement to emerge from the challenge of the new technology and become a more vibrant force.[19] Obviously, this has not been the case — indeed, in the US, we have witnessed the effective destruction of private sector industrial unions, both ideologically and organizationally.

But at the time, our local was plugged into a net of prestigious institutions and engineers which could not be easily dismissed by GE — or by union leaders who were willing to accept GE's intellectual and political dominance.

In 1980, the company introduced the Shop Activities Management System (SAM) according to GE to correct payroll errors. But continued questioning of management by our committee requests for information (from the Department of Defense which financed the system), yielded other knowledge.

In particular, the DoD sent us a huge manual which detailed how the system could monitor work performed and assign work among many other functions, including long-term planning. It was pretty clear the company deliberately misled the union as to the capacities of the system. In response, the angry membership demanded that the union do something — so Local 201 initiated the New Technology Committee. A leader of the more traditionalist branch of the local was chairman. I was appointed vice-chairman.

Our research allowed our union bargaining team – and the members – to understand the full scope of the SAM system and respond effectively. The team observed intensive monitoring by management does not produce a better product — and intensive surveillance may produce more unrest, but not necessarily increased productivity.

The SAM system of the eighties had the capacity, but not yet the installed capability of individual machine monitoring.[20]

Concretely, this meant the potential elimination of clerks and dispatchers. Thus, for the union to respond effectively, we needed both job protection language, as well as extensive access to data that described the new equipment, its capacity and intended use.[21] Our local demanded we have full access to the manufacturing database, production information, subcontracting — and any other relevant information (in addition to advance notice, so we could develop our response).[22] Most of these demands were rejected.

The union challenged GE throughout the eighties with regards to their use of monitoring systems, robots, direct numerically-controlled machines and tool crib distribution systems. Few locals in the U.S. did the same thing. [23]

These demands went beyond the narrow limits of "effects" bargaining enshrined in the National Labor Relations Act (NLRA), by raising the issue of prior notice and by implication, discussion of implementation — not just after the fact.[24] The issues of automation and the union's response would become a central issue in the struggle for union leadership two years later.

As time went on, GE upgraded The Shop Activities Management System with the Integrated Computer Aided Manufacturing system, Factory of the Future, and new Manufacturing Resource Planning (MRP) systems. MRP projects the entire number and type of components needed to build a product, along with the time needed for manufacture (or delivery). Using this document, it is possible to have a complete understanding of a firm's future product production plans.[25] In 1984, it allowed us to predict the eventual shutdown of turbine production, as well as GE's sale of the Wilmington plant a few years later in 1987.

IUE Local 201: The Technology Conference

In June of 1983, the SAM committee organized a technology conference whose major purpose was to show there were alternatives to the way GE intended to implement the new technologies. About one-hundred stewards and activists came to the conference, including representatives from UE local 506 — GE-Erie, PA.

Cordial relations between members of the UE in Erie, PA and Local 201 were of particular importance. The UE Local in Erie stayed with the UE during the anti-Communist blitz, while 201 went (barely) for the IUE. Our locally-organized joint discussions involving many union people from both locals were the first since the split occurred in 1950. The delegation from Erie shared with our local their detailed catalog of the effects of the flexible machining center as regards to job, income loss and rates of the job.

Local 201 officers were alerted to the potential effects of the "Factory of the Future" technology about a year before it was imported to Lynn. Officers, stewards and activists all attended the conference and were also exposed to the information. We had no idea a "Factory of the Future" proposal was in the works in June of 1983, but it is almost certain the "Factory of the Future" was already far along in the planning stages.

The conference proposed empowering union members by printing the technology agreements, requiring prior notification of new technology implementation, access to a tech library, and a monthly column by the technology committee.[26] The local was also urged to develop plans to organize technicians and work with the planners' and drafters' union as well as to meet with the IAM both at Pratt & Whitney and GE-Evendale. We also proposed a national technology conference to address new technology issues to be held one year before the expiration date of the 1982-85 contracts, so as to be prepared to make this an issue in the national negotiations.

Our committee opposed attrition as the way to cushion the effects of the new technology. We sought other ways to ensure that workers would gain some of the fruits from increased productivity. We went beyond explanation and acceptance of new surveillance and control systems to asking the basic questions of design and control.

In March of 1983, progressives won election to additional seats on the union's executive board, as well as the vice-presidency, holding six of thirteen seats for full-time officers — plus the occasional seventh vote from the non-progressives.

We had been instrumental in bringing the sex bias suit to a successful conclusion. And via the technology committee and conference, had demonstrated we had ideas for the future — not just acquiescence to the company's vision. Moreover, known leftists and union-conscious workers had led opposition to the national contracts and for items in those negotiations that made sense to other members.

In June of 1983, as the technology conference began, so did another battle for the leadership of Local 201. Business Agent Teel was moved to national staff. The president moved the Assistant Business Agent to the position of Business Agent. The Assistant Business Agent's position was suddenly open. With the support of our progressive group of board members and officers, I launched a campaign for the spot.

The campaign would function as a referendum on what type of union the members wanted.

Endnotes For Chapter Eight

1. When the GE was organized by the UE starting in 1938, the union set up a GE Conference Board. All GE locals belonged and this body made the recommendation to accept or reject the national contract. The negotiators for the union aside from the President and secretary treasurer were drawn from this group. The group also elected a chairperson and he was the day to day spokesperson for the unions far as GE was concerned. In 1949 when the union was dismembered, the IUE kept the same system. By 1979 there was an IUE conference Board and a UE conference board.

2. *The Weekly Worker* was the Communist Party's successor newspaper of the *Communist Party's Daily Worker*.

3. They secured the assistance of Nancy Gertner, later to become a Federal judge, but then a leading civil rights lawyer.

4. Kerkorian et al; Handbook detailing the agreement; Section V "Company Counter proposal Maternity Benefits and Leave Procedure" 3/18/82 10:25 PM Emspak Papers, WHS, Folder 8.927 "Benefits for disability arising from pregnancy and related conditions will be determined and administered under the weekly Sickness/Accident plan and such determination shall include a determination by the employee's physician that the employee's work presents potential harm to the employee or the unborn child". But the real challenge of course comes when the child is born. Here we made a major breakthrough "The Company will review requests, and under appropriate circumstances will grant personal leaves of absence to women employees for child rearing of their dependent newborns and for child care emergencies of their dependent child on a consistent basis without regard to sex".

5. There is a backstory here too. By about this time my wife Dolores had started her practice of medicine on the North Shore

and many of her patients were women from GE. The company was contesting all of her letters. One day as I went to call the company back to our negotiations, I walked into their meeting. The chief negotiator was facing the door, but his minions were not and one of them was explaining how they would never accept one of Dolores's letters. I inquired as to which one was going to perjure themselves once we filed a lawsuit. At that point, the chief negotiator, with great aplomb, noted that from then on, all of my wife's disability letters would be accepted.

6. The Cleveland GE complex was their lighting division. A huge proportion of the employees were women, and most of Hungarian descent. Cleveland had the largest proportion of Hungarians of any city in the world except Budapest. In 1990 after the fall of the Berlin wall GE moved its lighting division to Budapest.

7. There were about 13,000 women who worked in West Lynn between 1944 and 1983.

8. Krikorian et al vs General Electric; Local 201 v General Electric; initial settlement documents dated March 8, 1982; final settlement two weeks later pending decision of the federal judge which took place about a month later.

9. The IUE Conference Board was a body that included representatives from all locals under contract from GE. It was the body that made the recommendation to the locals to accept or reject the national contract. It was essentially the national negotiating committee. The business agents of the largest locals, like 201 were the actual bargainers.

10. I do not recall his last name, but Jimmy was from Tell City, Indiana and a former UE official.

11. The back story. John Shambo came from Schenectady. He was close to the family until he decided that his future lay with the IUE. After the GE and the NLRB installed the IUE in local

301 he became a business agent and then advanced to the key position of chief national negotiator. However he still kept in touch. One day when my father was up at his brother's cabin in the Adirondacks, John made a secret visit. I was too young to know what was being said- or even the significance of the visit. But I did meet him at that time.

12. I still have them, and in fact they are still accurate.

13. In the United States separation of the engineers from the workforce, as well as the almost zero participation of engineers in any union is the norm. In other countries engineers often have their own union or participate in the union in their enterprise.

14. David Noble was a professor at MIT and had written extensively about General Electric and its role in developing numerically controlled machine tools. His book "America by Design" outlined how technologies were developed with clear design criteria in mind, and that many of these criteria were socially determined, not a technological imperative. In this light General Electric was an important force. It specifically developed machine tools to eliminate skilled workers.

15. The manager of employee relations in GE Lynn Ray Holland, whatever his official title, was one of GE's corporate strategists when it came to the implementation of new technologies and it was he who initiated the pilot program. Over the course of the next 6 years I had occasion to speak with him- always informally about the issues of automation.

16. An important part of the program was to understand developments abroad, especially Germany. In September 1979, German projects, affiliated with the MIT program invited me I was invited to tour key industrial facilities and research institutions in my capacity as a fellow of the program.

17. The International Federation of Automatic Control (IFAC) is the largest association of professional engineers in the world

with 250,000 plus members. It is an NGO. There are multiple technical committees e.g. Aircraft Control systems etc. I was vice-chairman of the Technical Committee; the Social Effects of Automation1980 to 2000.

18. Guidelines for the Introduction and Use of New Technology, Guidelines for negotiations at local 600 of the UAW-Ford. Unsigned but written by Harley Shaikan, dated August 6, 1979. Emspak Papers, WHS, Folder 7.008.

19. "The New Technology: Who Pays? Automation and Collective Bargaining 1981,various publications; WHS, Emspak papers, Folder 7.006.

20. All of the contemplated functions and abilities plus instantaneous feedback for individual machines and hence the ability to adjust tooling would be commonplace 20 years later.

21. "S.A.M- Where Are We? Feb. 11, 1980, report to the Committee and Exec. Board of Local 201. WHS, Emspak Papers, Folder 7.008.

22. Draft-Negotiating Position for the local regarding the S.A.M system" 2/27/81 WHS, Emspak Papers, Folder 7.009.

23. " SAM Discussed in Everett" IUE Local 201, Electrical Union News, vol. xxxviii, Friday January 18,1980,Lynn ,Mass. Number 19,page 1; WHS, Emspak papers, Folder 7.009.

24. US labor law is designed around the concept of "effects" bargaining. Unions are given the right to negotiate the effects of management's decisions. The effects are outlined as "hours, wages and working conditions." Legally required intervention by the union in many aspects of design, capital investment; etc. are either not legal or prohibited. This is not so in most countries.

25. Complete Description of MRP WHS, Emspak Papers, Folder 7.015.

26. Proposals from the July Meeting of the New Technology Committee" WHS, Emspak Papers, , Folder 7.014.

Chapter Nine: The Battle for Leadership

The special election for Assistant Business Agent in that summer of 1983 was really a referendum on the kind of local that we could become. Unlike most previous elections which were personality driven, this one focused on responding to new technology, organizing the membership in defense of the contract, and a vision of how a union should be run using Wilmington as an example.

Progressive union ideals had gained ground in 1981, and again in the union elections of March of 1983 with several people winning seats on the IUE 201 Executive Board. Our distinguishing characteristics were support for the sex bias suit, increasing attention to the challenge of technology, and a commitment to democratic practice. In the context of IUE 201, that meant an end to the constant red-baiting that characterized the union, and an attitude toward the company which increasingly saw their interest as separate from the interests of many members.

A lot was at stake with this election. It would mean an avowed left-winger and class-conscious militant would become one of the four top officers of the union for the first time since the local was founded as UE local 201 in 1938. There was also the symbolism of a descendant of a UE leader running for office in IUE local 201.

While some union leadership would tolerate the advice provided by the tech committee, actual accession to power was another thing altogether. They fought it tooth and nail. The usual red-baiting was a feature of the conservative leadership, as well as attacks on me for being too supportive of women, especially when it came to harassment.

Our campaign was centered on the need to develop a union response to the introduction of new technology. We also called for vigorous enforcement of health and safety standards taking advantage of the union's funded positions. Finally, my reputation as an independent thinker and effective organizer allowed me to be a strong candidate. As a leaflet written by a longtime union activist in the River Works put it, "One overriding reason that Frank Emspak measures up to my needs is that Frank is independent of the internal power structure within the union....I strongly urge you to vote for Frank Emspak as a real alternative to business as usual at the union hall."[1]

Our progressive coalition was a coherent movement within the local for a more union-conscious, even class-conscious way to respond to GE. We were able to expose existing leadership as having no vision separate from that of the company. The "we" included almost all of the class-conscious people who had come to GE during the early and mid-seventies. The CP was part of this cohort and members did the hard day-to-day work talking with their fellow workers about the issues. Party members were already known as independent thinkers as regards to GE.

But in spite of strong support from many stewards and activists, the establishment won. The actual vote took place immediately after the summer shutdown. In the end, I lost by thirty-eight votes out of four-thousand-eight-hundred-thirty-four ballots cast.[2]

With the establishment victory, it was pretty clear to the union members and to GE that there would be no major changes in the union's approach to the company. Class consciousness was not in their lexicon. But the vote also demonstrated there was a large proportion of the membership willing to look at things differently. In our view, membership support was deep enough to allow for the effective challenge to GE's next vision — the "Factory of the Future."

In April of 1984, we continued our efforts to develop a union response to new technology. As a follow up to the 1983 Technology Conference hosted by IUE local 201, UE local 506 organized the UE Conference on Automation, Robotics and Jobs.[3] The sub-title of the conference report captures the tenor of the gathering: "Progress for GE is not Progress for us."[4] However, in contrast to the 1983 conference in Lynn, more key IUE locals, such as Schenectady-GE along with representatives from the Steelworkers, Machinists and IBEW came to the conference. The basis was to develop a strategy to deal with GE — but it would depend on the IUE as the largest representative of GE workers to support it.

Neither of the business agents came to the conference, which implied they would not support the conclusions of the conference. Sixteen Local 201 members attended. Our delegation was made up of E-board members, stewards and activists. The main suggestions to encourage job retention was to get organized. Organization of the membership to fight for jobs was the focus of that portion of the agenda, which we argued, must come from the shop floor and continue up to the International Union. In addition, the conference urged the unions to raise the issue of jobs and automation in the '85 contract negotiations.

Conference participants voted unanimously to ask the IUE, the largest union of GE workers, to call an international conference on new technology to develop a unified position around measured day work, electronic monitoring, elimination of piecework, salary and hourly job losses, video display terminal health hazards, and loss of skills.

Factory of the Future

A month later, in May 1984, the local's leadership was summoned to Washington by the International President to be told by GE that the company was willing to invest $51 million in Lynn ("an old union plant"), in a flexible machining center. "State-of-the-art" they said. Immediately, the union called it "Factory of the Future." The new plant would be located in West Lynn at the site of the soon-to-be closed West Lynn plant.

GE made it clear investment was dependent on the union agreeing to three items or the investment would go to the nonunion facility in Hooksett, New Hampshire. The three demands were:

- Broad classifications
- Day work with measurement [5]
- Two twelve-hour shifts (7 a.m. to 7:30 p.m. and 7:30 p.m. to 7 a.m.)

Broad job classifications meant the number of tasks a worker could perform included many things. For example, setting up different types of similar machines or sweeping the floor. In GE's case, broad classifications did not mean increasing the skill level. Piecework is payment by the piece. If one produced more, one got paid more. Daywork is payment by the hour, no matter how much one produced — daywork with measurement set standards for the amount one needed to produce during an hour. Thus, the firm might be able to get more production through various forms of pressure, but not compensate the worker for production over a specific amount. The company said the three demands would apply to the "Factory of the Future" only. But the union would have to reach an agreement with GE in thirty days, so they could break ground in July (subsequently, delayed until August). All of the company's demands contradicted long-held positions of the union. The design of the facility went in the exact opposite direction of any of the skill-building flexible automation discussions we had been having. With the "Factory of the Future" proposal, GE took advantage of the political and ideological weakness of the IUE nationally, and tunnel vision of the officers of local 201.[6]

The union could and did negotiate some minor points — training, clarification of pay for holidays, vacation shutdowns, and so forth. None of the fundamentals were discussed, however. Especially how the factory would actually take more skill and control away from the machinists and become a pretty inflexible place.[7]

The company's position was accepted by three of the top four officers of the local union, as well as all the International officers, prior to any discussion by the union's Executive Board or vote by the membership. There is no evidence the International Union raised any questions or objections. There was no attempt to get outside engineering expertise to evaluate the company's design and production estimates. Nor was there any attempt by the International or the local leadership to get copies of contracts governing similar machining centers at other GE facilities. This, of course, was deliberate blindness since our automation committee had some of these documents and had provided them to the officers.

Vice-President Ron Malloy, Board Member Charlie Corbett, Trustee Susan Shepard and I, opposed the deal. We objected to the lower rate and broad job classifications, the schedule, the way vacation time was calculated — pretty much everything.[8]

A long-service skilled worker and union activist (after noting his grandfather, father and mother all worked at GE West Lynn, as well as another four relatives who worked in the River Works) wrote, "My interpretation of this agreement is that GE has FINALLY taken away to R-19 machine operator rate and reduced it to R-17 "stager" — they have replaced the eight-hour day with a twelve-hour day; the forty-hour week to a forty-two-hour week; they have eliminated a complete shift with two shifts working measured day work; they have made the worker a human robot…The future at GE means longer hours, longer work week, more productivity at less wages. If this is the future, it looks like the 20's and 30's to me. They have wiped out all classifications and reduced them to three."[9]

The stewards' council also voted 63-30 against the proposal.[10]

The majority of the local's leadership and all local media accepted GE's threat GE would never again invest in Lynn if workers voted down the deal. Our group characterized the company's bargaining position as blackmail and noted the company had invested in GE Erie, PA without the imposition of the twelve-hour day and other onerous changes, once UE local 506 had made its position clear.

Because the changes demanded by the company required contractual alterations, the membership of local 201 had the right to vote on the proposal. But the deck was already stacked for support of the deal. It was one thing to support or oppose a person running for union office. It was quite another for people to go against the enthusiastic support of local GE management combined with the threat of losing out on investment forever.

The union leadership inflated the potential level of GE's investment while repeating the company's claims that a rejection was tantamount to sealing Lynn's doom. In leaflets to the members, the majority of the Executive Board and officers said,[11] "Do you want to be part of the future or go on living in the past? I for one say that we must have the Factory of the Future and control over it in our location".[12] The reality of plant closure was emphasized as the firm closed the West Lynn location"[13] and continued to move turbine work abroad.[14]

The final membership vote was three-thousand-nine-hundred-and-three for; and one-thousand-four-hundred-fifty-two against.[15] In the absence of any campaign by the leadership regarding investments except capitulation to GE, the members voted to accept GE's terms, motivated by fear of job loss. The most surprising aspect of this vote is the significant number of people willing to vote "no."

People who voted "no" did so because they opposed the new work rules, the company's arrogance and because they did not trust GE's assurances the new rules would apply only to the Factory of the Future. The greatest weakness (both then and thirty years later) is Progressives do not have an answer to address the issue of capital mobility.

The "Factory of the Future" had a very limited future. The company broke ground on Tuesday August 21, 1984. It started production about a year later. It was all over by 1992. Machining ended and the plant was used for another 4 years to train machine operators. GE mothballed it permanently in 1996, sold the land in 2016. It is now a grocery store. The corporation never was clear as to why it failed. But I think the reasons were linked to a corporate decision to begin to reduce dependency on Lynn; a turn away from manufacturing innovation in general as Jack Welch turned the company into a financial, rather than manufacturing powerhouse. As well as the inflexible nature of the "Factory of the Future" system (making it difficult to manufacture many different types of parts in relatively small quantities).

The groundbreaking was done by a robot controlled by a union member. At the groundbreaking Business Agent Murphy said, "If we continue to improve communications and work together in areas of mutual interest and concern, it will truly be a great day for Lynn…a great day for the IUE, and a credit to GE."[16]

High-minded as this is, the officers and negotiating committee members who recommended the agreement, also warned, "A few among the officers, executive board negotiating committee, stewards and members were gambling with our future. They have a right to dissent, but they should also be held accountable for the risk they subjected all of us to. Among them there are some who made it clear at a special membership informative meeting that they believed in another political and economic system and wanted to use this issue to advance their cause…."[17]

But support based on fear could only go so far. In March 1985, seven months after the "Factory of the Future" agreement was signed, almost every local union official who supported it was voted out of office.

Factory of Future Leaders Defeated 1985

After a couple of months of relative peace within the local, the fight for leadership began again. A progressive slate won the union elections in March as members became distrustful of the "Factory of the Future" agreement, especially as work continued to be outsourced from the River Works.

Our slate, headed by Vice-President Ron Malloy, emphasized that one had to have the courage to stand up to GE and be responsible to the local union membership, and thus independent in his attitude towards the International union leadership.[18] We implied that the leadership was suckered by GE, accepting their unsubstantiated claims about competing locations and their refusal to look at other locations with similar investments and better contract terms.[19]

The primary focus of attacks on our progressive caucus was our opposition to the "Factory of the Future" and claiming that our opposition threatened employment.

Our slate won by almost the same margin as the loss of the "Factory of the Future" vote. The plant was divided with about forty-percent willing to vote consistently for a more militant confrontational stance; forty-percent opposing that, and twenty-percent switching between the two. The arguments we made were the same ones we made eight months earlier. But this time the members felt they could express themselves without endangering their jobs.

The 1986 Strike for Respect

Over the next year, with the tacit support of the right wing of the local, GE-Lynn stonewalled any initiative of the union, making the progressive leadership look incompetent. The right wing demanded a strike over unresolved grievances — a risky proposition. After tense negotiations, which at first looked like a resolution was at hand, the company rejected all union offers of settlement. The local struck. For the first time since 1969, all segments of the local were called out. The strike lasted almost a month and achieved almost nothing.

Although the entire local, including Wilmington was to go on strike, the company immediately initiated efforts to split the local, as Wilmington was a separate bargaining unit. When the company and union met at the mandatory pre-strike negotiating session, GE agreed to all of the Wilmington bargaining unit's demands — even the ones where the company had already told us "NO." For example, they agreed to review the use of outside contractors doing maintenance, and reach out to the Lynn plant to see if there were union members available to come up and do the work instead of farming it out. Overall, GE agreed to take steps which we could verify to instruct their foreman to do everything they could to bring peace and harmony to Wilmington.[20]

GE made sure that the Wilmington bargaining unit had no legal basis to strike. The purpose was to undermine my influence, as well as to divide the local. To an extent, this worked. The contrast between the achievements in Wilmington and River Works could not have been starker.

A year later, in the March 1987 elections for union leadership, the progressive coalition was overwhelmingly defeated. By that time, Malloy had lost the moral authority he had at the time of the election in 1985. In January of 1987, GE began announcing the possibility of massive layoffs in Lynn, but the rumor was that if the union leadership changed to a less confrontational group, maybe some of the layoffs could be averted. Just prior to the vote allegedly for post-employment counseling (that is counseling by the company provided to employees who might be laid off), GE called in about twelve-hundred lower seniority individuals, but indicated that the employment situation might change. Democratic Congressman Nicholas Mavroules said there was nothing he could do to prevent layoffs. Even though he built his career on fighting for defense contracts for GE. He claimed he was unable to speak with anyone in the DoD or GE management about their plans.

I was well known as a supporter and associate of Malloy — and could have stayed in office in Wilmington. I had no opposition for either my Executive Board position or for the Conference Board. But I chose not to do so because I believed the principled thing to do was to support our vision of the union by running again for assistant business agent.

I knew from the first day of the campaign we were not going to win. The enthusiasm I received in 1983 in the River Works was simply not there — but the hostility from some of the workers there (including personal threats) was a regular experience.

The vote again switched and the Malloy slate, including me, was defeated by about the same margin as the "Factory of the Future" vote. The reasons were similar — fear of layoffs.

As in the "Factory of the Future" vote, the Left had no viable strategy to counter the company's threats of layoffs and workforce reduction. At the River Works, about two-thousand workers had been hired since 1983. What they experienced was a one-month strike and threats to investment in the plant — and thus loss of employment. Progressives talked about union democracy and unity against the company — issues which seemed foolish to this cohort, who were focused on employment. We were talking about the wrong issues at the wrong time and had no viable strategy to protect jobs.

In the two years prior to the 1987 election, our Wilmington organization continued to build the local. Wilmington stewards spent time reaching out to new people, bringing them into the union and doing our best to make them feel welcome. For example, we finally convinced the company to let us address new hires. We also produced cards in various languages explaining the union and an individual's rights.[21]

The intensive outreach and discussion brought union membership to just about one-hundred-percent. During much of this period, we did not have a union shop. Winning the union shop was a goal of the IUE in the 1985 national negotiations, and the union played up winning the agency shop as an answer to our problems. But in Wilmington it made little difference. We had already won it in practice.

While in office, the stewards and I worked hard to correct the remnants of the successful sex bias suit, addressing lower wage rates in some jobs sometimes as a consequence of well-planned, short strikes.[22] Sometimes, we were able to alert outside agencies, such as the Department of the Navy. In one case, we could hear the discussion as the Navy representative asked (incredulously) if the company was nuts denying fifty-cent-per-hour (for a total of three-dollars-per-hour) to these women and jeopardizing the Navy contract because of late deliveries. A few minutes later, we had a settlement in that strike.

The period after 1983 marks another major shift in my personal life. Dolores finished her internship and was hired at an Ob-Gyn practice in Beverly, MA. The practice served a number of women at GE. But the fact that we now had a significant income also changed our sociological matrix. My income contribution, while important, was no longer a life or death situation. I began to be concerned as I was making decisions about strikes and income loss for many, while we would not be suffering the same hardships. In retrospect, the change in income status did not seem to be an issue for my constituents in Wilmington. Members judged me by the efforts we made to advance our issues, and I was never attacked because of our family's change in economic circumstances.

Return to the Machine Shop and the End of GE for Me

The day after the elections in March 1987, I had a decision to make. But almost everyone in the plant, as well as the management, had already made it. They had decided that given my education and knowledge the likelihood of me returning to Wilmington was about zero. However, as an ex-union officer, I had the right to return to my job in the factory, as I had not broken service. On the Monday after the election, I arrived at work at about 2:45 p.m., pulling my tool box in a little wagon. As I entered the plant and was making my way to my work station, I received a standing ovation from the first-shift machine shop and the people just arriving for the second-shift. It was very moving.

But the political situation was difficult. In many ways it resembled what it was like before I was elected in that at about 2:45 p.m. stewards and grievants would also arrive at my machine station waiting to talk. Most people still looked to me for leadership. Essentially, not much of significance went on in the Wilmington plant without some involvement from me.

So, even out of my position on the Executive Board, I was a steward and still seen as a leader within our division of the local. Wilmington had a united and increasingly well-informed steward's body. We had some support from management, which saw the union as a fighter for work to stay in Wilmington. I organized small group of stewards to analyze the Manufacturing Resource Planning production and quality reports. Persons unknown left them in the refrigerator in my old department — which was labeled "Radioactive Isotopes." It was a secure location, so to speak.

I knew that I was in the end game of employment at GE when I refused the company's offer of a high-paid consultant job at corporate headquarters. GE often offered defeated union leaders foreman or low-level administrator positions. But this was something else, and a six-figure-income was nothing to sneeze at in 1987. As I explained to the company's spokesman, in my view, GE was the family firm as much as anyone else's. After all, someone in the family had been working at GE since about 1905. That being the case, as I was not being offered the CEO position and since taking the job offer would be a betrayal of everything I and the family believed in — I refused.

The corporate spokesman was shocked. The plant manager said, "I told you so. This was a complete waste of time." At this point, as far as GE management and the union leadership were concerned my future at GE was in my past.

In the spring and summer prior to my second shift at GE, I was working with a group at the University of Lowell studying advanced manufacturing. We had been developing a program that would result in my employment if the federal grant was funded. But by late August, it appeared we would not get the grant.

For some years, I had been advising the Massachusetts Department of Labor about responses to plant closings. As a result of union opposition from the District Director of the IUE, I was never placed officially on any of the panels. But senior Labor Department staff did encourage me to apply for a job to work on the issue of plant closures. I was invited to an interview in September, but heard nothing.

When I went back to work after my May interview with GE, I knew (as did everyone else with sense) I would be having trouble. And, indeed, the level of supervision increased. It got to the point where over the objections of my foreman, the more senior management attempted to suspend me for one trumped up charge or another. This, of course, was very stressful. From May through September, they made two or three such attempts, but each time my second shift co-workers generally stopped work until the situation was resolved. Clearly, this could not go on forever — and, indeed, it would not.

During this time, the stewards and I used our knowledge of the MRP system to track production. What was especially worrisome to us was that the amount of farm-out was increasing and seemed to equal or exceed what was being done in the plant.[23] It also suggested that the company had no interest in investing in a modern machine shop to be able to produce the farmed-out work — the usual indicators of a sale or closure. Ultimately, our knowledge saved the plant.

During the summer, I had been putting out leaflets attacking the farm-out and questioning the future of the plant. In August, union relations told me I would be fired if I put out another leaflet — especially one raising issues of the plant being sold. Someone in GE pointed out that several of the newer employees were from Guatemala, and would be fired and possibly deported if they walked out in support of me. As union supporters, their lives would be in real danger back in Guatemala.

At the end of September, we were able to conclusively show (using our purloined MRP data) that the company intended to stop production at Wilmington on December 31. If consummated, GE would be in violation of the union and Department of Defense contracts, as they had made no announcements (in fact, they were continually denying anything was afoot).

On about October 1, I printed a leaflet outlining the situation, describing what we had found, and demanding the company come clean and deal with the union. I signed it alone, so as not to jeopardize the other stewards. I knew I would be fired. We hoped the publicity would save the plant. We believed we had a good chance to maintain operations because we knew the defense orders and commercial orders were still strong. So, it was not a question of lack of work, but a question of who would do it and where it would be done.

As I was handing out the leaflets, the company HR person told me I was through. I said I was in my lunch hour and I demanded a meeting (pursuant to the contract) regarding my discharge. By that time, everyone knew what was going on; many had read the leaflet and the union hall in Lynn had been alerted. In addition to the machine shop, others on the second-shift had stopped work and many were calling friends on the first and third-shifts alerting them to the situation. People in the shop were extremely upset.

By around 10 p.m., Local 201 leaders arrived and we began serious discussions as to what exactly was going on. The issues were:

a) Illegal discharge of a steward for handing out a leaflet on his own time (not a discharge offense).

And...

b) GE ceasing production without contractually required notification.

After a day of tense discussions, the company admitted that they had sold the aircraft instrument division to the AMETEK Corporation effective on January 1, and that no provision had been made to recognize the union or maintain the contract. In addition, the defense department's Department of Contract Administration (DCAS) had not been informed.

GE, faced with violations of their contracts with the DoD, violations of the national IUE-GE contract regarding notification and plant closures, and an increasingly restive workforce, agreed to the following settlement with the local.

1) AMETEK would recognize the union and maintain the contract in place for at least a year;

2) There would be no discipline as regards to any of the activities surrounding the publication of information;

3) I would not be fired, but IF the state of MA hired me as Director of the Center for Applied Technology, I would be allowed to leave the company on an indefinite leave of absence for community service, but since there would be no GE bargaining unit, I would not be expected to return once that was over (I retired from General Electric on my sixtieth birthday in 2003 still on my leave of absence for community service). I had refused to resign and the company would face an arbitration which they would lose if they fired me.

Peter DiCicco, president of IUE District Two, who had blocked my appointment, announced the state had agreed to hire me. DiCicco speaking for IUE also said they did not expect me to be involved in, or run for office in local 201 once I left the plant.

On Friday October 23, 1987 I left the Wilmington plant for the last time as an employee.

The contract was intact, none of my friends or supporters had been disciplined, and all of us could be proud we had stood up in a positive way to GE and, at least for a while, maintained our dignity and standard of living.

As far as local 201 is concerned, GE slowly but surely reduced the scope of products, phasing out businesses and people along the way. Investment almost ceased. Union membership at GE dropped from about eight thousand in 1987 to about one-thousand-one-hundred-ninety in 2021. The plant is clearly in danger. The defined benefit contribution pension plan is gone for new hires. The retiree medical insurance plan has been abolished. I don't think any worker is planning on a future with GE.

A worker view of technology and a clear commitment to democratic practice in the local reached its high point with the "Factory of the Future" discussion and subsequent repudiation of those who supported it. But in the end, the company's fierce opposition to meaningful worker participation in control of the work — plus absolute company control of capital — overwhelmed the progressive forces in the union. Central to our defeat was, and remains, the refusal of the trade union movement and its political allies to propose any meaningful political or practical opposition to capital mobility. That requires a class-conscious labor movement. And that brings us back to the origins of the IUE and the strategic victory of companies like GE who succeeded in extirpating most class-conscious workers and their organizations from the heart of manufacturing in the U.S.

Looking back, I did not regret any of my activities as a union activist and officer. Overall, I think I found ways to use my intellectual ability on behalf of the people I worked with. They appreciated it and I appreciated their wisdom and support.

My greatest regrets are that we were unable to build the type of union movement that could effectively take on GE. We strove for independence intellectually and politically from GE, and at times we achieved it. But we did not have the ability to transform our movement into the aggressive union-conscious organization it needed to be to defeat a firm like GE. I was and remain extremely proud of our sex bias suit victory, as it forced GE to give some recognition to women and offered pathways for advancement to others.

What I and most of my colleagues in the labor movement did not recognize in 1987, was that we were at the peak of our influence. People had the fortitude to go out on strike in 1986 because we thought we could do better. It was not primarily a defensive strike to preserve benefits or wages. The same was true for our various work actions in Wilmington in the 1980s. Wilmington is almost gone — Ametek reduced employment to about sixty workers. But most of the benefits we won at Wilmington are still in place for the remaining Ametek employees.

In the most basic way, the structures built by workers — our union and its political system — were not able to protect, never mind enhance, the gains that had been made up until that point. At the same time, progressives were not able to build a movement that could effectively challenge the root causes of destruction-capital mobility. Instead, the Democratic Party and trade union leadership chose to ameliorate the immediate suffering via long-term unemployment insurance, some medical insurance protection and job training. Even the most minimal efforts to force firms to pay back subsidies they might have received to stay in communities were fought by the political leadership, and generally not supported by the trade union leadership for fear the business climate might be harmed.

CODA: Fast forward to 2006. I was on my way to New Hampshire with Dolores when I decided to stop in at Wilmington. There were about sixty people still employed there. Almost all of the work, however, had been moved to Mexico. But in order to get FAA certification, the aircraft instruments were shipped back to Wilmington for final tests and repairs if needed. I had always felt guilty about leaving Wilmington, but that feeling was ill-founded. I knew all of the people who were still there. They still had their pension, medical, cost-of-living and their union. As they said, "Why negotiate against ourselves? Sooner or later, they will close this place. There is no reason for us to make it easier."

Endnotes For Chapter Nine

1. Leaflets in support of Emspak Ron Malloy "An Open Letter from Charlie Ruiter" WHS, Emspak Papers, Folder 8.936.

2. Given that the election was held when a significant number of people were out of town, and little or no information was provided as to how to cast an absentee ballot, the turnout was close to 80% of eligible voters.

3. Automation, Jobs and Our Future-Report and references UE Conference on Automation, Robotics and Jobs, Erie PA April 28th 1984 WHS ,Emspak Papers, Folder 7.017.

4. The GE advertising slogan was "Progress is our most important product".

5. Day work with measurement meant intense supervision and measurement per a standard of production. In piecework standards were set via time study, and could be adjusted. If one produced more pay would increase. Day work offered no such production incentive. Measured day work with supervision (or machine pacing) tried to achieve productivity increases by reducing the standards-the time to make each piece- but without compensation for additional production.

6. The IUE always focused on trade as the issue. In spite of many plant closures they never engaged in or mobilized any effort to deal with issues that might expose GE's aggressive and predatory capital mobility strategy.

7. Negotiating Minutes factory of the Future and GE Labor-Management relations WHS, Emspak Papers, Folder 7.023.

8. Lynn Item Monday June 25-1984 vol. 213, no 15 page 1 and 12; WHS, Emspak Papers, folder 7.025.

9. Statement by Joe Fleury at Special call Steward's council meeting of Factory of the Future agreement 6/22/84 WHS, Emspak Papers, Folder 7.022.

10. Malloy objections: replace days off with hours off- has negative effects throughout the contract-nots that instead of 3 days off for death in the family they would get 24 hour or two days off; also disturbed by the elimination of modification termination clause which allows either the union or company to unilaterally reopen negotiations with 30 days' notice Lynn Item Monday June 25-1984 vol. 213,no 15 a page 1 and 12 WHS, Emspak Papers, folder 7.025.

11. LYNN Item Friday June 22 Vol 213.no 13; pg. 1, WHS, Emspak papers, Folder 7.025.

12. Ibid.

13. Ibid.

14. During the summer of 1984 we were able to ascertain that no new rotors for turbines had been ordered. Given that there was an 18 month lead time, it seemed certain that medium steam turbine manufacturing and assembly would end about 18 months later. The BA and ABA chose not to take this information seriously.

15.Special Edition, Electrical Union News Friday June 29, 1984.

16. Electrical Union News Friday August 24, 1984 vol. xliii number 7 pg. 1 Emspak Papers, WHS, folder 7.024 Evelyn Murphy Secretary of economic Affairs for the Commonwealth of MA also spoke. Ironically she hired me 4 years later.

17. Leaflet, unsigned entitled "Vote of Confidence" first sentence indicates it is from the officers who supported the agreement. Undated but after June 26th and before August 24th 1984 Emspak Papers, WHS Folder 7.022.

18. I had no opposition as Wilmington Board Member or as delegate to the Conference board in 1985.

19. Leslie Schneider, Charles Levenstein, Charles Richardson, Fred Sperounis The Center or Productivity Enhancement, University of Lowell Working paper 87-6 March 1987 folder 7.026 "Since the factory of the Future negotiations between GE and Local 201 the company has declared that the agreement would serve as a model for future agreements… The authors also concluded "The Company's demands for altering the traditional work rules were not mandated by technological constraints, nor by some innate characteristics of the technology rather a decision was made which would change the social territory on which the struggle for control is carried out" Ibid. Pg. 43.

20. Notes of pre-strike negotiating session, dated 2/26/1986 WHS, Emspak Papers, Folder 8.966.

21. Translating some words was a real problem- "grievance" and "arbitration" among them. These words, at least in the industrial context did not really exist in Laotian or Cambodian.

22. Maria DaSilva, a diminutive activist from Portugal who told us how to really go on strike. At 5:30 AM as we began our picket, she sat down in the middle of the long entrance road to the plant, just as a huge tractor trailer pulled up. He stopped and several people stepped out of the bushes on each side of the road. I asked the driver to turn around (which he really could not do) and call his dispatcher to say he was in danger. He noticed that the ball team had bats but had forgotten the ball. As he was doing this other trucks pulled up. After about 20 minutes the highway Route 62 leading to the interstate was blocked. A bit later the Northbound and Southbound lanes of I-93 were down to one lane. At about 8:30 AM the governor's office called. Around 9:00 AM we had a settlement.

23. Extensive farm out research folders WHS, Emspak Papers, 8.999; 9.000.

Chapter Ten: New Technologies Promises and Defeats

Center for Applied Technology

The Center for Applied Technology (CAT) was a division of the Massachusetts Centers of Excellence, one of the economic development/industrial retention agencies of the state of Massachusetts. Its goal was to stem the accelerating deindustrialization then underway.

While it was clear capital flight was a root cause of job loss, most policy discussions focused on financial assistance to firms or covering the costs of worker training, rather than impeding capital flight. Policy proposals that impeded firm mobility were rejected by both the business and labor community, as they thought that such ideas encouraged firms to leave a business unfriendly environment.

Instead, the needs of these firms were defined as a lack of capital; lack of marketing ability; a need for worker training, and technical support. The state launched the Center for Applied Technology to provide that technical support. In essence, I was supposed to figure out ways for small and medium manufacturers to adopt new technologies for manufacturing without displacing workers.

CAT also worked with specific unions to help them develop an understanding of the new technologies and be able to articulate those understandings from their point of view. So, in addition

229

to skill development amongst management, we also needed to develop expertise within the labor movement.

The MA Secretary of Labor and the Secretary of Commerce were my direct reports and employers. Leading hi-tech firms such as Prime Computer were on the board, as were prominent educators and union officials.

I was hired as the first executive director for CAT because of my prior connection at MIT, and because I had been working with members of the Dukakis administration on industrial retention issues for some time. For political reasons discussed earlier, the New England District of the IUE had blocked my appointment. But in October 1987, both the union and GE wanted to find a way out of the crisis at the Wilmington plant, and so all opposition to my employment evaporated. In fact, GE became a public supporter about a year later.

What differentiated the CAT and its projects from other industrial retention schemes is that it sought to support manufacturing through something other than the public paying for the consequences of layoffs, or through tax relief. In its essentials CAT strove to make worker centered criteria equal to traditional business centered criteria as the basis for deciding which projects to support.

At CAT, we organized industry, labor and university partnerships as the way to promote new technology and innovation."[1] These "partnerships" often meant mobilizing public resources (universities) and political support (organized labor) to provide political and financial resources to a business defined set of projects. The recipient of the services were the co-operating firms in industry. CAT would identify and subsidize technical expertise coming from the universities. Unions approached CAT with projects and pushed their employers to participate. Unions, if they were present, had to be part of the project team in order for firms to access support or advice. We called the program "Results Oriented Technical

Assistance". New technologies meant implementing new computer-based metal working tools, or new methods of manufacturing and organization, or production of new products.

My office was on the first floor of a building that Lafayette had used way back in 1790 or so. Historic? Yes. Poor lighting? Yes. View of the Boston Common? Really great! And the sanitary facilities had improved a lot since 1790.

CAT required workers be part of the technology selection and implementation process. We buttressed our arguments using the experience in Lynn, with the Pilot Project and the research from IFAC,[2] as well as work from the University of Lowell in MA.[3] The research and experience showed that worker participation, meaning actual decision authority, resulted in better and timelier outcomes. There were just too many problems with programming, tooling and organization to be addressed effectively without worker participation.[4]

We insisted the scope of technical solutions had to be broadened from a Tayloristic vision of a job, to one that used the tacit knowledge of the workforce. In other words, the workers had skills and ability — and implementation of new manufacturing ideas worked much better if one worked with and used those skills and ability rather than simply getting rid of the people. As the CAT board stated, "We want people who are experts in using computer driven systems, rather than expert systems." To the greatest extent possible we sought to implement new technologies in ways that enhanced skill as well as productivity.

CAT only granted technical assistance to companies that agreed to include the workforce.[5] If there was a union present, the union and company both had to agree to work with our staff to develop a path forward. Secondly, the firm could have no outstanding employment violations pending from either state or federal agencies. CAT also undertook to train technical assistance providers in consensus-building techniques — that is how to really speak with and value working people.

CAT developed criteria for success which went well beyond simple firm survival. Projects were designed with explicit improvements in employment and job content in exchange for worker participation that would yield increased productivity. To be a success, employment levels had to be the same or greater. We opposed attrition. Greater productivity achieved could not be translated into reducing the workforce, but rather a push for increased market share. We also sought to improve the job content of the new jobs in terms of skill, health & safety and, of course, compensation.

Our employment, worker participation and technology design criteria distinguished the CAT from other technical assistance centers then being developed. National models in North Carolina, Michigan and Minnesota attempted to implement some form of direct assistance to firms. But CAT was the only one that insisted on criteria regarding technology design; maintaining total employment, and the need to achieve consensus – not just involvement of the workforce.

We launched the technical assistance project with a conference at Worcester Polytech University on February 19, 1988. More than a hundred people attended — professionals interested in providing the technical assistance, union leaders worried about plant closures, and manufacturing managers looking for productivity improvements. Much of the discussion revolved around our ideas regarding technology and decision-making, with a focus on concepts like skills-based automation.

I emphasized that CAT employed a skills based method for applying appropriate technology.

Skills based change meant:
- Draw on the knowledge of the workforce in planning for change;

- Include the workforce in technical design and manufacturing criteria for product and for process innovation;
- Design in worker skills and shop floor decision making for flexibility, quality and efficiency;
- Make workforce training and knowledge development part of technological change;

To be perfectly clear, we also defined "Results Oriented Technical Assistance," which involved the management and the employees developing a common mission and including measurements of success. We noted that that there can be distinct interests, for example, employment levels and profit — but both had to be satisfied by the project to proceed.[6]

By 1990, CAT had assisted about twenty firms in improving their product and production processes. We had also assisted in the creation of other twenty or so partnerships with universities to help them understand how and why to involve the workforce in the design and implementation of the projects. These projects consisted of applying new technology in CAD/CAM, intelligent systems and CNC technologies.

Our biggest project, which we conducted with the University of Lowell, was the Pneumatic Scale Company. Located in North Quincy Massachusetts, the firm built the scales and associated equipment to ensure the exact amount of product was in each box or bottle sold by a firm. For example, the exact amount of Cheerios in each box. In 1988, the company faced huge challenges as it switched from a mechanical measuring-based system to an electronics-based one. Local 444 of the Retail, Wholesale and Department Store Union (RWDSU), with two visionary and committed leaders in   Charles Colby and Terry Manly, represented the workers. Ed Mulkern, the HR manager, led the company's efforts. The initial project focused on changing the way production was organized. [7]

Pneumatic Scale illustrated the best that could happen in this type of project. The union was energized and involved, and stuck to their criteria of maintaining the same level of employment as before the adoption of the new tech (no attrition). But the company was also willing to find ways to move forward with a complete reorganization of production and maintain employment.[8]

The project included the revamping of the scale measurements systems from mechanical to electronic with the concomitant changes in production and skill. The department that actually assembled and tested the scales was the most skilled and senior. In what I thought was the greatest achievement, all workers in the department were given the opportunity to go to the Wentworth Technical institute to take classes   to acquire the skills needed to produce the new products. The company paid for the classes, as well as a portion of the wages (some of the classes took place during the workday). The class took more than a year — but all sixty people who took it passed (except for two nearing retirement, who were excused). The result was a transformed company that used the most modern machining technology to build a state-of-the-art product. It was proof positive that incorporating the workforce in key decisions and offering high quality training in new techniques could work.

As the Pneumatic Scale project was proceeding, I began to focus on the process of joint company-union decision-making, especially techniques to make it possible for the workforce to participate in strategic planning meetings as equals to the company. I had begun working with Mike Brower, a consultant. Brower had developed a training system which helped workers better understand the relationship of complex and competing interests within the firm. In essence, Brower's system was a class-conscious one. The Brower system did not try to convince participants they had a common purpose with management (all in the same boat), but rather taught how people actually came to reach a conclusion and then applied those insights to conventional problem-solving tools. Various Japanese initiated problem-solving tools were being widely utilized by the late eighties. Brower repurposed them, especially the plan, do, check, act tool as aids to help unions develop consensus and plans of action. We added the concept of "ableness" to this model, as well as a rigorous evaluation aspect to the ideas of "check" or evaluating the results of an action. The objective was to maximize the possibility of a group reaching consensus. We wanted to make sure consensus meant workers had enough tools and understanding at their disposal to really achieve consensus, not just acquiescence.

But all good things come to an end. Governor Dukakis lost the presidential election to George Bush in 1988. Almost immediately, more conservative Democrats in the Massachusetts legislature moved to defund all of the projects that Dukakis had created—including the Massachusetts Center of Excellence. In order to continue, CAT had to become more self-sufficient by the budget year of 1990. We did this by marketing ourselves to out-of-state union-management groups. Two long-term projects emerged. UAW Local 5,[9] representing workers at AM General in South Bend, Indiana wanted the AM General Company to initiate a civilian version of the Hummer, the military's all-terrain vehicle. The union also wanted to work out a joint process to deal with issues regarding layoffs.

At about the same time, union activists from the International Brotherhood of Electrical Workers employed in the maintenance department of the SD Warren paper company in Westbrook, Maine also reached out. They and the other unions in maintenance wanted to begin a process that ultimately transformed the maintenance department from a cost center to a profit center for SD Warren. Projects like this could bring in enough income- to satisfy the state legislature and impress the new governor.

In 1990, the citizens of Massachusetts elected conservative businessman Bill Weld governor.[10] Firms (and unions) that we had helped convinced the governor not to defund CAT. Pneumatic Scale was particularly influential in this regard. However, I did not see how I could continue to work in such an administration.

In the early summer of 1990, anticipating the possibility of a Republican election win and responding to the funding cuts being carried out by conservative Democrats, I had applied to the School for Workers based in Madison, Wisconsin and was subsequently offered a job starting in April 1991.

The Technology Innovation Policy World 1988-2000

Between 1985 and the year 2000, there were a web of organizations within the U.S. and abroad involved in trying to implement new manufacturing techniques. I was asked to join several of them based on our relative success at CAT and my subsequent work at the UW School for Workers. The UW Extension School for Workers had a reputation as being one of the only labor education entities in the U.S. with an emphasis on engineering and technology issues. One of the foci of the SFW was worker participation and employment guarantees. As a consequence, I was asked to participate in various governmental technology initiatives.

For example, the National Institute for Standards and Technology, a division of the U.S. Department of Commerce, funded the annual Malcolm Baldridge Award for Manufacturing Excellence and identified standards to achieve manufacturing preeminence. Some firms liked to advertise their relationship with this entity as examples of their forward-looking approach to technological implementation. I and others made vigorous efforts to get the Baldrige people to include some favorable mention of worker involvement, and to an extent, this happened. However, their recommended standard was weak and did not insist on consensus or the education of either the workforce or management in the capacity of the new technologies.

Congress also established the Office of Technology Assessment (OTA) to evaluate new technologies and their effect on the economy. OTA study panels included union-friendly researchers as well as some union research department staff, but also a substantial number of business organizations. While the studies recognized the importance of involving workers without serious regulatory measures, the research was used by unions to advocate their positions and incorporated in some state projects. But there was no national regulatory follow-up. However, participating on the various OTA panels introduced me to staff associated with the National Institute for Standards and Technology. These studies were used by progressive members of Congress to support their proposals for more dollars for job retraining. Republicans won control of the House of Representatives in November 1994. They abolished the OTA a few months later. An equivalent has not been restored.

Within the federal bureaucracy, the National Institute for Standards and Technology was designated as the agency within the Commerce Department to focus on manufacturing. They funded manufacturing extension centers and the NIST Advanced Technology Project, which eventually hired me. For a brief moment, the AFL-CIO had persuaded NIST they should have some project that involved consideration of workers-centered automation, using tacit knowledge as a design criterion. After strenuous lobbying efforts, NIST offered me a position.

The National Electrical Manufacturers Association (the industry group representing manufactures of electrical equipment from turbines to light bulbs) organized the Automation Forum. Its function was to identify best practice plants in the U.S. and publicize them as one means of encouraging innovation in manufacturing. I was asked to join because they had heard about CAT.[11] The Forum wanted someone who had some knowledge of the issues unions were concerned about. I was asked to join the program committee, where I remained as a prominent member for the next ten years or so.[12] I insisted the forum go to unionized plants, (GM's Saturn Plant) as well as to their favorite nonunion plants. What the Automation Forum did allow me to do was to actually see management's vision of advanced manufacturing. We visited an average of three facilities a year, and participation was limited to senior management.

During most of this time, the AFL-CIO Technology Working Group was meeting regularly and trying to develop a labor-oriented approach to new technology. It was composed of staff from the International unions and activists. There were no national elected officials, and while the group had some standing with the AFL-CIO, it was not a funded department. The goal was to arm unions with information to strengthen their ability to resist the negative impacts of new manufacturing. What it did do was function as a place where it was possible to discuss the technological developments in specific industries. It served as a lobbying group within the AFL-CIO, urging the unions to take more nuanced and aggressive positions while negotiating over new technology issues — especially regarding job content and employment. To this extent, the dialogue about best practice plants was of interest. This group was also influential in pushing the AFL-CIO to designate me to work within the Advanced Technology Project (ATP) of NIST.

The International Federation of Automatic Control

The International Federation of Automatic Control (IFAC) is the largest organization of professional engineers in the world. It enjoys non-governmental status at the UN. In the late seventies, responding to the requests of engineers dealing with factory automation and the new computer systems, the organization agreed to form a technical committee — the Social Effect of Automation. In the world of IFAC this committee was on par with the long-established groups that dealt with chemical engineering or aircraft design. As a committee it organized regular international workshops and symposia bringing together engineers once a year, generally. Every three years or so, there was a world conference. As such, IFAC became a place for engineers concerned about the social impact of their work to have a world class forum to discuss issues. For example, the safety issues in a two-person airline cockpit, instead of the three-person systems in place during the seventies.

The Social Effects committee studied the consequences of new designs as they related to skill and employment. IFAC opened a new vista for me in that the annual symposia discussed examples from all over the world. Eventually, I became vice-chair of this committee. But in practice, the IFAC connections meant that we at local 201, or in the state of Massachusetts, were plugged into the network of people and ideas dealing with the social effects of automation.[13] The "Factory of the Future" was an example of one type of design which limited skills, innovation and creativity. Although we could not defeat such a retrograde system, the fact is because of the Social Effects Committee; our group possessed the intellectual tools to challenge it. When it came to the formation of CAT, we could call on this network for advice and support. There were many IFAC members from MIT, including a leader in the factory automation area. As the president of MIT was also on our board, it made it a lot easier to reach consensus regarding our adaptation of a skills-based automation approach to manufacturing as the basis for the technical support we intended to provide Massachusetts industry.

Generally, unions in the United States were not engaged in dialogue with engineers or Centers of Excellence when it came to discussing the effects — never mind the design of new factory automation systems. This was not the case in Scandinavia or Germany. In both places, unions were participants in governmental efforts to support manufacturing.

Germany labor law for example, specifically the works council and codetermination legislation,[14] mandates union participation in discussions of proposed investments — especially their social effects. There were also a number of research centers tied to regional universities with relations to local industries where professors worked with the union and management to implement ideas using tacit knowledge. IG Metal — the German Metal workers union — was particularly active. In addition, the union also participated in the regional centers financed by the central government. It was in these centers that the nuts and bolts of concepts like skills-based automation or computer-aided craftsmen were developed and put into practice in various industries. IG Metal's participation in the Social Effects Committee, along with the engineers working with them in these regional centers, meant that their innovative efforts to involve workers in the development of new technologies were included in the IFAC discussions.

Starting in 1991, while at the School for Workers as well as serving as vice-chairman of the Social Effects Committee in IFAC and the AFL-CIO Technology Working Group, I endeavored to bring this information to the unions and firms that were willing to listen and implement them. Although there were real efforts both from a technical design perspective, and in some quarters a union perspective, in fact, our efforts of the eighties and nineties did not produce any change in the way technologies are designed or implemented. To the extent that there were proposals for change, they have centered on individual rights and protections. In this regard, as in others, the workforce is either ignored or treated as a variable with no autonomy.

Most of the innovative European projects came to a halt by the year 2000. Several factors accounted for their demise. Many of the engineers were employed by the Scandinavian and German Automobile companies

In the Scandinavian case, the firms were purchased by American companies.[15] When that happened at Volo and Saab, the projects were terminated. In Germany, auto firms changed their investment strategies and began heavy investments if what they termed as the "low wage, low skilled" U.S. South, and saw no need to continue to find new ways to manufacture in Germany.

A third reason was with the collapse of socialism in Eastern Europe. Firms felt there was no need to invest in projects under the rubric "humanization" of work to demonstrate that working conditions in the west were superior to anything in Eastern Europe. It was more profitable to move production to the low-wage but high-skilled locations in the Czech Republic, Poland or Slovakia. Most of the German projects lost government funding. These losses occurred as the manufacturing trade unions in Germany and Scandinavia began to hemorrhage membership as basic industries declined, and hence, resources evaporated.

Today in 2022, the situation — as regards to worker participation in how systems should be designed and how they should be implemented — resembles the American model. On both sides of the Atlantic, workers have lost their voice at this important table.

1. Massachusetts Centers of Excellence Corporation: Center for Applied Technology; 1988 WHS, Emspak papers Folder 18.000 The CAT Board recognized that the process must be an inclusive one with the workforce and management working with engineers and other technical specialists to achieve an upgrading of the traditional manufacturing sector The CAT understands that the model of successful technology transfer is through skill enhancement, so that the skills of the workforce would increase with the complexity of the equipment. We want people who are experts in using computer driven systems, rather than expert systems.

2. In 1987 I attended the World Congress of International Federation of Automatic Control, and exchanged information with project managers and researchers-information that we used in our presentations to the MCEC board.

3. The University of Lowell Center for Productivity Enhancement was a precursor to the Center for Applied Technology. In July of 1987 I was a visiting Research Assistant.

4. Emspak, Frank; "*The Strategy for the Center for Applied Technology*" February 1988; WHS, Emspak papers Folder 18.000.

5. Memorandum to MCEC Directors, December 15, 1987 pg. 3 WHS, Emspak papers, Folder 18.000 Controlling Documents; legislation and justification for CAT WHS, Emspak papers, folder 18.001 The CAT will encourage and support management if it decides to innovate... [CAT] will pay particular attention to new and innovative ways to engage the workforce as an integral part of technological innovation and application.... We recognize that the road to technological excellence is not through concessions in our workplace standards but through the elevation of workplace skill and knowledge.

6. Center for Applied Technology, no date; WHS, Emspak papers Folder 18.003.

7. See "Pneumatic Scale" Meeting Thursday November 17th 1:30 PM North Quincy MA. I functioned as the sort of mediator facilitator. WHS, Emspak papers, WHS, Emspak papers Folder 18.007 Folder contains minutes of numerous meetings as the project continued.

8. Ibid.

9. UAW Local 5 was originally the Studebaker local. The UAW had its first convention in South bend Indiana. The factory still was known as the plant with the million dollar floor. During WWII the plant made aircraft parts out of aluminum which were soft. Hence they put in a wooden floor, so when parts fell, they would not be deformed. The UAW local 5 office has a mural with each section describing the local president's accomplishments.

10. As he put it, he was so blue blood that the family's servants came over on the Mayflower to prepare their cottage.

11. Aside from the MIT connection, and the publicity surrounding what we were doing due to the presidential campaign, Kathy Cote, a senior director of Prime Computer was on our board and interested in manufacturing issues.

12. On one of the study tours we looked at some plants along Route 128 in Massachusetts. At lunch I met the HR director of one of the plants, Terri Mackzenis. She was the human relations person who processed my employment application and officially made the hire at GE Wilmington about 16 years previously. She told me that as soon as the Lynn HR discovered that I had been hired they immediately attempted to get me fired. They also wanted to blame someone, so they fired her. She bore me no ill will. It was directed at the stupidity and vindictiveness of the GE.

13. Emspak, Frank; Noble, David; *Automation and Labor Policy; Report to the Science, Technology and Society Program*; MIT September 1980, WHS Emspak papers Folder 6.802.

14. In the 1960's the West German parliament passed a series of laws guaranteeing worker representation on the boards of directors of companies. The workers were elected thus in strong union locations those workers tended to reflect the views of the union. The works council was the organizational expression of this system at the plant level. IG Metal devoted considerable resources to train their members of the works councils, so that their participation would be meaningful in the sense of being able to effectively advocate for the needs of their members. This turned out to be successful in some places, and not successful in others.

15. Saab was purchased by General Motors in 1970. Volvo by Ford.

Chapter Eleven: The School for Workers

I first became acquainted with the School for Workers (SFW) as an undergraduate at the University of Wisconsin. The SFW faculty, unlike those of other departments, had been friendly and supportive of our student workers' movement.

Years later, while organizing the 1983 Technology Conference with IUE Local 201, I learned that the School for Workers was one of the few places where faculty was beginning to focus on the possible impacts of new technology on the workplace.

The School for Workers, officially the Department of Labor Education-School for Workers, has a long history at the University of Wisconsin. The first iteration of the program was called the Summer School for Women Workers, which launched in 1925 after a trial run in 1924. The YWCA of Madison had been advocating for such a school to meet the needs of the working women they served, and the Summer School for Women Workers filled that role. The first class was comprised of eight women from Madison. By 1930, there were sixty students, but The Depression drove enrollment down to forty by 1936. The composition of the school changed, too. It was intellectually aligned with the American Federation of Labor and thus, tended to have a very narrow focus on union administration and grievances. The school also transitioned from the "Summer School for Women Workers" to the "Summer School for Workers" and saw a concomitant drop in female enrollment.[1]

In 1930, the university hired Ernest E. Schwarztrauber, who taught in the summer school and became a year-round educator a few years later. Schwarztrauber, originally from the Portland, Oregon labor college, became the director of the School For Workers, retiring in 1950. An advisory committee dominated by the Wisconsin AFL advised the school as regards to curriculum and its orientation towards the labor movement. The school believed everybody, including and especially workers, deserved an opportunity to receive an education. Schwartztrauber believed collective bargaining would soon become as common as in Scandinavia. "Collective bargaining," he wrote, "implies certain common interests of employees and employers. The School holds that the differences that exist and give rise to recurrent conflict can largely be eliminated around the conference table… the success … is easily attributable to an intelligent, informed approach to co-operation between union and management."[2]

In practice, this meant a concentration on the technical aspects of bargaining and contract enforcement. This vision did not include political mobilization or the development of class consciousness. It did include efforts to provide bargaining committees with reliable information about the economics of their industry.

Given my experience at the University of Wisconsin, I was surprised when, in 1991, the School for Workers was willing to hire me to focus on labor-management cooperation, with the goal of reducing plant closures. I was hired under a specific budget line dedicated to training in the area of labor-management cooperation.[3]

When I was hired a political and cultural shift was underway in the department. The intellectual focus of the department's relatively narrow focus on grievances handling was broadening to encompass more of the challenges facing the trade union movement, such as health and safety and technological change. Younger leadership in the trade union movement was coming to the fore,[4] and the same was happening at the School. There was a doorway to new ideas which was opening — and I was able to slip through it.

The School for Workers had a reputation as a union source for industrial engineering consulting and training, and was developing an expertise regarding new technologies and work organization. It was also expanding its work in labor management-cooperation, a direct response to requests from unions who had adopted that strategy as a means of preventing continuing downsizing and closures. Given my experience as Director of the Center for Applied Technology, and with successful projects at S.D. Warren and A.M. General, I fit in with the strategic objectives of the institution.

But although I talked about the same topics, I was using a different language and had a completely different frame of reference for understanding trade union dynamics of the time. The language I used to define labor-management cooperation focused on equality of decision-making and knowledge, and thus the education of the union, so the union and firm could participate as intellectual and organizational equals. This was not simply a process issue, but an issue of power.

The second area of difference related to the way productivity benefits were shared; in my most successful projects, the businesses shared productivity gains by retaining employees.

My different perspective on how the School should interact with unions and employers was illustrated in part by the following: Soon after my arrival, I was asked to participate in a time study project — that is, the study of the time it took to accomplish a particular task. I had worked piecework both at United Shoe Machine and GE, and thus understood time study in real life. One of my areas of expertise for Local 201 was to find ways to maximize worker income. For example, on one machine it was possible to set the visible feeds and speeds at the rates called for in the method sheet, but operate the machine at the minimum feeds and speeds which would still allow it to cut metal, thus increasing the time allotted for the work. I thought this was great. My colleagues were horrified, and for the next seventeen years of my employment with the SFW, I was never again asked to participate in a time study project.

I had a similar distrust of job evaluation studies based on my experience with the sex bias suit at GE, where the outside consultants that were hired proposed lowering some wage rates. Usually, the company or the joint committee hired an outside job evaluation consultant after a political settlement was reached between the company and the union. The hiring was the result of that settlement. Often, if the union was strong enough, a firm was willing to be flexible on rates paid. In those cases, the consulting firm would produce job evaluation studies to justify an eventual agreement with the union.

At the School for Workers I pursued four pathways aimed at strengthening working class power:

a) Developing the technical means to place the worker at the center of production.

b) Initiating robust, joint decision-making techniques between the employer and union.

c) Adding class-conscious content to our teaching with an objective of helping unions develop tools to go on the offense.

d) Self- expression, that is, effective use of the media.

We had some successes, such as at Waukesha Engines and S.D. Warren Paper Mill — as well as defeats such as at Tower Auto. At Tower (previously the A.O. Smith Company), workers and the management of the Milwaukee factory conducted a remarkable series of joint meetings and consensus decision-making wherein they proposed major changes in the way products were produced. Local management, as well as the Federal Mediation and

Conciliation Service, and I as the lead consultant, believed we had senior management's agreement to the results of the joint process. But at the mass meeting of the employees and management, Tower executives from Detroit announced they expected the process to be a "zero-sum" game, rejected the work of the Milwaukee workers and management, and announced potential layoffs and walked out of the meeting. A strike vote followed.

It is clear, at least up as of this writing (2020), that the capitalist class has been successful in marginalizing the union movement, especially as far as the new twenty-first century technology firms are concerned. It would be nice to say that in all aspects, the relative standard of living of most working people has improved since 1980. But this is not the case. Therefore, we need to assess the efforts I and others made to alter the balance of forces in labor's interests in the light of what actually happened.

New Technologies to Build Worker Skill and Control

Early in my tenure at UW, I was able to use my connections with the International Federation of Automatic Control (IFAC) to bring the concepts of the computer-aided craftsman to the U.S. With the support of the School for Workers In 1992, I organized an IFAC International Symposium "Total Quality Management and Skills Based Automation."[5] It was the first symposium of its kind in North America and brought together a significant number of American engineers, their European counterparts and some union specialists.[6] It helped open up the discussion of new ways for unions to interact with new manufacturing. Seven years after the "Factory of the Future" loss, we were able to show actual examples of successful skills-based new manufacturing projects.

In our most successful projects — the Waukesha Engine Company and S.D. Warren, the joint labor-management committee used that intellectual framework as they worked through the issues of work design.

For those of us trying to bring the ideas of skills based-work organization forward, the early 1990s were a time of considerable optimism. The Technology Working Group of AFL-CIO staff was advocating funding at a federal level to support research into this area. The Machinists Union had adopted the concepts of a "High Performance Work Organization" as its principal strategy to prevent plant closings and job loss. The Office of Technology Assessment[7] (OTA) organized seminars and research projects to address this topic, while the newly revamped National Bureau of Standards (now renamed and repurposed as the National Institute of Science and Technology) was tasked with developing new manufacturing techniques and funding the mechanisms for transmission of those ideas. These centers of innovation — the Hollings Centers — were similar to, or based on the work we had done at the Center for Applied Technology, with the notable exception of meaningful worker input or union participation.

In late 1993, after a huge lobbying effort on the part of Brian Turner working with support of the Federal Mediation and Conciliation Service and leaders of the AFL-CIO, I was appointed to the Advanced Technology Project (ATP) of the National Institute for Standards and Technology under the Clinton administration.[8] The ATP was essentially a research and evaluation organization focused on specific industries such as automobile manufacturing looking at ways to implement various technologies.

On January first 1994, I had begun my yearlong appointment at NIST. From my perch in D.C., I pressed UW extension and the SFW to challenge the management-driven manufacturing centers. I noted, "No manufacturing center works with unions as independent entities, but all see workers and unions as appendages of management." I proposed "the School should develop a strategy with the goal of becoming the major provider of training for workers involved in the various state and federally supported extension programs…we should insist that the SFW be accorded equal status with any other university based experts when it comes to assessing the issues to be addressed at any particular firm. Thus when firms agree to involve outsiders in assessments the SFW would be a prominent provider of the services."[9]

I suggested providing all of our classes for shop stewards with material about the modernization efforts process, and that we work with the chancellor's office to provide expertise to labor in grant-writing, and consider directly approaching the AFL-CIO nationally and at the state level as a provider of technical advice.

These ideas were in keeping with expressed concerns of leaders at the AFL-CIO — and with the chancellor. However, embarking on a project such as this would upset the individual piecework nature of the SFW system of calculating salaries based on individual hours taught — and also place the school in a more political and professional relationship with the university and outside companies, as well as with a federally-funded agency.

This was too great of a challenge for the School for Workers, and while the School never exactly rejected these ideas, it never adopted them, either.

I had a unique position at NIST. I was not simply an advisor; I was the only senior staff member clearly identified with the union movement, and the only labor person in the Commerce Department who might actually have control of a significant budget.

I officially was still an employee of UW-Extension even while on contract with NIST. I got the job at NIST because of the prestige of the UW, but mostly because of the determined effort by AFL-CIO and union staff based in D.C. who were concerned about the effects of new technology on the workplace. I advocated for a project funded at $20 million to design and develop techniques for skills-based automation. The AFL-CIO and Automation Forum supported the proposal. I found allies within the Department of Labor — but most surprisingly within the Manufacturing Technology Project (MANTECH) within the Department of Defense. The DoD wanted to maintain the capacity to build a warship in the U.S. in its entirety, but the capacity was rapidly disappearing in 1995 (and now no longer exists).

Prior to the purchase of Bath Iron Works by General Dynamics in 1995, the IAM and Bath developed an extremely innovative project of joint discussion and decision-making. Their report, entitled "Labor Negotiations through Teaming IAM and Bath Iron Works," became a model for other IAM activities, including my project at Waukesha.[10]

A defense preparedness lobbying group met periodically to ensure the DoD funded new tech development and implementation. They were interested in what I had to say about how workers could be involved in the process of innovation and implementation. One day, I received a call to come over to their Virginia headquarters and have lunch. To my utter astonishment, the chair of the meeting was General Richard Ichord — the same General Ichord from Vietnam who blamed those of us who were against the war (and in particular me) for the loss of his troops in the Ia Drang Valley in 1965. Obviously, he knew who I was. The other attendees were somewhat in the dark.

He explained the difference of opinion (to put it mildly) that we had regarding the war in Vietnam, and asked if we could move beyond our past animosity, and on to saving American industry. A few weeks later, Bath Iron Works invited me and others up for a review of their efforts and to discuss their report.[11]

My objective at NIST was to acquire funding that would allow us to test the concepts of the computer-aided craftsman at American companies —- and with the participation of the workforce and/or union. Twenty million dollars was the internal budget within the Advanced Technology Program for projects of this nature. To get an initiative funded through NIST, the manager of the specific initiative organized regional meetings of stakeholders (in my case, unions as well as corporations and think tanks) in order to assess interest. I arranged for seven meetings, all in tech centers, including Atlanta, Georgia, which was beginning to be a tech center, but also had an increasingly vibrant union presence. I insisted that organized labor be present at all of these events — and be furnished with background papers and educational material so they could participate meaningfully. The IAM, among other unions, helped recruit unions and NEMA helped recruit the leading firms to showcase their technological excellence. Over two hundred and fifty potential stakeholders participated in meetings to discuss the proposed project called, "Integrating Design Engineering and the Workforce."

NIST, however, was not enthused. They were discomfited more than I suspected by my insistence on labor's participation, and unsettled by my obvious ability to network with all kinds of people. Without any forewarning, my direct supervisor told me he was canceling the meetings — and incidentally, that I was through.

My termination was totally unacceptable to the organizations that pushed for my employment in the first place. The AFL-CIO called and NEMA arrived at NIST the next day. Shortly after their arrival and a brief but vigorous discussion, my boss called me in and retracted the termination. He never did agree to hold a meeting with Atlanta stakeholders. But we had enough locations for NIST to go forward and make a decision.

The end result was not so positive. In November of 1994, the director of NIST, Arati Prabhakar, convened a meeting at the under-secretary level of the Cabinets concerned— Commerce and Labor. Tom Donahue, Secretary Treasurer of AFL-CIO came, as did Peter DiCicco (from Lynn!!),[12] now the Director of the Industrial Union Department of the AFL-CIO and a strong supporter of the initiative.

The level of disaster became evident a few minutes into the meeting when Arati asked Tom Donahue exactly who he represented. She observed that only about ten-percent of industrial workers were organized, so exactly what was his role in this meeting? It was pretty clear where this was going. I was not going to get $20 million for the project, period.

I could still keep my appointment at NIST, but the content was eviscerated. The main reason that NIST canceled the project was the Republican election victory of November 1994. NIST was nervous about funding and they were not enthusiastic about funding something that had to do with unions. In December 1994, one year after arriving at NIST, I drove back to Wisconsin to resume my position at the SFW, where I continued to work with unions and firms on technology design issues. But we were no longer on the offensive. No other opportunity to get federal support for a project specifically identifying the design of new technologies in ways that might include working people has been funded since.

Failure to Win Public Policy Support

Despite our valiant attempts to prove that it was possible to restructure the workplace in ways that were profitable — while also enhancing the workforce and unions — in the end, we were not able to achieve any significant public funding or negotiated contracts that supported this restructure of the workplace. In spite of some management interest, there was simply not enough institutional pressure, especially pressure from the union movement, to change the way in which software and machines were being designed, and systems implemented to center worker's needs. The dominance of quarterly measurement of shareholder value was, and remains a strong deterrent to any long-term industrial strategy. Maximization of shareholder value, rather than valuing other aspects of a company, reflects the dominance of the speculation-financial wing of the ruling elite.

While it is easy to understand why management and neoliberal theorists in the U.S. would rather export production rather than undertake any efforts to make significant changes to manufacturing, it is not so easy to understand the role of unions in this equation. After the push and defeat at NIST, union momentum evaporated with the exception of the IAM and their High Performance Work Organization (HPWO) initiatives. I attribute this to the long-term effect of ideological and political defeat of the left in the late forties and early fifties. The enthusiastic support of GE's vision of the future and our subsequent defeat on these issues at GE were an indication of the real mindset of the national union leadership.

The legal framework of collective bargaining in the U.S. also is an impediment to unions acting on broader issues of design or investment. U.S. unions are constrained by law to engage in "effects bargaining" only — that is, they can bargain about wages, hours and working conditions — but with limited ability to negotiate over business decisions, including the implementation of new technologies. Demanding that the union become involved in the actual design of work — and hence, the structure of manufacturing and *then* address wages, hours and working conditions — was totally at odds with the thinking of generations of union leaders, company HR people and legislators. But there is more. The left, Communists and others who had a vision of workers controlling the means of production, has been extirpated from the major industrial and service unions since the forties and fifties. By the time the new computer revolution began, even though there was a significant cohort of newly-arrived class-conscious people within the unions, the various progressive projects never congealed into an organization capable of pressuring the system as the Communist Party and the left had done in the thirties. Many of those who understood the politics from a political point of view — e.g. more democracy — were not able to integrate the theoretical concept of "control of the means of production" and build a movement to actually fight for that as the means of survival to respond to extreme capital mobility.

The failure to pose a challenge to industry in the U.S. is not simply another example of American exceptionalism. Because of the initial strength of Swedish, Norwegian, Danish and German unions, as well as a more class-conscious ethos, they were able to initiate the development of a significant number of university-corporation-based projects that analyzed work. They especially focused on the potential for computerization to simultaneously increase productivity (wealth) and create thousands of high-skilled manufacturing jobs. Overall, their vision of the environment was a highly productive, high-skilled, superior-quality production system. In that sense their work provided examples that unions could use in many places — here in the U.S., as well as in Australia, Japan — and maybe even in what was then the Soviet Bloc.

The highpoint of the new manufacturing trend was between 1985 and 1995 in Germany, fueled by a push from below and German governmental support. But by 1995, the push from below evaporated as did governmental support. Up to about that time, the German government supported a vast humanization of work initiative. They did so to show that the workplaces of Western Europe were superior in every way to the equivalent workplaces in the East — especially East Germany, Czechoslovakia and the U.S.S.R. In this regard, various initiatives received enthusiastic support from within the Social Democratic trade union movement.

However, this balance of forces ended with the collapse of the U.S.S.R. and the socialist countries of Europe. European workers who had been shielded somewhat from the ravages of capital mobility saw jobs and investment going to the low-wage and relatively high-skilled former Eastern Bloc. At the same time, German tax law changed, enabling the major auto companies to take German profits and invest them in the low-wage but stable U.S. states of North and South Carolina. Last but not least, independent European auto producers such as SAAB and Volvo, which had been at the heart of many humanizations of work projects, were purchased by U.S. companies who simply canceled those projects.

From my point of view as a believer in socialism, and as a person committed to finding a way to strengthen workers and our unions on the shop floor, these developments were certainly depressing. The end of the German projects confirmed my belief that unions could not defend the working class effectively until they dealt with the issues of capital mobility and investment — not just because it might be politically expedient to do so — but because there was no other way to guarantee the survival of a decently-paid working class in the U.S. (or any other relatively high-wage country).

Labor-Management Co-operation

The second group of initiatives that the SFW pursued was what was then called labor-management cooperation — often shortened to "WIN-WIN" bargaining. It was based on the theory that ultimately the interests of management and the workers were congruent, and if ways could be found to bridge personality, cultural and other impediments in the labor management relationship, then equitable contract settlements were achievable.

There was considerable tension within the SFW regarding the actual content of labor-management training and the apportionment of the fruits of productivity gains. I advocated for a form of labor-management cooperation that really boiled down to enforceable company commitments to share the fruits of increased productivity with the workforce in terms of employment — not attrition, a principle the SFW never adopted widely.

A second source of tension was the character of joint decision-making in and of itself. When I moved from the shop floor and union hall to the world of education and consulting, one of my objectives was to strengthen the ability of unions to make decisions. As part of that process, unions needed to be able to clearly understand and express their interests as opposed to the interests of management. In my view, once the union clearly understood the needs of its members, only then could meaningful agreement be reached regarding work design or technology implementation. WIN-WIN bargaining assumes a congruence of interests. I did not assume that, I assumed that joint decision-making meant an understanding of the balance of power and a method to evaluate and derive solutions ultimately driven by that balance. Concretely, "WIN-WIN" often became a means of lessening the pain of concessions in trade for keeping the facility open.

My intellectual core at SFW came from the "Committee Effectiveness Training"[13] developed with Mike Brower when I was at CAT.[14] The training empowered the union participants so they had the skills to clearly define their interests, and on that basis reach consensus with the company. This training became part of all of my labor-management work, as well as the strategic planning projects for unions.[15] This vision opposed the practice of accepting the company's agenda under the faulty assumption that "we are all in this together." The more or less official training package the School for Workers used was derived from the basic idea that the company and union shared basic needs and thus could work together.

The leading exercise to establish this framework was the lifeboat exercise where, as might be obvious, everyone had to put aside their differences in order to survive. Once this was accomplished, then the specifics could be worked out. In practice this meant that company survival (and hence your job) was tied to putting aside issues and finding ways to agree on "getting to yes." Criteria like skill and productivity-sharing, other than attrition, were simply out of the question.

However, for the first several years at the School for Workers, I was able to facilitate several long-term projects which yielded positive results. I continued the SD Warren and UAW Local 5 projects and initiated projects at Waukesha Engines and with the unionized nurses at the UW Hospitals and Clinics.

In those cases, we were able to maintain the framework of worker participation and technological innovation that emphasized skill and maintaining employment. These SFW projects utilized the CAT criteria.

1) Productivity gains would be shared by workers and management in the form of employment — no attrition — which in practice meant the number of workers at the beginning of the project would equal the number of workers at the end. If more products were produced, it was the company's responsibility to market them.

2) Equality — especially equality of information. The union partner had to have access to all relevant financial and technical information. This exchange of information went well beyond labor costs, which in general, were the smallest portion of any project. Often our joint work had to pause for training so that we could understand the firm's accounting procedures (some of which were news to the foremen as well as the workers).

3) Consensus based decision making, starting with defining which decisions would be guided by this process, e.g. investments, training or work organization and into areas of determining manufacturing strategy –skills based automation for example. The concept of consensus required the union management relationship to go into the areas of understanding the capacity of the manufacturing or information systems so it would be possible to have a

discussion based on all aspects of the proposed systems not simply a discussion based on a limited understanding of immediate effects.

At both SD Warren and Waukesha, the union and management effected substantial changes to the way work was performed. The companies agreed to go far beyond "wages, hours and working conditions" — that is, effects bargaining. They agreed to a consensus process to define the actual design and content of the work.

In the Waukesha case, the willingness of the IAM local to strike over some of the issues (which, in fact, happened) and the IAM's willingness to go out and organize the plants to which Waukesha Engines farmed out work, helped keep the company on track. The IAM also supported the project nationally, as it was committed to the implementation of the High Performance Work Organization (HPWO), and the Waukesha project fit the bill. Automation Forum was particularly impressed with the huge gains in production efficiency and the direct positive result it had regarding the market position of the firm. The result was that Waukesha saved itself from being driven out of business by the heavy equipment and diesel manufacturing company Caterpillar. The union and Waukesha management detailed the project in a study tour organized by Automation Forum.[16]

Meanwhile, huge changes occurring in medicine sparked the development of a labor-management committee at the University Of Wisconsin Hospital. Nurses were facing increasing complexity of care, as well as additional pressure to do more to capture patient data. The university was considering implementing a medical information system to track all aspects of patient care based on what had been a billing system developed by the behemoth Madison-based medical software company Epic Systems.

The nurses organized the "Nurses Information Systems Design Group." A key criterion for design was their desire not to be distracted by data entry that made them have to turn away from the patient. They also expressed the need for more horizontal communications among nurses. These traits were more or less the opposite of the EPIC system implemented a couple of years later.

Although the committee had the strong support of the nursing leadership, the union was not successful in convincing the hospital administration to accept the conclusions of the joint committee. The surgery department, which dominated decision making, preferred a top-down, inelastic system. Sexism and the concomitant disrespect for nurses was also a factor in the determinations of the hospital. Representatives of the committee were invited to Berlin to present their paper describing the project at the Social Effects of Automation Committee of IFAC.[17]

Our biggest failure was with Tower Auto in Milwaukee, the former AO Smith Plant which illustrated the limits of "jointness" in the absence of enforceable laws limiting capital flight. Initially, all parties agreed to the joint decision-making process, and it seemed to allow productivity increases to be reflected in maintaining employment. The company and union made a significant commitment to the process — all thirteen-hundred workers in the several unions on all three shifts received training in decision-making, the financial operations of the company, and introduction to new manufacturing ideas. But at the meeting called to ratify a new contract with the new owners (Tower Auto) management made clear it was a "zero sum game" (as they put it), and in front of the assembled workers, union leaders, our team and the Federal Mediation and Conciliation service — rejected the plans out of hand and made clear the future of AO Smith Milwaukee was in its past. They then walked out. Shortly thereafter, Tower Auto suspended and then closed operations in the plant, the largest employer of Black workers in Milwaukee at that time.

Even the more limited version of cooperation, which did not plow the fruits of productivity back into the workplace, was by and large rejected by the firms after George Bush's election in 2000. In general, the ideological offensive of the companies was successful — reinforced by continuing capital mobility. Concession-bargaining became the norm, with unions negotiating defensively in the face of reduced wages and benefits.

What is a Union? Stewards and Activist Training

For much of my tenure, I was the only faculty member who had spent significant time in the factory or in the union movement as an elected steward and leader. By the time I was hired, I was no longer a member of the Communist Party, but my intellectual framework was a Marxist one and my trade union orientation was much closer to the industrial union approach of William Z. Foster than any other twentieth century trade unionist. I was also steeped in the culture of the UE with its emphasis on membership participation and involvement.

An important, but declining portion of the SFW work was community classes. These classes, held around the state, were generally held once a week for two hours, over the course of five-weeks. They were the outreach part of the SFW. Most faculty taught two or three such classes three times a year. While they were really the lifeblood of an extension organization, they were also the least lucrative. Union locals were the sponsors and /or recruited participants and paid the tuition.

In community classes, I first wanted to instill union and class consciousness. Secondly, to demonstrate how working collectively was the key to winning grievances. And finally, for workers to develop the tools and the self-confidence to advocate publicly for the union and fellow workers.[18]

I used my experiences at GE and United Shoe as the basis for the stewards' classes. I tried to build union and class consciousness by helping the students to develop an understanding of the power inherent in collective action and building the skills needed to speak on one's own behalf. Developing the consciousness to frame ideas from the worker's point of view, and not accept management's framework, was a fundamental skill as far as I was concerned. I also knew a more actively involved membership often meant a more vibrant internal political life in the union, which ultimately could lead to challenges to the local leadership.

There was some tension with my approach. The Wisconsin union culture was more conservative than the all-out civil war which seemed to characterize relations with GE. It took some time for me to relate those experiences in ways that made sense to smaller locals with fewer resources.

I also believed that the steward had to have heart — they had to believe in the union and its mission. But you can't teach heart. An emphasis on "heart" and troublemaking was at variance with the grievance-oriented, legalistic approach of some of my colleagues, even if it was attractive to the more activist members of the unions.

Another aspect of the training was the development of a strategic planning package both to plan for negotiations with the company and to organize the local internally. It was based on some of the tools we used in the training which prepared unions to participate in labor-management discussions. We taught this as the basis to assist locals to understand the resources they would need to conduct any type of action, and thus help them move from a defensive grievance oriented frame of mind to one where the union might be on the offensive.

The machinist's concepts of a High Performance Work Organization as a means of fighting for jobs and increasing wages and benefits was an example of the intellectual framework which resulted from a strategic planning, union consciousness approach.

The High Performance Workplace Organization concepts became part of my collective bargaining classes as an example of how unions could move off the defense and on to offense by proposing new ways to serve the membership. Overall, HPWO advocated a more democratic and hence, productive workplace. The key elements were:

1) Worker control over production, especially regarding issues of design. A first step is an understanding that there are alternatives, which implied an understanding of the new technologies.

2) The means and methods of decision making (committee effectiveness training) and how to reach consensus.

3) Within the workplace, an agreement to move beyond effects bargaining. Oppose attrition agreements, and in exchange for increases in productivity, go for maintenance of employment. Try to force the management to do its work and grow the business.

The HPWO concept was a direct response to the shareholder value offensive and concomitant concession strategies of the major companies.

The HPWO idea mirrored the thinking of the computer-aided craftsman from Europe.

If the intellectual disputes were not enough, I organized two projects at the SFW which drew attention to the school and also raised eyebrows — at least in the eyes of my fellow faculty, threatening funding.

From War to Peace

The early nineties were a time when it appeared progressives might begin to move the economy away from defense and on to other things. At the local level, these discussions usually took place within the context of labor-management cooperation, and so was acceptable as part of my work as far as the SFW was concurred. The concept of defense conversion fit well within my vision of an empowered labor movement.

To this end, a coalition of conversion advocates, the IAM, and

I, organized two national conferences (each attended by about eighty people) to discuss what we then called Defense Industry Conversion. The first was in 1992. Unions representing defense workers were the main sponsors and it produced a handbook on conversion for defense industry workers.[19] The IAM was a key player in this conference — as they related the need to change the way work was organized (using HPWO) and what was being produced to bring about a more stable economy. The IAM General project was a specific example of how a progressive local union — UAW Local 5 — could try to get the firm to build civilian HUMVEES. Designing a civilian version was not too difficult and it was a small step to modify the manufacturing process.

The crunch came with the Defense Authorization Act. Although some money (one-percent) was set aside in contracts for alternative production, the language stated a firm "**may**" use the dollars for the purposes of conversion — not "will."

Can Markets Govern? Should They?

By the mid-nineties, the public sector unions were under increasing attack as public sector management aggressively pursued privatization. Some of the School for Worker's biggest public sector clients was affected. Consequently, we wanted to develop tools to fight privatization. We also emphasized the deeper significance of privatization, in terms of the ability of citizens to actually govern. We organized two conferences in successive years to evaluate responses to privatizations.[20] There were three tracks.

The first track was an affirmation of democracy. Our view was people should govern and privatization took governance out of the public's hands. We asked, "Can (or should) Markets Govern?"[21] And answered "No."

The second track took on the widespread belief that the private sector was more efficient and cost-effective than the public sector.

To really deal with this ideological belief we devised a tool to measure the true costs of privatization. With the financial support of AFSCME, the NEA, SEIU and the AFT, my colleague Rolland Zullo developed an Excel-based spreadsheet that would allow anyone to evaluate all the costs (obvious and hidden) that would occur if a function was privatized.[22]

The third track was a series of workshops and papers from unions describing how they had resisted privatization.

There were strong objections by Republican lawmakers to these conferences culminating in an editorial in a Sunday edition of the Wisconsin State Journal by the Lieutenant Governor demanding my termination. As I did not have tenure yet, this was a serious threat. However, the Executive Director of the statewide AFSCME Council 24 made it clear that his organization, one of the largest and most politically active unions in the state, strongly objected to such a move. Our conference went on — with a new leaflet no longer depicting the public being hung by privatization, and I kept my job.

Ultimately, the state of Wisconsin agreed that our cost evaluation system was accurate. We also did three or four pilot projects with our union sponsors. However, almost no one used the program because effective implementation required extensive membership mobilization to acquire data and help analyze it. This was a far cry from the bureaucratic grievance model practiced by most public sector unions. Another barrier was the absence of strong ties between the union and community in defense of public services, an absolute necessity to win a privatization fight. In 2011, with the passage of Act 10, the consequences of the insular and bureaucratic nature of public sector unions came home to roost with the almost total annihilation of public sector unions in Wisconsin.

Madison Labor Radio

Teaching media was a means of empowering working people to

build a movement for social change. Working people have stories to tell about work, their lives, oppression, vision, victories and defeats. Building media skills meant building on the issue of self-confidence — a sense that what you had to say was valuable and just as important (if not more so) than the comments of "experts." Self-confidence is a key aspect of leadership. After all, if you don't value your own ideas, why should anyone else? I therefore added to my standard curricula exercises aimed at improving listening and writing — both for a newsletter and for radio.

In 1995, in cooperation with other labor activists, especially Ellen LaLuzerne of the Wisconsin Education Association, we launched Madison Labor Radio, which by 1998, had evolved into a thirty-minute news program broadcast at drive-time on Fridays. As of this writing,(2020) we estimate almost one-hundred people have cycled through the reading, reporting and production staff. We produce about 200 stories per year.

The existence of Labor radio allowed me to use the opportunities at WORT 89.9 FM-community radio as an extension of my classes.[23] Thus, using media skills was not just theoretical as we could involve the class right away — members, who had something to say, could say it on the air.

What is in general missing from both commercial and noncommercial broadcast is the presence of working people as subjects, not just objects. At WORT and later with WIN (Workers Independent News) we wanted to give working people their space without mediating the content through our lens of class or race.

• Working people have aspirations, ideas, concerns and experiences different from and specifically related to the fact they are in the working class.

• The working class has needs, desires and a vision different and distinct from, and in many ways, in opposition to the ruling class.

It is pretty obvious I was on a different wavelength than many of my colleagues. One part of that difference was a commitment to organize the faculty and academic staff of the university — excluded as they were from coverage under Public Sector bargaining laws. Nonetheless, since 1935, United Faculty and Academic Staff Local 223 of the American Federation of Teachers, has persisted as a representative body for faculty and staff at UW. I became president of the local and also elected a vice-president of AFT Wisconsin. Throughout the time I was at UW, we maintained a local of two-hundred to three-hundred people constantly agitating for fair procedures, pay and recognition. Over time, we organized a "right to decide" campaign which challenged every UW academic and staff assembly to support the right of UW faculty and staff to decide if they wanted to have a union. Ultimately, we won support in all of the bodies and split the Madison faculty senate that was opposed to collective bargaining. In 2008, just as I was retiring, we won the legislation.

Endnotes For Chapter Eleven

1. Ernest E. Schwartztrauber, *Workers Education-A Wisconsin Experiment*, (The University of Wisconsin Press, Madison WI 1942,) pg. 24-29, 1.

2. Ernest E. Schwartztrauber, *Workers Education-A Wisconsin Experiment*, (The University of Wisconsin Press, Madison WI 1942), p.124.

3. About three years after I was hired, Jack Barbash, who had opposed my PhD, asked me to lunch with him and Owen Beiber, recently retired International President of the UAW. Beiber told me he had arranged the lunch because Barbash had something to say. Jack told me he had been privately contacted by Extension regarding my hire but declined to block it. He also apologized for his behavior at my PhD defense.

4. Not just younger leadership, but the balance of power changed within the Wisconsin labor movement to public sector and private industry leadership and this a diminution of the trades dominance.

5. "TQM and Skills Based Automation" Symposium, Madison WI September22-25, 1992.

6. Automatic Systems Based on Human Skill (and Intelligence) IFAC Symposia series 1994 #14 Eds. Noel Harvey; Frank Emspak.

7. The Office of Technology Assessment was an entity request-ed by a committee in the House of Representatives and charged with assessing the new technologies and their effects on the economy. When the Republicans won a majority in the House of Representatives in 1994 they abolished it.

8. The National Institute for Standards and Technology (NIST) was an agency within the Department of Commerce. My appointment was unique in that I also had the right to meet members of congress without a chaperone, a rare privilege enjoyed only by the Director and her most senior staff. UW was compensated for my time, so I maintained my employment relationship with UW thus keeping me on the tenure track.

9. "The School for Workers and Manufacturing Extension Centers" April 6, 1994 written for UW Extension and for the SFW.WHS, Emspak papers, Folder 19.710.

10. Labor negotiations Through Teaming IAM and Bath Iron Works 1994 WHS, Emspak Papers, Folder 20.300.

11. 1994 Labor Negotiations through Teaming IAM and Bath Iron Works, WHS, Emspak papers, Folder 20.300.

12. Peter DiCicco had been District Director of IUE District Two and was the person responsible for blocking my appointment to the position of Director, Center for Applied technology. He was the ideological and political leader of the administration and in our view, company minded forces with in the IUE.

13. Michael Brower, a consultant based in Boston developed most of the tools in these curricula. My modifications were not that great, but the groups I worked with, and our objectives differed significantly. Brower and I worked together on the SD Warren Project, and on the UAW Local 5-AM General Project. The SFW declined to use his material or involve him in training faculty for labor-management projects.

14. Michael Brower founded the North East Labor Management Center later known as the Massachusetts Quality of Working Life Center. Brower worked with both labor and management to encourage more collaborative and worker-empowering organizational values and structures.

15. Frank Emspak, *Strategic Planning: A Comprehensive Approach to Problem Solving.* WHS, Emspak papers, Folder 22.200.

16. Frank Emspak, *Combining Technology with the Skilled Workforce: Waukesha Engine Division Dresser Industries and Eaton Cutler Hammer;* (Automation Forum August 1997) WHS, Emspak papers, Folder 20.200.

17. Emspak, Frank, Sharon Trimborn . NISDG *The Nursing Information Systems Design Group: Collaborative Design of Healthcare Information Systems* Federal Mediation and Conciliation Service) WHS, Emspak papers Folder 19.023 Trimborn, Sharon, Ruth Robarts. *The NISDG: A Collaborative Design of a HealthCare Information System* 1998; Trimborn, Sharon, Frank Emspak. *The Nursing Information Systems: Collaborative Design of HealthCare Information Systems.* AI and Society, vol12, issue 1-2,March 1998 pp.64-70.

18. Most of us taught 2 or 3 six 2 hour session community classes during the spring fall and winter.

19. *Defense Industry Conversion: Strategies for Job Redevelopment-A Handbook on Conversion for Defense Industry Workers,* Miriam Pemberton, ed. School for Workers, Continuing Education Division University of Wisconsin Extension and The National Commission for Economic Conversion and Disarmament. March 1993 Principal contributors Greg Bischak; Frank Emspak; Miriam Pemberton Jim Raffel; Editors Miriam Pemberton; Production Editor Noel Harvey.

20. Challenges to the Public Sector, September 1995, Madison WI; followed by a second " Challenges" December 1996 Emspak Papers, WHS, Folder 22.100.

21. Frank Emspak, *Should Markets Govern?* Paper delivered at the CWA HealthCare Workers Conference, San Antonio Texas, January 26-27, 1997. WHS, Emspak Papers, , Folder 22.106.

22. Zullo Roland, Frank Emspak. *A Comprehensive procedure for Comparing the Cost of Public and Private Services*, , (School for Workers 1996(WHS, Emspak papers, Folder 22.101.

23. "Media Skills Training" course material WHS, Emspak papers, Folder 23.001.

Chapter Twelve: Workers Independent News

I came to the media world by writing union and anti-war newsletters for the UE, IUE and various anti-war organizations. When the opportunity presented itself in the early 1990s at WORT 89.9 FM, we launched Madison Labor Radio.

Workers Independent News (WIN) grew out of the thirty-minute labor newscast that we developed at WORT. The initial WORT radio program came from the realization that there was practically no coverage of working people, and especially the labor movement, in the commercial press. Wisconsin Public Radio was also negligent in covering working people, a large segment of their statewide audience. *Union Labor News*, the print publication of the South Central Federation of Labor, was not distributed to the general public; it was available only to existing union members. All that being the case, I thought it possible to place some labor commentary on the local community radio station WORT.

I was not alone in that belief. Station management, as well as Ellen LaLuzerne, another union activist who had initiated a project on cable-TV, also thought it a good idea.

We launched Madison Labor Radio in January 1998. The all-volunteer effort focused on the issues and concerns of working people (not just unions). We were able to arrange a 5:30 p.m. thirty minute time slot on Fridays — we have been broadcasting there ever since. A rotating group of about a dozen volunteers work on the program. Over the years, we have involved well over one-hundred volunteer readers and reporters, all of whom were active in their local union or community organizations.

Once we started broadcasting, we immediately found other progressive labor broadcasters, many of whom belonged to the Union Producers and Production Network and Labor Voices (UPPNET). The project was part of a group effort by class-conscious progressives to get labor's voice into the mainstream.[1]

In 2000, the American labor movement had no regularly-scheduled news voice on any commercial or noncommercial radio network anywhere in the country. From a historical perspective, labor's disappearance from public view was remarkable. In the early 1900s, there were over two-hundred newspapers (in English and various other languages) both nationally and locally that were avowedly working-class publications. Gradually, however, they disappeared and by 1970 there were practically no labor-oriented press available. The Black press, which dealt with the issues of the Black working class, had almost entirely disappeared. Commercial television never had a news program devoted to working people. Mass circulation newspapers had all but eliminated their labor beat by 2000. The last labor beat person from a national paper retired in 2012.

There were some flickers of life in radio. After WW II, the United Electrical Workers(UE) sponsored a regular radio show, as did the United Autoworkers. The UE's program was off the air by 1950. The UAW's show disappeared a few years later. By 2000, there were some labor programs left on local community radio stations (like Madison Labor Radio), but as far as a national news presence was concerned — there was nothing. AFL-CIO sponsorship of "Edward P. Morgan and the News" which was a general newscast on public radio ceased in the late sixties with the launch of PBS and the evening newscast "All things Considered." There were some progressive talk radio shows, but they did not identify as "working class" or union. There were, however, two groups of labor activists that had been exploring ways to develop a labor presence on the air waves — each utilizing this emerging new thing called "the Internet" as a means to distribute news.

But one important impediment to a labor newscast, in any media, was the editorial content. What positions were they willing to broadcast on air? In other words, was the paper a house organ for union leadership, or should it be open to dissenting views within the movement? Would they host debates over contracts, internal democracy, and the relationship between employers and the union? Unions financing media were especially reluctant to include alternative views on those subjects.

To a great degree, the 1940s had settled some of these issues. The progressive editor of the *CIO News*, Len DeCaux was charged with being a Communist and fired.[2] The newspaper increasingly became a house organ for the CIO — and later, the AFL-CIO. Politically, it supported the Democratic Party. A similar evolution occurred at the local and state levels of the union movement, since many of the union papers were founded as a voice for workers who were organizing the union. For example, the newspaper of IUE Local 201 was called the *"The Electrical Union News"* and advocated for the organization of GE along industrial lines. But as the unions won exclusive bargaining rights, the agitational aspect of these papers declined, and they tended to become more and more internally focused and have less and less news about the labor movement generally. As the internal politics of the unions became less democratic with the ouster of radical leaders and workers, the papers reflected that evolution — and in truth — became less and less interesting. It was very rare, indeed, for opposition voices to national union policies, leadership or contracts to receive space in any organ of the AFL-CIO at any level.

It is important to bear in mind that the unions were operating within a general atmosphere of opposition. Contracts were often hard-fought affairs. So, the overall environment was not one where open discussion was valued; it was seen as a weakness. This was particularly true when it came to contract mobilizations and elections.

WIN had the same challenge. Unions financed WIN and we faced pressure to restrict our coverage to conform to the interests and opinions of union leadership. Civil liberties and press freedoms did not seem to be of particular concern.

Two events stand out as particularly stark examples of this problem.

As a commercial product, WIN had a chance to become part of the morning newscast on WBZ radio — the largest station in New England. A major international union —Service Employees International Union (SEIU) — had agreed to sponsor our show. As the regional director was preparing to sign a six-figure check for the first few weeks of the broadcast, he mused aloud that writing the news every day would be a challenge for him. We explained, not for the first time, that we wrote and edited the news — not him. He tore up the check.

In 2008, as part of my work as a Professor at the University of Wisconsin's School for Workers, I reviewed books that dealt with the labor movement. I gave a positive review to one book that dealt with the efforts of a group called Teamsters for a Democratic Union to change the entrenched political culture inside the International Brotherhood of Teamsters. During the middle of a live broadcast of the Barack Obama inauguration from Washington, D.C. (and an accompanying live event in Chicago) — I was told over the phone that the IBT would not be paying their share of the costs (or our regular contribution) because of that positive book review.

The political and economic terrain for a daily labor-focused newscast was forbidding. And yet, WIN managed to broadcast every weekday from February 2002 to mid-November 2017 — reaching hundreds-of-thousands of people daily — sometimes even a million. At its peak, WIN was broadcast from about one-hundred-fifty stations nationwide. We were the longest-running labor newscast ever in the U.S.

Antecedents of Workers Independent News — UPPNET

Union Producers and Production Network (UPPNET), was a group of class-conscious union-oriented producers of labor media. Most of the members were activists in their unions, generally leading efforts at democratic reform and opposing concessions and the company-minded union leadership which dominated many unions. UPPNET members came from all over the country and were mostly involved in electronic media of some sort.

In January of 1998, in collaboration with UPPNET, Madison Labor Radio[3] circulated a document to progressive producers outlining the reasons for, as well as the means and costs, of getting a labor voice on the air.[4] In November, as a means of increasing support for a regional or even a national network, UPPNET, SFW, the Illinois Labor Forum and WORT all co-sponsored an event called the Midwest Labor Conference. Larry Duncan from *Labor Beat/ Labor Express* in Chicago and I were the keynote speakers.[5]

The huge demonstration against the World Trade Organization in November 1999 — known as the 'Battle of Seattle" — made our point. Progressive media groups had followed the protests and brutal police response closely, using the Internet to mass distribute the information. That coverage was widely considered to have forced the mainstream media to cover the Battle of Seattle more fully and treat the protesters more favorably. These events seemed to validate the UPPNET approach of using community-based media organizations and the Internet as the means to leverage our media presence.

Based on the Seattle experience, on January 15, 2000, the UPPNET Board proposed a media strategy to the AFL-CIO.[6] UPPNET made special note of the fact that CNN began using the independent media's site as a source for news and altered its coverage to both allow the demonstrators to explain their objectives, but also covered the police violence. UPPNET reported that over one-million people logged into the media site which was established by independent media groups to provide news feeds to both commercial and noncommercial broadcasters. [7,8]

The AFL-CIO declined to act on the proposal.

In response to the inaction of the AFL-CIO, UPPNET organized a conference to bring together labor-oriented media people and discuss ideas for the future. The "Labor Solidarity through Labor Tech: Building New Global Unionism Through Labor Media" conference took place from December 1-3, 2000 in Madison, Wisconsin. As we put it: "At each step of the way corporations have sought to impede, destroy or disrupt worker to worker communications…We encourage the participation of any person who is interested in getting the word out about working people, our culture, issues, goals and struggles."[9]

We emphasized the mutually-supporting aspects of TV, Internet and print — the tools of the new millennium. And we noted that the Seattle media center, in its coverage of the Battle of Seattle, had proven independent media had the power to break the stranglehold of "media conglomerates" and introduce a progressive perspective.

Almost two-hundred-fifty people from all types of media came to Madison. Both progressive labor media organizations — UPPNET and Labor Voices[10]— supported the conference.[11] Other sponsors included Wisconsin State and local AFL-CIO, as well as the Wisconsin affiliate of the NEA.[12] Of immense importance was the strong presence of organized labor, with about ten International unions, the AFL-CIO, as well as important regional organizations like the California and Connecticut Federation of Teachers supporting our cause.[13] International labor media activists from Korea, Pakistan and Japan (among others) joined us as well.[14]

Our conference showcased the entire media spectrum. We screened the Midwest premier of *"Bread and Roses,"* filling the seventeen-hundred-seat Orpheum Theater in downtown Madison. We turned our conference dinner into dinner theater with a performance of *Walmartopia* – an irreverent political satire of big business and eternal smiley faces.

The Decision to form a Labor Radio Network

Twelve different radio projects made presentations during the conference. The general consensus was that labor needed a national platform equipped for regular broadcasts. Several people agreed to form a national steering committee, and I agreed to start organizing our network in Madison.

We met on January 7, 2001, and mapped out a plan for content acquisition and distribution. We decided to pull our material from existing audio sources like *Madison Labor radio*, the *Heartland Labor Forum*, or *Labor Express* and present it in a unified news format syndicated nationally.[15]

In an innovative move, Liz DiNovella, then WORT News Director, successfully recruited the U.W. School of Business to conduct a study of the U.S. radio market. That data indicated radio had huge news market penetration, especially among working people and among the working-class Hispanic audience in particular. The study demonstrated that radio was inexpensive relative to other forms of media, and using the Internet, it was easy and economical to distribute programming.

I became the Executive Producer, or CEO, of Workers Independent News. The job lasted for almost sixteen years. Howard Kling of the Labor Education Service at the University of Minnesota became the Chairman of the initial project, and then board president of the non-profit-Public Economic Information Service which "owned" the news broadcast. He remained in that position for the duration of the program's existence. Ellen LaLuzerne eventually became the President of our for profit commerical wing-Diversified Media Enterprises.

We launched on the air mid-February 2002. WIN produced some stunning interviews and the most widely-circulated CD of the Wisconsin uprising of 2011. Between 2002 when we went on the air, until mid-November 2017 when we ceased broadcasting, we never missed a scheduled day.

From the Internet Radio Network to WIN

In the early phases of the program, we envisioned content flowing to WIN from the existing labor radio programs, college stations, NPR affiliates and community stations to be distributed via the same avenues, as well as through individual access via the Internet.[16] The Internet Labor Radio project became Workers Independent News as soon as we began trying to market ILRN. But while the name changed, the class focus remained the same — working people are our own best representatives. Our creation would:

- Have a strong labor focus.
- Be accessible through multiple formats.
- Reflect a strong working class culture content.
- Build union democracy.
- Supply the most accurate news available concerning working people.

We had clear objectives:

- Raise the profile of working people in the public consciousness.
- Provide comprehensive news about the labor movement and working people.
- Fill a current void in reporting about economic and legal issues affecting working people.
- Build the capacity of local activists to access the news media
- Empower workers to make their own media.
- Raise the profile of organized labor.

Initially WIN was a project of the U.W. School for Workers. WIN agreed to reimburse the U.W. For staff salaries and the School for Workers agreed to make significant "in kind" support in the form of office space, high-speed Internet lines and clerical services. The School for Workers would also be a fiscal sponsor. WIN was always conceived as a unionized entity; the staff chose to be represented by AFTRA the American Federation of Television and Radio Artists.

The School for Workers was a department within U.W. Extension — a division of the University of Wisconsin system. Wisconsin Public Radio (WPR) was also part of the Extension. I thought there might be a possibility of getting some of our material broadcast by WPR, either as a standalone or as a part of the regular newscasts. We couldn't have been more wrong. As far as Wisconsin Public Radio was concerned, news focused on labor, from a labor perspective, was biased and hence could not be used. When we pointed out they were broadcasting *Marketplace* — a pro-management three-minute feature (at that time financed by General Electric) — it made no difference. The WPR decision foreshadowed the decision of the Corporation for Public Broadcasting, whose director conveyed that PBS would never broadcast our news because it was too pro-union and Congress would defund them. He also said they had told stations to be careful. And, indeed, our news was never broadcast on any PBS station in the U.S. Except one (briefly) — located in New Mexico. When we attempted to buy time on *Marketplace* they refused to sell and would never use a story of ours.

We discovered anti-union bias in other, more unexpected places.

The National Federation of Community Broadcasters is the organization bringing together PBS affiliates, Indian radio, many community radio stations, as well as producers and programmers. As a producer, we were welcome to participate in the organization as supporters of community radio. But when it came to doing workshops about the need for news focused on working people that was another story. We found it very tough going. History was okay. Songs were okay. But a regular newscast? That was another issue altogether.

Community stations that took content from Free Speech Radio News[17] often used our newscast. Most of the strongest community stations broadcast Free Speech and so we were on in Berkeley, Los Angeles and Washington D.C. (among many other places). All told, about seventy community stations broadcast our news regularly.

We conceived WIN as an organization that could help build community/independent media. To accomplish this, we paid stringers who were already working for community radio stations. The infusion of cash would help support either the individual or the community station they worked with. We were able to maintain this arrangement for about five years.

Sponsored News Commercial Broadcast

Our vision was to reach the working class with a nationally syndicated daily radio news program. Our analysis of news consumption performed by the UW Business School demonstrated that all ethnicities of the working class accessed their news primarily through commercial radio; therefore we needed to find ways to get on commercial radio.

We thought we would face overt political censorship in the commercial radio sector, since that had been our experience with public radio. But that was not the case. The first and only issue for commercial radio is money. Conservative stations even took our material if we paid for the time — in fact; most reported their listeners liked it.

In addition to financial challenges, we faced a type of organizational censorship — our news was never placed in the news department. It was always considered sponsored content. But within that framework, the largest news and talk stations in the U.S. were willing to play Workers Independent News or our local variants. The stations included 1010 WINS in New York City, KMOX in St. Louis, WLS in Chicago, and several others.

Paying for it was the tricky part. All news is sponsored by someone. In most commercial three-minute newscasts there are two or three commercials. Commercials by national advertisers usually go to finance the national content. The individual station takes the news feed from some organization, pays for it and in turn collects advertising from the local sponsors.

That we were able to broadcast in major markets over extended periods of time is a testament to the level of union support, vigorous sales and the high quality of our news. In almost every case, managers at the largest stations in the U.S. (including conservative stations) found our news rated higher than almost anything they had and asked the owners to take the news directly from us, pay WIN and then the station would undertake the sales effort for sponsors. But the owners of major stations would not agree to this arrangement, so we were left with the responsibility of raising all the advertising funds by ourselves and simply pay the station.

The successful project in New York City illustrates the effectiveness of a focused news broadcast influencing political behavior. Many of our broadcasts on 1010 WINS in New York City dealt with the problems faced by the Building Trades. While we could not guarantee a direct link between a news story and action, we could show that City Council leadership began referencing some of our stories. We believed that, in the end, the almost daily focus on the problems of unskilled workers in city housing rehabilitation did make a difference when the City Council voted to require rehabilitation projects of city-owned apartments include at least one journeyman. But it took more than two years. In this aspect of the nexus of news and politics, the right-wing showed it had much more of an understanding than the left. As evidenced by the now massive reach of conservative and evangelical talk radio, the right-wing understood that developing a media audience was a multiyear project.

One morning, I went up to a construction site on Amsterdam Ave and 66th Street and asked the foreman if I could talk to a couple of the workers. He reluctantly agreed. But when he told people who I was, people stopped work or yelled down from the crane that they listened to our newscast. I told the guys to let their business agents know since they were paying for it. Sponsorship on 1010 WINS was no small item. The cost for one minute was approximately $800.00. We were on 1010 WINS for almost four years, four days a week, at about 9:01 a.m. (really drive time, but at the much lower morning rate).[18]

WIN stories played a positive role in political campaigns. We reasoned that working people might want to hear real news rather than just commercials about issues of concern to them. After all, the whole point of Fox News was to deluge potential voters with news and an interpretation counter to their interests with the hope of encouraging a right-wing vote. We worked directly with the Office and Professional Employees International Union (OPEIU) to arrange sponsorship in Iowa (prior to the 2008 primary), Virginia and DC. as a lead up to the gubernatorial election in 2014. We maintained our position in D.C. for another two years.

We could not break the cycle of having to pay for news broadcasts. We accepted the terms of the situation because we thought it more important to get on the air than quibble about the means of payment, but we recognized the dangers in this arrangement and the insult to our work. We also recognized the total control of the mass media exercised by those opposed to organized labor.

Had the progressive network Air America been successful, it is possible that we would have been able to establish a precedent (Air America did accept our news and broadcast it on their network). However, we discovered that they would cut stories without notice, regardless of the terms of our contract. Our sponsors were reluctant to continue and we withdrew from arrangements with Air America shortly before their bankruptcy and demise in 2010.

In addition to the structural censorship and outright political censorship, WIN also faced legal challenges. In 2002, the media conglomerate VIACOM moved to get an injunction against Workers Independent News Service — or WINS as we were known then. VIACOM claimed that listeners would not be able to distinguish between WINS and their station, the largest in the U.S. — 1010 WINS. We were not even on the air in New York at that point.

To our advantage, the Communications Workers of America and the International Brotherhood of Electrical Workers were on the WINS board — and they intervened on our behalf with VIACOM. VIACOM agreed to drop the injunction efforts if we agreed to eliminate the word "service" from our name.[19]

A much more serious legal offensive against WIN occurred a few years later, in 2009. WIN was sponsored on WLS radio in Chicago by several unions where we provided a short newscast and anchored a Saturday morning talk show. All told, I think we were on the air at WLS for about six months. As it turned out, and unbeknownst to us, every broadcast of WIN was being monitored by a right-wing think tank in Washington. D.C.

When, through a technical error, WLS neglected to mention that the news was sponsored, the think tank contacted the FCC and the FCC went after WLS.

The usual fine for an error of this magnitude is $400. The FCC charged WLS $44,000. The size of the fine caught the attention of Talkers magazine — the trade publication of Talk Radio. They, in turn attacked WIN as "fake news" because of our sponsorship arrangements. Needless to say, WLS was not thrilled. Initially they did try to appeal, but dropped the whole issue after paying the fine. WIN was not charged, nor did we have any specific legal expense. But "everyone" in the business knew about the incident, which did not make it any easier to make arrangements with commercial radio.[20]

Under Federal law, scholars have access to the FCC files in a case like this. John Anderson, one of our original producers, by 2009 a professor of Broadcast Journalism at Brooklyn College, asked for the file. He was told that it was in excess of a thousand pages. This was weird in itself. Initially, the FCC agreed to give him access — but then stonewalled. He and a leading journalism professor from Georgetown University went to the FCC to physically look at the files. After being greeted and allowed into the building, and determining that the files indeed existed, they were escorted from the building by security. Ajit Pai was the FCC commissioner dealing with WIN. Pai went on to serve as the chair of the FCC under the Trump Administration.[21]

Meanwhile, should we wish to get the files, we were told we had to initiate a legal action through the First Federal District Court in Washington, D.C., an enterprise that would cost thousands, and which had no real expectation of a positive outcome. So, I guess we will never find out why a simple fine of $400 turned into a $44,000 attack, who was really behind it all and the justification for the FCC actions.

The right wing had made a success of right-wing talk radio. In the view of union presidents and communication directors, the way to go was to emulate right-wing talk. Unions put a great deal of money into individual hosts whose style and format copied right-wing radio stars. We (WIN) argued that a constant drip, drip, drip of labor oriented news, heard as "news" by listeners rather than "talk" would have more influence on those not already committed. We did not succeed in convincing most communication directors of this strategy.

Content, Programming and Staff

The most exciting aspect of our producers and stringers was their tremendous creativity, which appeared in a few different ways. For example, every day on the radio we hear the Dow-Jones stock market report. We thought workers should have our own daily economic report. Statistic of the Day sounded deathly, so we named our product the "Dow-Bob."[22] All of the material was vetted for accuracy. By far our most popular Dow-Bob was entitled "Is Your Boss a Psychopath?" The basis for this piece was an article in a Canadian Medical journal which showed that, indeed, many of the hard-driving Type A, take-no-prisoner-bosses — were psychopaths.

WIN covered just about every major labor story of the decade.[23] But one in-depth interview made history. Producer John Hamilton discovered the last remaining member of the Taft law firm (responsible for the Taft-Hartley Act) alive and well in Cincinnati, Ohio.

John interviewed J. Mack Swigart, one of its authors. He described why they wrote the law in the way they did. The authors did not think they could abolish unions completely, but they did think they could weaken unions to the point of insignificance. He emphasized that the idea was to impede the growth of U.S. unions, thus ultimatelyleading to their demise.[24]

In early 2011, the Scott Walker administration in Wisconsin passed Act 10. The legislation effectively crippled public sector unions. It limited the subjects of bargaining and wage increases only to the increase in the cost of living. It banned dues check-off (that is the ability of members to pay their dues with a deduction from their paycheck) and it also eliminated union representation entirely from the University Hospitals and Clinics. It further required unions to re-certify – or show that they represented a majority of workers at any location via a vote each year. However, unlike most elections, the union had to win more than fifty-percent of the votes of all members in the bargaining unit — not just those who voted. Nonvoters were counted as "NO." The result has been a precipitous decline in union representation at state, county and city institutions in Wisconsin.

Hundreds of thousands of pro-union Wisconsinites turned out to the Capitol to demonstrate against Walker's plan, with hundreds occupying the State Building for nearly a month. Republicans prevailed, but the people of Wisconsin led a grueling and brave opposition. One of the most dramatic moments in what would come to be termed the "Wisconsin Uprising" occurred when students at East High School walked out in support of their teachers. Producer Jesse Russell called in to say he was with the students walking down East Washington Avenue, so he could interview and film them as they marched to the state capitol about two miles away. Hundreds of students participated.

About an hour later, in the midst of thousands at the capitol, Molly Stentz of WORT and I interviewed the students as part of a live broadcast. Standing on a bench in front of a whole bunch of kids, I asked if anyone was willing to talk on the radio. They all volunteered. We got great, heartfelt outpouring of support for teachers. These interviews and many others became part of the CD WIN and WORT produced entitled "This Is What Democracy Looks Like." Among other clips is one of producer Doug Cunningham pounding on the capitol's doors, which had been closed, barring reporters from entry. As we intended for him to enter no matter what, we expected immediate arrests. Mike Goodwin, then president of the OPEIU International and present in Madison that day to support the demonstrators, agreed to pay the bail if necessary.

It was these moments of exceptional reporting from the front lines that buoyed our reporters and staff. The archived material is also a record of labor's struggles, defeats and victories. One can feel the emotion, dedication of the many people we interviewed. Those voices are the real America.[25]

WIN and the School for Workers

When we launched WIN, it was as a project of the School for Workers. But a news service was simply not part of the SFW culture. The SFW was an absolute necessity when we began. The school provided the initial physical space.[26] Union media directors said they would not have met with me, except that I was coming from the School for Workers. I think it is highly unlikely that the Ford, Rockefeller, Schuman and MacArthur foundations would have been willing to assess our project except for my faculty status at the UWEX-School for Workers.

However, the School for Workers was not willing to finance WIN, nor was that our expectation. In 2004, WIN terminated as a SFW program.[27] The Republican legislature demonstrated its opposition to WIN in July 2006, asking Extension to censure me for allegedly using the UW e-mail system to solicit funds (something we did not do). Nor did the university administrators provide me with a copy of the alleged funding request. UW Extension administration did go through with the censure with the acquiescence of the School for Workers. In response, I opted to develop a combination of teaching and leaves of absence, retiring in March of 2008.[28] Dolores and some friends organized a great retirement and fundraising party. Of real importance to me, my brother came out as did people I worked with at the United Shoe Machine company. My friends thought leaving the SFW would make a huge positive contribution to my mental health — and they were right.[29]

Great Expectations!

When we launched WIN, the feeling among labor media people was one of optimism   (in spite of the victory of George W. Bush). There had been a great anti-world trade demonstration the year before where environmental activists and union people were in the streets together — "Turtle-and-Teamsters." There was relatively newer and younger leadership at the AFL-CIO. It seemed as if the huge concessionary attacks on working people had eased and certain gains were being achieved in organizing health care workers, flight attendants and others. So, it was not completely crazy to think that a nationwide voice for workers was possible. And some unions, like the UAW were beginning to experiment with radio, for example, with their ie.America network from 1996-2004, which was then replaced by Air America. There was also an increasingly vibrant community radio movement — and the Internet offered new and inexpensive means of communication.

Finances were always a challenge. During the more than sixteen years of WIN's existence, we raised (on the average) between two-hundred-fifty and three-hundred-thousand-dollars per year. The vast majority of that came from the international unions, of which twenty-two provided support for some period. So did over one-hundred local unions. WIN raised almost $2 million from the Internationals. Maintaining this stream of income was extremely labor intensive and time consuming, not to mention soul destroying.

Some of the unions that initially founded WIN and were its earliest supporters, stuck with the project throughout. IBEW, IUPAT and OPEIU were outstanding in this regard. While many international unions wanted to have an increased media presence, that did not mean they wanted a news organization that might be critical. The tension between public relations and news was a longstanding issue and the conflict in WIN was an extension of that huge difference in perspective.

In the end, WIN was never able to get to the point of financial stability. We never won organized labor as an institution to the notion they needed a national daily news voice rather than PR or talk radio. While some communications people did understand that and did support it — we never achieved a regularity and level of support that we needed to plan and grow.

Nor did WIN garner any significant foundation support. We had many lengthy discussions with all the major foundations involved in media projects. Many were interested in "workers" or poor people or specific ethnic projects. None were interested in unions. As far as I can tell no foundation has ever helped organize a union in any private sector workplace. Almost every foundation we went to said essentially this: "If labor wants a network, let them pay for it".

One of the things about American society is that most working people are not rich. WIN did develop a relatively large number of small donors — but to really grow this to a sustainable level (about 5,000 in our case) was beyond our capacity. Perhaps, if we had convinced some of the state AFL-CIO's to support WIN with the vigor in which they supported the United Way, we might have been successful.

Instead of a long-running and consistent news program — unions committed their money to political organization and advertising. WIN was looking for about one-percent of the funds unions spent in any one place for PR or media for political mobilization. In our view, instead of episodic and clearly self-serving political advertising ad programming, we would have a continuous high quality and daily newscast, which we believed was more effective. Funding was an ideological question, not a resource question.

The eventual (and maybe inevitable demise) was evident as we approached the election of 2016. In September of 2015, a year before the 2016 election, AFSCME told me they were going to reduce their commitment to WIN — probably to zero due to the financial demands of the election. Although other unions were not as explicit, we had a very difficult time in reaching our usual (and insufficient) goals. The 2016 election was like a giant sponge sucking up resources.

After years of trying to sell the news, I personally felt I had nothing more to offer and any creativity I might have had was being drained out of me because of the constant grind of fundraising. Instead of being a news producer and writer, I became a glorified fundraiser. It is one thing to have a vision; it is another thing to know that every time you went to a union you needed to get some cash. The rest of the WIN leadership also felt that we had reached an endpoint. Moreover the retirement of key union media figures left us without powerful voices in D.C. OPEIU President Mike Goodwin's retirement had the same effect in New York.

In September of 2016, I had made the decision to leave management of WIN as soon as we could find a successor. After much discussion, the Board decided to restructure and ask a private concern called Altus, who had been working with us on data issues and distribution, to take over management of the enterprise. They did so in April of 2017.

Altus was unable to maintain the advertising base and had a contentious relationship with the staff. The financial situation became untenable. We ceased broadcast on November 17, 2017. It was a sad ending for the longest running labor radio news service.

ASSESSMENT

Certainly I regretted the end of the service. I also recognize many mistakes in the way we managed WIN, raised funds and related to others. But overall, given the resources at our disposal — political, financial and intellectual — my assessment of the effort is positive. WIN succeeded in doing the right thing for a long time.

Our experiences illuminated a contradiction which we barely addressed — never mind solved. How and where could we discuss major issues facing our movement? This was especially true when unions were in campaigns to organize or facing state repression.

In those cases and many others we were privy to, or came to understand, fatal flaws, mismanagement or fundamental political misjudgments as the various campaigns were in progress. My feeling then (and now), is that if WIN reported what we knew, our news service would have been over very early as evidenced by what happened with the IBT and SEIU. This assessment leaves the "how" to finance independent labor journalism unanswered — but it points to developing a funding model that is widespread and not dependent on institutional union support.

The funding and format issues were made obvious with our coverage of events like the Wisconsin Uprising and attack on public sector unions by Governor Walker in 2011. Our news focused on the huge outpouring of popular sentiment against the attack on collective bargaining.[30] We made editorial decisions that emphasized the scope of the mobilization. But we did not report that the state leadership of all the public sector unions were meeting across the street from those occupying the capitol and never met with them. We did not report that WEAC's massive effort to reach every teacher in the state, while successful, was with a message NOT to engage in any work stoppage — but only come to Madison on Saturday. We did report that Madison Teachers Inc., a WEAC affiliate, had figured out a strategy to close the schools. We did not report that the AFT-W — with thousands of members within walking distance of the capitol — never even asked their members to think of taking a long lunch just as a show of force so that the Republicans would have an idea of the value of state workers.[31]

A headline news service, while important, is not enough. We need to find a way to move to a class-based news service. The last time that happened in the U.S. was at the height of the CP's *Daily Worker* circulation (with all of its contradictions). The discussion of how one covers labor, and also has meaningful analysis, is part of the discussion that has gone on inside the International Labor Communications Association over the years.

Our challenge now, remains the necessity to build a nationwide multimedia labor news service — one robust enough to enable discussion of our movement(s) and how best to advance the working class.

If the working class is going to win, we need voices with a significant presence across the electronic spectrum. It is worth fighting for — and we can win.

Endnotes For Chapter Twelve

1. Kling, Howard. "Suggestions for a New Labor Media Strategy" Report to UPPNET members and others. Howard Kling, Labor Education Service, University of Minnesota November 7,2004.

2. DeCaux's real sin was that he was a supporter of Henry Wallace and a supporter of the Progressive Party. After being fired by the CIO news and blacklisted in the industry he eventually became a typographer and worked at that trade until retirement.

3. The document was written by me, Norm Stockwell and Ellen LaLuzerne.

4. Emspak, Frank. "The World of Radio: An Approach for Labor" WHS, Emspak papers, 1998 folder 23.026.

5. Midwest Labor Media Conference, November 7,1998 WHS, Emspak papers Folder 23.003.

6. UPPNET, "A Media Initiative for AFL-CIO"; sent 01/15/2000 WHS, Emspak papers Folder 23.024.

7. Media Centers became a popular tool for organizing for democratic change in many countries. For example in 1990 the one in Prague became one such center urging progressive policies on the newly established non- communist Czech government. The center was closed a year later.

8. UPPNET NEWS; winter 2000 page 2. WHS, Emspak Papers Folder 23.024.

9.UPPNET News Summer 2000 page 1; WHS, Emspak papers Folder 23.024.

10. Labor Voices was also a group of labor media activists, with strong participation from Cornell University's School of Industrial and Labor Relations. Many of the participants were staff of different unions and tended to be closer in their thinking to the union leadership than UPPNET members.

11. Sponsors were UPPNET, The School for Workers, Labor-Net; the Labor Education Service of the University of MN the Wisconsin Federation of Teachers, the Wisconsin AFL-CIO and others.

12. ILCA, Leaflet-Registration "Labor Solidarity Through Labor Tech; Building New Global Unionism Through Labor Media December 1-3,2000" in WHS, Emspak papers Folder 23.031.

13. List of Presenters, Labor Tech 2000; WHS, Emspak papers Folder 23.031.

14. To ensure the safety of the Pakistani participant in the conference, conference participants mobilized and contacted the US State Department and the government of Pakistan to assure his safety.

15. Participants Howard Kling, Judy Ancel, Larry Duncan, Julius Fisher, Wes Brain, Kuzumi Zeltzer; Frank Emspak, Carl Bryant; WHS, Emspak papers, Folder 23.033.

16. The actual digitized version of the founding meeting is corrupted. We will use "The Internet Labor Radio Network" proposals to foundations and unions as the source document. All quotes are from this document. WHS, Emspak papers Folder 23.033.

17. Free Speech Radio News was the daily newscast of Pacifica. It launched in the year 2000, and went off the air first in 2014, and then was able to be in news distribution again but finally closed for good in April of 2017.

18. Marvin Naftolin, of Union Communications in St Louis was the prime salesperson for WIN in New York (1010WINS) and Chicago (WLS).

19. BUT- and this shows the level of ignorance at that time- they asked us to remove all traces of WINS from the Internet- something that was and is truly impossible. Finally we convinced their lawyers that this was impossible. We also were cautioned to be careful with our funniest feature- the DOW-BOBS. Later about that- but VIACOM owned DOW-Jones at that time.

20. Emspak papers, Folder 23.606 for the FCC complaint; articles from Talkers Magazine and Radio Ink and the WIN response.

21. Alit Pai represents the most conservative views regarding media consolidation and Internet access. As of January 2020 he still believes ending Internet Neutrality is a brilliant idea. (VICE; January 8, 2020.

22. We have been able to retrieve many of them and they are part of the sound archive available at the WHS.

23. WIN conserved most of the stories and features produced since 2002. They have been donated to the Wisconsin Historical Society.

24. The recording is available at the Wisconsin Historical Society.

25. For analysis and comments by Frank Emspak: " This is What Democracy Looks Like" CD, 2011;; " The Wisconsin Up- Rising" in Wisconsin Uprising, ed. by Michael Yates; Monthly review Press NY NY 2010; "Labor, Social Solidarity and the Wisconsin Winter" with Paul Buhle in It Started in Wisconsin, Verso (London and New York; 2011 and the video "Divided We Fall" Katherine Acosta, New Day Films https:// www.newday.com/film/divided-we-fall.

26. Emspak Papers, WHS, Folder 23.107 Memo "WINS" overview of technical needs and who would be supplying them. Ultimately WINS was located in #3 Lowell Hall Rooms 414 and 534, rooms assigned to the SFW.

27. Report to the WINS Board of Directors, May 3,2003 page 3, WHS.

28. WHS Emspak papers Folder 19.586.

29. Capital Times; Weekend Edition Feb2-3 2008 page B-1; WHS Emspak papers Folder 23.305.

30. "This is What Democracy Looks Like" Cd produced by Workers Independent News and WORT-Back Porch Community Radio, April 2011. Produced by Frank Emspak and Molly Stentz.

31. "Divided We Fall" New Day Films. https://dividedwefall-movie.com/ Katherine Acosta producer, 2016. See my candid comments regarding the Wisconsin Uprising.

Chapter Thirteen: IT WAS WORTH IT

Donald Trump's rise in 2016 shocked political observers and drew the attention of mainstream media to the rightward shift of working class whites.

But the political realignment did not happen overnight: It was the object of a long-term campaign by elements of the Republican Party to stoke racist beliefs among white workers and mobilize them on that basis.

This strategy has been successful so far because of the stagnation of real wages and loss of benefits by industrial workers, as well as the end of upward mobility experienced by that same group. A great motivator for the post-WWII generation was that their kids would do better than they — and, in fact, that happened. But after 1975, that train came to a halt.

The conservative campaign to denigrate poor people — and especially poor Black people — receiving any kind of public assistance stoked white feelings of resentment: "They are getting something that I worked for." The physical deterioration of cities caused by capital flight has been an additional source of resentment.

And that nagging sense of insecurity is constantly fed by the mass media, especially local news. "If it bleeds it leads" is the mantra of local news reporting, which, increasingly starved of funds, turned to prurient and violent coverage rather than informative reporting.

In response to the real economic and social needs of vast numbers of people, the political class provided less and less in terms of real support — and nothing when it came to the preservation of manufacturing jobs. For example, in states like Iowa, Nebraska and Minnesota what had been decent-paying jobs in meatpacking turned into killer jobs as unions were gutted.[1] The political class in these states proved either unwilling or unable to do anything to protect health & safety standards, pollution regulations, or use whatever leverage they had to pressure the meatpacking companies to maintain wages and working conditions.

The Democratic Party tried to address the growing dissatisfaction of the working class via policies and programs which did not result in the benefits advertised — but did spare companies pain. Various job training programs often took longer than the benefits subsidizing them. From the outset, the definition of "success" was eighty-percent of the affected workforce would get eighty-percent of their previous income — benefits not included.

The North American Free Trade Agreement (NAFTA) was touted as the solution — in theory, encouraging investment by eliminating barriers to trade. It did encourage investment — but in Mexico where U.S. firms used tax and investment protection language to build new production facilities and move work previously done in the US. The work included automobile production and high-skilled commercial aircraft maintenance, as well as aircraft instrument manufacture (the work done in the Wilmington, Massachusetts GE plant, for example, was all moved to Mexico).

Meanwhile, NAFTA's agricultural policies caused the bankruptcy of thousands of small Mexican farms and a resultant huge influx of economic refugees to the US. In turn, this refugee crisis was used to motivate racist attacks on the immigrants who were blamed for the collapse of wages and "stealing jobs" in the U.S.

Frank Emspak

Between 1960 and 1970, thousands of people from my generation joined the labor movement. They were the "red diaper babies" — sons and daughters of the prior generation of labor activists and Communists. They were also the young people who, motivated by the civil rights and anti-Vietnam War movement, saw labor as a potential source for progressive change.

By the sixties, the Communist Party was no longer the hegemon of the left and movement activists also came from the Progressive Labor Party and segments of Students for a Democratic Society (SDS). They (we) saw the working class as crucial to the success of any progressive political movement. In part, this understanding was driven home by the constant refrain from the right of the "silent majority" — the theory that the majority of white middle and working-class people supported the Vietnam War and opposed the upward mobility of Black people, especially when that meant the integration of schools and neighborhoods.

But all of us had a vision it would be possible to rebuild a strong, progressive labor movement with enough economic clout to move society forward. For many, underlying our model was the Flint sit-down strike or the huge strike wave after WWII. Flint inspired because it showed a relatively few organized workers in a key spot — the primary manufacturer of engines for the General Motors empire — could sit-in, stop production and bring GM to halt, thus launching the United Auto Workers. The strike wave after WWII (primarily in the spring of 1946) involved millions of workers in all of America's basic industry and shut down the auto, steel and electrical industries, among others. But most importantly, unions were not destroyed and won some major concessions from the industrial ruling class. Maybe, many of my cohorts thought, we could do it again.

But you can't step in the same river twice.

The world we faced in the 1960s and 1970s differed fundamentally from the cultural and political world of labor in the generations prior. U.S. capital was much stronger financially. Production was dispersed, so geographical concentration, which helped when it came to mass mobilizations, was vitiated. All of the major manufacturing firms had overseas affiliates, production capabilities and income. Finally, almost every successful tactic used by workers and their unions in the 1930s — such as jurisdictional strikes, wildcat strikes, solidarity or political strikes, secondary boycotts, secondary and mass picketing, closed shops, and monetary donations by unions to federal political campaigns — was made illegal with the passage of the Taft-Hartley Act in 1948.

Anti-democratic practices were a key aspect of the Taft-Hartley Act. In order to participate in the NLRB process, the Act required individual union officers to sign non-Communist affidavits. If one signed and was known as a Communist, perjury indictments and termination of employment often followed. If one didn't sign and was known as a militant and progressive leader the same routine followed. The result was a significant cadre of progressive union leadership was eliminated. Union members no longer had the option of selecting leaders of their choice. The United Electrical workers initially opposed the Taft- Hartley Act on these grounds specifically.

The left unions were the most advanced unions on issues of race. The CP had a considerable Black membership in places like Alabama and Virginia where a Black female Communist had been elected president of the thirteen-thousand-member Tobacco workers union. The implementation of the Taft-Hartley Act, and the enthusiastic support of the non-Communist oath sections by the right wing of unions who used it to raid the progressive unions, resulted in the destruction of some of the largest Black-led local unions in the South. This included the destruction of the Mine Mill and Smelter Workers near Birmingham, Alabama, and in the cigarette industry of Virginia with the destruction of the Food and Tobacco Workers Union.

Meanwhile, the fights against racism and for equal wages by the United Packinghouse Workers of America were led by a coalition of CP members and trade union militants. As conservative forces moved to one-party-rule, Black workers were forced to choose between working with longtime allies and being attacked for leftist sympathies. One consequence was a weakening of the Black-white unity needed to fight racism, and fierce resistance to Black and white progressive coalitions.

The Taft Hartley Act and its state expressions in the form of "right to work" laws were designed to not only impede union growth by forcing unions to represent non-paying employees covered in the bargaining unit — but shape the way unions could organize by making illegal almost all the tactics unions successfully used to gain victories in the thirties (such as secondary boycotts). The law was a strong push in channeling union resources off the shop floor and in the direction of complicated and endless litigation.

At the same time, the elimination of a militant cadre of workers in many industrial locals during the McCarthy Era cut the transmission of history to a new generation of workers who had not experienced the heady early days of union organization. Those who did the organizing were gone and could not pass on their experiences, and many of those who stayed got the message "don't put your head above the trench line."

The actual transmission of history did survive in a few places, such as New York City and San Francisco — but in the main it was gone in industrial centers like Schenectady, Lynn and the steel towns of the upper Midwest.

While in the formative years of the CIO militant unionism and progressive politics had been part of working class political culture, those currents had become scarce by the sixties. While some aspiring union activists (like myself) had deep family ties with the industry, most had to overcome both generational and tribal resistance, as well as the normal political opposition.

The repression of the forties reduced the CP — a nationwide, working class, class-conscious political organization capable of conducting coast-to-coast mobilizations — down to almost nothing.

Absent was the presence of people who had learned how to organize and deal with it. Absent also was an almost automatic hatred or rejection of "the boss." While radical soapbox orators and union activists of the thirties might not have been accepted by their audience, workers generally believed that the ruling class — the boss — was no friend. By the mid-seventies this automatic assumption was gone and often replaced by the idea that industry leaders provided jobs. In part, the automatic assumptions were gone because for almost a generation, the trusted voices who reflected that vision were gone. Workers heard only the constant refrain that corporations provided jobs. They did not have access to the message that it was the workers who made profits possible in the first place.

The Disappearance of the Working Class in the Mass Media

The working class tended to disappear from the culture starting after the Second World War. For example, analyses of the 2020 election often used educational attainment as a stand-in for defining "working class," while income levels were sparingly discussed. There was no mainstream discussion of the working class defined in terms of the functions that workers perform in our society — namely, the creation of wealth or its manipulation for some social or personal end. If a class, by and large, does not really believe or understand that it is creating wealth, then it will not demand that it share in the wealth.

After WWII and the huge strike wave of 1946, the framing of "workers" and "working class" in the mass media began to shift. Increasingly, the population was divided between "rich," middle-class and poor. Workers began to disappear as a distinct group, being instead subsumed under the banner of the middle class. A growing consensus among white people, if unspoken, was that the poor were, for the most part, people of color and not "real workers."

The fact that most people in poverty in the US were white and most were working as many jobs as they could to make ends meet was not part of the dialogue.

In the media, "jobs" were almost always portrayed as gifts provided by the company to the community, encouraged perhaps by tax breaks, subsidies or socialization of job training costs. There was no consistent linkage to the notion that a worker was contributing to the wealth of the employer one way or the other.[2]

In other words, there was no place in the mass media for a worker to go to hear about their problems from their point of view, articulated by workers in similar positions. Not just once or twice in some special show — but daily, many times a day, for years. In the absence of exposure to any solutions except those approved of by management, is it any surprise that white workers would support a candidate who came along and seemed to speak directly to their racialized fears?

My generation of activists entered the workforce when the deep cultural identification including a real sense of pride and accomplishment in being a worker was eroding. And this erosion was encouraged by yet two other factors.

Preceding the attack on the intellectual community by the red scare crew, and the acquiescence of (or the active support) of most liberal Democrats,[3] the right wing in the labor movement mobilized against the left. Among others, the right wing of the movement pushed the idea that management would make all fundamental decisions and that the role of unions is only to deal with the negative effects of those decisions.

American labor prided itself on this model. Indeed, the system seemed to work as the standard of living for workers (especially those in the highly unionized basic industries) increased almost year by year from 1945 to 1975. A model which avoided pitched political battles and mobilizations for universal benefits, like healthcare, seemed to work for the union's members — and thus, provide a reason for workers to join a union. The story the left told of a need for class-based solutions did not seem to make sense, especially when combined with severe repression for those who advocated political and social mobilization.

It worked until management determined that continued investment in unionized facilities, or even within the U.S., was no longer in their interest. Capital flight, in particular out of the U.S., began to be noticed by some unions in the mid-seventies as highly capital intensive industries like steel production began a rapid decline. At this point, unions (in the main) were totally unprepared ideologically or organizationally to deal with this challenge. Rather than a political mobilization to try to impede capital mobility, many chose accommodation and various forms of labor-management cooperation in an attempt to placate the firms — tacitly accepting the basic company argument that somehow the costs of labor, though constantly falling as a percentage of overall costs, were responsible for capital flight. The Democratic Party, which by the seventies was the sole political organization supporting "organized labor," provided no leadership. One perfect example being U.S. Representative Mavroules, who as described earlier, told Local 201 members there was nothing he could do as GE announced layoffs.

During this period, and accelerating from the seventies on, the Democratic Party was moving away from responding to the needs of working people — for many reasons. In 1960, JFK showed with his victory in the West Virginia primary that candidates could use television to appeal directly to voters. By the mid-seventies, as media-led campaigns became more dominant, the ward and precinct organizations (loci for the mobilization of working people) became less and less of a factor — and hence, less and less important to the Democratic Party. Money became the driving force in politics.

Among other factors, this change in the balance of forces meant that upper middle-class and wealthy people had more to say about the policies of the Democratic Party. The Democratic Party walked away from working people in their time of need — when faced with escalating attacks by the corporations in the seventies and eighties — stagnant real wages and the rapid de-capitalization of the U.S. industrial economy.

Essentially, the Democratic Party bought the neoliberal ideas that rising shareholder value was the measure of economic success and that the role of government was to encourage that measure through investment policies, tax laws and deregulation. These capital strategies were accompanied by huge efforts to dismantle the public sector via privatization, which also has an anti-democratic aspect.[4] The Democrats moved increasingly to identity politics, which in and of itself, weakened the ability to mobilize the working-class in their interests. To be clear, by identity politics I mean the slicing and dicing of the electorate into specific groups based on race, gender, sexual preference or ethnicity — and the concomitant organization of political mobilizations focused on specific groups to the exclusion or downgrading of more generalized class interests like Medicare for All.

Meanwhile, my efforts in CAT to build a response to capital mobility by attempting to impose meaningful conditions on government subsidies was defeated — and not by a right-wing attack, but by a coalition of mainline Democrats in Massachusetts and the active agreement of organized labor. The movement failed because the unions were ambivalent and almost all progressive political forces (now led mostly by middle and upper class college educated individuals) contented themselves with the social welfare model in which unions fought for expanded benefits at no cost to the company. However, CAT was successful in three projects which included provisions that productivity gains would be shared with the workforce by maintaining employment. Each project also had a joint decision-making process which was based around consensus and went beyond wages, hours and working conditions. These examples indicated that such provisions could be implemented if the company was challenged enough and the unions were committed.

While the labor movement and progressives within the Democratic Party fought for various benefit extensions, these extensions did not fill the tremendous hole in the psyche of individuals, or the economic hole in the community when plants closed.

Factories like United Shoe, GE-Lynn, and the auto plants of Detroit were not only the economic linchpins of the community, but psychological and ideological ones as well. Members of the community could see the physical manifestations of wealth production. Everyone could see that people went to work and were producing something. People could not really believe that these multi-generational mainstays of their community could simply disappear. But when they did, welfare (no matter how generous) could not assuage the feelings of being made useless and dependent — as well as the reality that the skills and techniques learned over many years in a factory were of no value.

These deep trends overwhelmed efforts by radicals to bring about a resurgence of the labor movement. As plants closed, relatively low-seniority militants were laid-off. Again, severing the working class from a source of intellectual and political information. But even if individuals survived, the unions were often so debilitated that they could not have the scope and vigor of a resurgence that one would need to fight plant closings successfully.

At the same time, firms aggressively implemented new technologies in the machining and other production industries. Most American unions stood by their original adherence to effects bargaining — that is, the framework which gave management the right to run the business — and unions the "right" to deal with the effects in regards to wages, hours and working conditions. Unfortunately, this framework was totally inadequate to the task of dealing with the challenge of new technology. The unwillingness and/or inability to lead — or even strongly support any meaningful discussion about how things should be done — contributed to the notion that the union movement was intellectually all used up. Workers understood this and began to look elsewhere for answers to the employment crisis.

Within the progressive scientific and engineering community (especially in Europe), the discussion about how to organize work and production to maximize human skill and value was gaining strength. By the mid-eighties, some major firms Siemens, Volvo, Saab and John Deere among them, were beginning to adopt worker-centered practices. Several streams came together to push the firms to change their manufacturing practice and take up the computer-aided craftsman approach. First, there were efforts by unions such as IG Metal — the German metalworkers' union. There was, at the time, also significant government support driven by the political decision to demonstrate to the workers of Eastern Europe that western capitalism provided better working conditions.

And there were tax laws that made it more attractive for firms to maintain employment and invest in Germany. When these outside pressures dissipated (in large part because of the fall of the socialist governments of Eastern Europe), companies and most governments ended support for worker-centered technology experiments.

The 1994 NIST adventure was a highpoint of this movement in the United States. In the absence of strong pressure from the working class, the progressive engineering gaze shifted to the climate. In the case of NIST, aside from their anti-labor predelictions, leaders were concerned that the Republican victory in the House of Representatives would endanger funding if any project that explicitly worked with organized labor was financially supported. Within the union movement (with the exception of the International Association of Machinists) no union had warmed to the notion that their job was to challenge the organization of manufacturing. Joint labor-management cooperation was the order of the day with most unions agreeing to the corporate framework as the means to save employment.

Another consequence of our inability to build grassroots, democratic organizations based in the working class, was that the American liberal democratic system was derailed by a right-wing autocrat leading a predominantly white, racially motivated anti-democratic uprising. It appeared as if, in spite of a huge growth in the scope and racial composition of the progressive wing of America, all might be lost.

And then, 2020 happened. Black-led protests in Minneapolis against the police murder of George Floyd blossomed into a multiracial uprising that touched every state in the country. White people, in greater numbers than ever before, began to hear what Black Americans were saying about racist police violence. Millions marched — a far greater number than was ever involved in the civil rights movements of the 1960s. But so far, this tremendous outpouring of commitment to justice has not been matched by an organizational form that can continue to give voice to this movement.

Mentally and intellectually, the organized working-class movement remains on the defensive. In the U.S., organized labor was never able to overcome the political decapitation (self-inflicted and otherwise) of the forties and fifties. It was never able to connect culturally, politically or organizationally with the tremendous energy of the civil rights and peace movements of the sixties — which saw their reflection in the rank & file movements in the steel and auto industries (among other places). The real mindset of the AFL-CIO began to more and more resemble the craft-minded, undemocratic, politically-narrow and defensive mindset of the AF of L of the twenties.

The trade union movement, too, resembles the twenties in that the new industries of the late 20th and early 21st centuries remain almost one-hundred percent nonunion — as did the electrical, auto and steel industries of the earlier century. Even when the unions finally organized the most productive sectors of the U.S. economy — the trade union movement never challenged capital mobility — the firms retained total freedom to relocate production to parts of the world where labor costs were cheaper. Without a legal framework to resist capital mobility and in the presence of a refusal to organize mass-based political resistance to it, unions have been systematically stripped of their ability to advance the needs of their members.

While it is not necessary to have a union structured like the traditional AFL-CIO unions, or a political party structured like the Communist Party, it is necessary to have a movement or organization capable of disrupting the means of production — or the creation of wealth — if one is to get the attention of those who control society. The Teamster strike of 1997 demonstrated that. This strike paralyzed the United Parcel Service, but it also won popular support because one of the key issues was improving the conditions of part-time drivers and eliminating wage & benefit disparities. A union showed that one of the largest companies in the world could be beaten.

Widespread protests are great. Millions marching for social change are even better. But without the ability to disrupt the means of production, demonstrations have not succeeded in winning economic and political objectives, either in the U.S., or in any other so-called liberal democratic state.

One measurement of this failure can be seen in the increasing wealth and income disparities in all wealthy countries. The increase in inequality in all cases is tied directly to a decrease in the ability of working people to halt the production of wealth in some meaningful way.

So, at the end of the day, why keep going? Why be optimistic?

I believe that humanity wants to survive the climate crisis facing us and that desire is   fueling ever more widespread and effective efforts to question capitalist political domination and modes of production. The movements to deal with climate change have a deep philosophical resonance with some of the ideas that underlay the concepts of   human-centered automation or the computer-aided craftsman, which treats the worker as a whole person — a human being — not as an addendum to a machine. The climate change movement is by definition a holistic approach to our society. Dealing with global warming requires changes in production methods of what we as a species produce — not just the use of fossil fuel. The crisis calls into question consumerism and its concomitant waste of resources and generation of pollution. Millions of people in the generation currently coming of age are looking for answers and are in motion to find them.

That philosophical approach means that we look at production from the point of view of enhancing a person, eliminating pollution, ending work schedules that destroy and dehumanize. In other words, if we are to solve the climate crisis, the way in which we organize work will also have to be addressed.

My source of strength and enthusiasm is speaking with this generation of people who have a holistic view of society. They may not embrace my version of Marxism, but they do embrace the need for their generation to speak truth to power. There is an understanding that their needs as citizens, as human beings, and as working people are different and may be in contradiction to the "Me first, profit maximization" ethos of the rulers. In the U.S., the willingness of a significant number of this generation to confront racism, sexism and gender roles is a huge step in the direction of building a movement that can express our human and ethical values.

Over the span of my life, I think I have contributed to this consciousness building. Maybe not as much as I would wish. Maybe not so successfully — look at the trade union movement or Workers Independent News.

Participating in movements that encouraged people to grow and decide that they were ready to demand the equality they deserve was a great gift. I wouldn't have it any other way.

Endnotes For Chapter Thirteen

1. The Hormel Company of Austin MN effectively defeated the UFCW local P-9 of the United Food and Commercial Workers. Thus accelerating the destruction of standards in the meat packing industry.

2. According to Wikipedia, *The Honeymooners* was one of the first U.S. television shows to portray working-class married couples in a gritty, non-idyllic manner, as the show is mostly set in the Kramden's' kitchen in a neglected Brooklyn apartment building. The show ran for two years-1955-56.

3. An example of one such democrat was Hubert Humphrey D-FLP of Minnesota.

4. It is worth noting that just as Blacks became a major force in the Steel industry and won a consent decree mandating that discriminatory seniority lines be abolished that the steel industry entered a period of massive contraction wiping out thousands of jobs- the ones that Blacks had been aspiring to. There is a parallel development of the public sector with privatization- but not as widespread.

About the Author

Frank Emspak is a Professor Emeritus, School for Workers, University of Wisconsin. So workers could speak for themselves Frank and other labor media activists founded Workers Independent News a nationwide labors news program which Frank directed (2000-2017) A machinist and union activist, Frank sought to use his education (PhD History, BA Zoology) in the service of his class. He and colleagues sought to develop strategies to fight plant closings. (Director, Center for Applied Technology (MA) 1987-91) Although many other centers provide technical assistance none instituted a requirement that workers and/or their union must be involved in decision making (not just advice)

Frank sought to restructure the design of work to enhance skills through the development of skills based automation. He did this both within the union movement and within various scientific organizations, including MIT Program Science Technology and Society, The National Institute for Science and Technology (NIST);The International Federation of Automatic Control technical Committee-The Social Effects of Automation and Automation Forum.

Frank was also a member: Joint task force of the Ministry of Education and the Economic Ministry, Federal Republic of Germany 2000-2012.

A union activist all of his adult life, Frank was President of United Faculty and Academic Staff Local 223 AFT,(1998- 2008) Executive Board member IUE Local 201 1979-1987, Executive Board local 271 UE 1974-75, union steward and organizer.

At the time of publication Frank is co-producer of Madison Labor Radio, WORT 89.9 FM Community Radio Madison WI.